D1615375

The Art of Work

The Art of Work
AN EPITAPH TO SKILL

Roger Coleman

PLUTO PRESS

First published 1988 by Pluto Press
11-21 Northdown Street, London N1 9BN

Distributed in the USA by Allen & Unwin Inc.
8 Winchester Place, Winchester
MA 01890, USA

Copyright © Roger Coleman 1988

Typesetting: Ransom Typesetting Services,
Woburn Sands, Bucks

Printed and bound in Hungary by Interpress

British Library Cataloguing in Publication Data

Coleman, Roger
 The art of work: an epitaph to skill
 1. Industrial Sociology
 I. Title
 306'.36   HD6955

 ISBN 0–7453–0168–1

Contents

For Frances and Ivan

*Nothing should be made by man's labour which is not worth making;
or which must be made by labour degrading to the makers.*
William Morris – 1884

Preface

Before there were ever artists and sketchbooks, skilled workers kept their own working notebooks: patternbooks in which they recorded useful pieces of information, sketches of other people's work, notes on how to solve specific problems or achieve particular effects – a working record of their own studies and investigations. In this way the theoretical and experimental side of the practical arts was built up and preserved.

What follows is my own 'patternbook', a collection of pointers and ideas, and an attempt to think through some of the problems that surround the future of both art and work in a world where technology (in the West at least) seems poised to eliminate or transform them both beyond recognition.

Patternbooks are not part of an academic tradition any more than this book is. They are rooted in the older practices of skilled work, and very much the products of practical and enquiring lives. In putting this book together I have drawn on much of the experience of, and written directly about, some of the people who taught me most of what I value today. I would like to thank them for their example, and all the other people who should, but for lack of space do not receive a mention.

Thanks also to all the friends who encouraged me in what at first seemed an impossible task, and in particular to Hilary Picardie, Gwyn Prins and especially Christopher Cornford, who read a series of garbled drafts, and whose criticism and encouragement has been invaluable; and to Bill Powell, who gave me the idea for the first chapter.

As I have not written this book primarily for an academic audience I see little point in including a conventional bibliography. Instead I have added a short note at the beginning of each chapter, which I hope will act as a guide to why I wrote it and what it is about. Specific quotations are numbered and the references given in full at the end of the book. Suggestions on further reading are included with the references.

Roger Coleman,
Hackney, London, October 1987

1
Introduction –
The Fall of Daedalus

The history of art is really the history of skilled work – no more, no less –
and when we marvel at the products of other periods and cultures, we
marvel at the achievements of a tradition of skilled work, not 'art'. This
confusion has been responsible for a form of snobbery that makes most art
intellectually inaccessible to the majority by pretending that it contains
inscrutable qualities discernible only to those with cultural education and
finely developed sensibilities. From here, it is but a short step to the
museum charges that symbolise the abandonment of any remaining
pretence that art works constitute a freely available heritage.

Attitudes among art historians have changed, and some particularly
enlightened and enlightening studies have been published over the last
ten or so years, but they have not changed basic assumptions about the
nature and history of art which I intend to challenge in this book. My
primary concern is the development of ideas about work and art in the
West, as to my mind, the cultural assumptions implicit in much of
available art history distort our understanding of the nature of work and
art to such an extent as to make the products of non-Western cultures
largely inaccessible to people in the West. The unravelling of the
confusion surrounding the nature of work is an essential first step towards
an understanding of creative activity and, I hope, a more useful definition
of both art and work.

Once art is defined as a special, refined and valuable commodity, it
moves out of the sphere of everyday life. Galleries and museums cease to
be places where examples of a popular tradition of skilled work are
preserved. Instead attention is focused, not on the skill that went into
hand production, but on a semi-magical quality – art – which is supposedly
inherent in very special objects and reflected in their often fabulous price.

If art works are the almost priceless holy relics of the modern world,
then this leaves the artist – as producer of the unproducable – impaled on
the horns of a very nasty dilemma. On the one hand there is the open door
and fat cheque-book of the gallery system for those who are prepared to
make the Emperor's New Clothes in which the art market trades, and
compete for its unpredictable patronage. On the other hand there is the

missionary vocation that follows from accepting the role of 'cultural worker' engaged with the processes of social change.

I cannot pretend to be an artist in any conventional sense. Much of what I have done has had a clearer social purpose, and I would not want to claim it as art, but I have never lost an early faith in the power of creativity to challenge, inspire and transform. I think creativity is possibly the most significant of human talents, whereas the charade that much art has become succeeds only in diverting our attention from the innovative potential of creative thinking. Unfortunately we are still locked in patterns of work and production that are at least a century old and largely inappropriate today. Around these we have built up stultifying social stereotypes, desires and aspirations.

Unemployment is one symptom of the deep imaginative failure of modern society, and neither monetarism, nor Keynesianism, nor any other political or economic palliative, will cure the symptoms of this imaginative failure. Before we can put people back to work we have to rethink what we mean by work and how that affects the detail of our lives. We have to put creativity, imagination, innovation and invention back to work; we have to put art back to work and back into work, and to do that we have to start somewhere.

One October morning, in the North of Crete, I watched a flock of young birds of prey rising from a rocky hillside nearby, and wheeling above the sea under the tutelage of a few patient, dark-plumed adults. The ease with which the adults hung on the rising air currents contrasted with the energy-wasting pleasure of the young birds, and inspired me with that same, age-old envy of the power of flight that has made the myth of Daedalus and Icarus unforgettable.

Daedalus and his son Icarus were imprisoned on Crete after Daedalus had fallen out of favour with his royal patron King Minos. A simple moral is commonly drawn from this story. Icarus, doomed by his own vanity (or was it youthful, energy-wasting enthusiasm?), imagined himself god-like and invulnerable. Pride came before a fall; Icarus

disobeyed his father's instructions and began soaring towards the sun, rejoiced by the lift of his great sweeping wings. Presently, when Daedalus looked over his shoulder, he could no longer see Icarus; but scattered feathers floated on the waves below. The heat of the sun had melted the wax, and Icarus had fallen into the sea and drowned. Daedalus circled around, until the corpse rose to the surface, and then carried it to the near-by island now called Icaria, where he buried it. This island has now given its name to the surrounding sea.[1]

But the tale has other, more intriguing meanings and overtones, for Daedalus was the legendary craftsman/scientist of classical mythology personified: a Greek Leonardo da Vinci. The Daedalus myth tells us much about the prehistoric origins of art and technology, and the overweening arrogance that certain artists and technologists have fallen prey to, believing they could imitate and even improve on nature.

The terrible consequences of pride and jealousy run through the story of Daedalus. Icarus his son (and presumably his apprentice and chosen successor) was killed through his own folly, while Daedalus himself had been exiled to Crete from his native Athens. Envy had driven him to murder Talos, his sister's son, who had been apprenticed to Daedalus and who threatened to outshine his master at an early age.

Behind these stories we can glimpse the fierce pride and intense jealousies that breathed temperament and vitality into a tradition of skilled work and invention that made much of Greek art and architecture, and indeed much of Greek culture and civilisation, possible. The Greek tradition eventually migrated across Europe, providing both the technology and the inspiration for the major artistic and commercial achievements of Western civilisation. This tradition was built on apprenticeship and artisanal production: the family workshop in which a deep, practical knowledge and understanding of technology, science, technique and, above all, of the sensitive manipulation of materials, was passed on from generation to generation in an oral tradition and a heritage of inestimable value which eventually spread out from Minoan Crete to inspire the workshops and trade guilds of classical and medieval Europe.

Just as the craft skills and traditions of Minoan Crete spread out across Europe to provide the technology on which Western civilisation was built, so Daedalus too is remembered in myth and legend. His name changes, but the stories are similar. In the Norse myths Wayland or Weland the Smith is imprisoned by a king, makes wings to fly away, and kills not his sister's son but the king's two sons. Along with the gods, the famed artisan was also immortalised in these stories.

My travelling companion in Crete – Bill Powell, a goldsmith who comes from a family of blacksmiths – lent me an old book which relates the story of Weland Smith and points out the similarities with the Daedalus legend:

in the middle ages the popular belief in a skilful artisan was spread over a great part of Europe, but especially in the North. They represented this individual as having excelled in all that then constituted art, that is to say, the mechanical as well as the fine arts. Thus he was a skilful goldsmith, armourer, smith, statuary, engraver, founder. This skill was accompanied with a little magic, and a great deal of malevolence ...

But antiquity presents us with a more striking analogy with the North, in the fables which relate to Daedalus, and we do not hesitate to believe that it is the history of this Greek artist, altered and disfigured, adapted to the manners and creeds of the people of the North of Europe, which has given rise to the romance of Weland.

At first the word Daedalus was, among the Greeks, like that of Weland among the scandinavians a generic name. Δαιδαλλω signified to work artistically, as Vœlundr signified a smith in Islandic. Daedalus was, like Weland, pre-eminently the artist and the workman. This word was a proper name only because they attributed to this mythologic being all the perfections of the art.[2]

Daedalus did not drown, indeed, in his role as craftsmanship personified we could claim that his flight has lasted some 5,000 years, but the daedalic tradition of skilled work and knowledge acquired through practical experience that Daedalus represents is on the verge of extinction. In this sense the fall of Daedalus is imminent and its consequences could well have repercussions far more serious than the volcanic eruption that destroyed a large part of the Cycladic island of Thera between 1500 and 1400BC, and seems to have brought an abrupt end to the Minoan civilisation that Daedalus served.[3] The fall of Daedalus will herald the final triumph of a narrow, science-based, mechanistic culture over the more human traditions of skilled work. This materialistic, all-consuming culture is obsessed with so-called 'new technology', and convinced that, despite the problems of pollution and ecological damage to which it gives rise, science can and will solve all problems. It is a form of blind faith in science and technology mirroring the medieval belief in the literal reality of the angelic choirs of Heaven and the eternal fires of Hell.

When the much depleted gene pool of skills, techniques and practical knowledge is finally discarded in the name of progress, when that unique repository of intimate knowledge and understanding of natural materials and processes, which provided the technological base on which recent generations of innovation and technical discovery stand, has vanished, we will have suffered an irreparable loss and have committed ourselves to a path from which it will be difficult, if not impossible to retreat. To abandon this rich tradition would be a disaster comparable with the wholesale destruction of natural forests and wetlands which already poses a serious threat to the world ecology and climate. The loss of the practical technologies, arts and skills will be as final as the destruction of the tropical rain forests, and, I believe, of equivalent long-term significance.

The legend has it that Daedalus buried his son on Icaria and then flew on to Cumae near Naples and eventually took up residence in Sicily under the protection of King Cocalus, and later in Sardinia, where he enjoyed great fame and erected many fine buildings.[4]

But Daedalus left Sicily to join Iolaus, the nephew and charioteer of Tirynthian Heracles, who led a body of Athenians and Thespians to Sardinia. Many of his works survived in Sardinia; they were called Daedaleia.[5]

Although scholars dispute the historical basis of the myth,[6] the accuracy or otherwise of the legend cannot detract from its potency and charm. In Daedalus we should look, not for an historical person, but the personification of craft and skill – the daedalic tradition. His wanderings point to the spread of these skills outwards from Bronze-age Crete, which can well be regarded as the cradle of Mediterranean civilisation. For some 1,500 years, up to about 1400BC, Crete was the centre of the first naval power known to history, boasting a culture associated with the name of the equally legendary King Minos. This Minoan culture can fairly compare with its contemporaries in Asia Minor, Syria, Mesopotamia and Egypt.[7]

This period was remembered in Greek folk-lore as the series of myths associated with King Minos and the fabled Labyrinth ascribed to Daedalus, where the Minotaur – the man headed bull, and offspring of Minos's wife Pasiphae – lived. With the help of a hollow wooden cow fashioned by Daedalus, Pasiphae conspired to couple with the white bull that had risen from the sea in answer to a prayer of Minos, and gave birth to the Minotaur as a result. In these myths Minos and Pasiphae personify some 1,500 years of relative social stability, and Daedalus in turn personifies the achievements of the brilliant artisanal tradition that flourished during this prehistoric golden age.

The fact that so many of the real and fabulous marvels of prehistoric Greek art and architecture are attributed to Daedalus makes it all the more reasonable to assume that he was mythical rather than real, whilst the god-like perfection accorded to his achievements points to the level and sophistication of skill seen during the Minoan period. 'So lifelike were his statues that they had to be chained down in order to prevent them running away.'[8]

So Daedalus is the archetypal craftsman: inventor and engineer; architect and builder; artist and sculptor; designer of labyrinths; maker of wings; problem-solver and toymaker. In short, the virtuoso exponent of all that is skilful, inventive, constructive and creative. In Daedalus we can see not just the origins of an artisanal tradition of great richness, but the flowering of 1,500 years of technical innovation and consolidation. A technology that made the Acropolis in Athens and the Coliseum in Rome possible, provided the structural engineering skills that built the Roman aquaducts and the Gothic cathedrals, nourished the Renaissance and fed the rich vein of inventiveness tapped by the Industrial Revolution. We must remember that each of these successive high-points of Western achievement originated in the skill and expertise of working people, preserved and perfected within the traditions of the practical arts or trades. The history of art is really a very short one. The history of skilled work is altogether different.   Daedalus was, as we have seen, artist-craftsman, engineer-inventor, designer-maker, before such skills were separated out from each other, and in Daedalus we can see the workshop tradition which was the original repository and guardian of knowledge in a time when knowledge and understanding were orally transmitted, essentially practical, and locked in an intimate relationship with the physical world.

It is ironic that the Renaissance should have revived, or rather codified, the separation between hand and brain which has become endemic in our culture. Plato and other Greek philosophers conspired to separate intellectual and manual work, legitimising the slave system which made the existence of a leisured class possible. In the Renaissance the revival of such ideas, wedded to the growth of a money economy and the burgeoning of a factory style of production, enforced a fatal division between art and skill, between hand and brain, which has led to an almost irreversible separation between the aspirations of human society and the needs of the natural world: to a greedy materialism which has made Western civilisation arguably the greatest threat to life on earth.

The wax on Daedalus's wings started to melt when the Renaissance tempted him with the semi-divine status of 'artist' and 'genius', which it accorded to Leonardo and Michelangelo. The Industrial Revolution and the less than human conditions of work in the factories of the nineteenth century sapped his strength, but Daedalus flew valiantly on into the twentieth century, and even today some vestiges of this great tradition of skilled work survive. Unfortunately the demands of a technology which has lost the human dimension that nurtured it are rapidly outstripping our ability to control, and the planet's ability to repair, the damage.

Unless we act to try to halt the loss of this 5,000-year-old tradition, we will see an end to Daedalus, his wings burnt out in the ultraviolet glare of an ozone-depleted atmosphere. If we hope to see a world in which people are active participants rather than passive consumers and spectators, then somehow we have to rescue the idea of work as something worthwhile, something if not enduring, then deeply humanising. But this implies changes in our attitudes to work and our understanding of its content: what work is and could become.

The pointless, national-service-style job creation people envisage as a sop to unemployment, and the utter boredom of repetitive, production-line work have nothing in common with the tradition that Daedalus represents, which is one of skilled inventiveness built on a deep understanding of the nature of materials and processes, of time and weather, of use and usefulness.

It was the Industrial Revolution that finally distorted our understanding of the daedalic tradition by demanding an absolute distinction between work – labour that could be exploited in the factories and fields of the nineteenth century – and an art that was to be revered and idolised as close to genius. In its original use the word art meant skill and the exercise of skill – we still use the word in this sense – but it was only in the late nineteenth century that the words art and artist developed their modern meanings. At the same time another word – artisan – was coopted to distinguish the skilled manual worker from the intellectual, imaginative or creative artist, and artists emerged as a very special category of cultural workers, producing a rare and marginal commodity – works of art.[9]

I am convinced that the answer to the artist's dilemma is to be found in the practices and traditions of skilled work. Skilled work, the daedalic tradition, has always respected the experience gained from practical experimenting, and the crafts and trades can best be described as the accumulated experience of generations of practitioners. Early in this century of great promise, capitalising on the potency of mythology, James Joyce combined the tradition of the first Christian martyr – Stephen – with that of the greatest inventor of pagan times, in the name, if not the character, of Stephen Dedalus, who represented the young Joyce in *Ulysses*.[10] In the latter days of the twentieth century we need a modern Daedalus, a new myth to celebrate the achievements of skill and creativity and remind us that science and technology cannot provide us with all the answers to the problems currently facing society.

2

The Art of Work

In this chapter, by examining the complexity and subtlety of the practical skills involved, I am trying to take a fresh look at what is an old debate concerning the roles of architect and builder in producing the buildings around us. This is part of a larger debate concerning the division of labour between hand and brain: a division which has taken place relatively recently, but has acquired such significance – underpinning as it does both class divisions in our society and attitudes towards technology, automation and human skill – that I think it is important to redress the balance in favour of the combination rather than the increased separation of practical and intellectual knowledge.

I am trying, therefore, to argue by example that prior to the modern division of labour between hand and brain there were people who commanded immense practical skills, and worked within a vital and complex tradition which we can barely glimpse in the few vestiges surviving in record and craft practice. To my mind, the professional/academic lobby has made a good job of denigrating the importance of skill as a component of technology. It is my concern to pick a way through some of the evidence, and various interpretations of it, and point to the complexity of skill and understanding which informed classical and medieval building methods.

In ancient Greek the word *arkhitekton* meant chief builder. The sea-change the Greek chief builder has undergone to become our modern architect is comparatively recent, as is the division between hand and brain in the building industry. For centuries the chief builder rose through the ranks of the crafts, and learnt a trade like any other skilled worker. Writing about building in classical Greece, J.A. Bundgaard comes to the conclusion that, not only were Greek buildings highly conventionalised, but the chief builder was paid little more than a skilled craftsman, and acted more as a coordinator at a site agent level than as an independent artist: 'the leader of the work can be allotted only a small share of the credit for the incomparable effect produced by the Greek columned buildings. His real sphere is the organisation of the work.'[1]

We are so used to the idea that buildings are designed by architects and merely executed by whichever builder wins the contract that we find it almost impossible to conceive of large and important public buildings being designed and built by collective effort. Yet the vast majority of buildings – Polynesian long houses, country cottages, terraced town houses – have always been constructed on traditional patterns. Until recently most so-called architecture, both private and public, was built according to conventions which did not involve architects. The basic form was known in advance and the construction carried out on a collective basis by workers who knew their own and each other's roles in that process: a collective working method we have the greatest difficulty in understanding or accepting because it is so far outside our present experience of work as an externally disciplined, regimented activity.

Until recently the form of a building was established by tradition, like the cruciform plan of the Christian church, and the orientation by earth-measuring – geometry. Both the structure and the building method were based on trade practices embodied in a tradition of orally transmitted, practical skills learnt by apprenticeship. Few decisions, apart from practical ones, had to be made about a building once the site had been chosen, other than the size, the degree of elaboration, and the inclusion or otherwise of any special features of ritual or symbolic significance. For long periods of history, going back at least as far as Stonehenge, and including monuments like the Pyramids, the most important features of public buildings were their siting, orientation and symbolic purpose – elements that linked the building with cosmic forces in a spiritual geometry of ritual significance. Under these conditions, the chief builder or coordinator could rise quite naturally from the ranks of the trades, and would thus have acquired the practical knowledge necessary to understand the process which had to be organised, practical knowledge which contemporary training in architecture does not include.

This is exactly what happened in Greece, as Bundgaard noticed:

> When one studies the Parthenon, where the stiff, rectilinear, temple design has been modified with an almost incredible delicacy, it seems only reasonable to assume that a very elaborate and carefully worked out design must have formed the basis for its execution ... These subtle divergencies show only one thing with certainty, however, namely that the workmen who executed it had working habits of amazing precision; this is not surprising, since the Attic masons of that period had behind them several generations of work with a material which not only permits, but actually requires the greatest exactness in finishing it – the fine grained, shining white Pantelic marble. So great is the degree of precision in reality that a design that was to be of any help to those specialists would have to be actual size.[2]

In fact masons and woodworkers have always prepared their own full-size drawings to work from, drawings which define precisely the details and relationships to be expressed in the finished work. Essentially ephemeral and therefore rarely preserved, few examples of working drawings by building workers of any era exist,[3] but there are enough to infer – along with the evidence of traditional practices preserved in the building trades themselves – that drawings were an essential part of the building process and originated on the site, not away from it.

Bundgaard also points out that in existing Greek documents and contracts the buildings were not described and drawn in miniature as they are today; instead, only the essential information required by the craftsman to perform the task was given.

> We have now followed the creation of the column from the time work began on the blocks till the very moment when the column was completed in the form we admire to this very day, and can work out the information required by the mason:
> In cutting
> 1   The full height of the column, and its lower diameter.
> 2   The general tapering.
> 3   The maximum degree of curvature at the entasis.
> In erection
> 4   The inclination of the upper surface of the first drum, determined in relation to the horizontal plane.
> In the final working over: None.
> All the rest is part of the artisan's training and can be assumed as known.[4]

The process is not one of reproducing an existing design, and is therefore completely different from modern building procedure. Instead it is an organic and cooperative method in which the building type is known and the final details emerge from the process of building, a process which reminds Bundgaard of 'an elegant solution of a mathematical problem'.[5] The craft basis of this system is obvious: certain known principles and working methods are applied to the problem at hand in order to produce a specific solution – in this case a particular Greek temple – within the framework of a general type of building.

The medieval building process was very similar, and the skills that were brought together to construct the Gothic cathedrals of Europe were virtually identical to those used to build the palaces and churches of the Renaissance. Renaissance architecture could not have existed without the medieval trades, but by persistently attributing the achievements of classical and medieval builders to hypothetical architects, rather than exploring the alternative tradition of the master masons, historians have effectively distorted our understanding of those periods, and of the part played by craftsworkers in constructing the great buildings of the past. Traditional skills have lost their significance to such an extent that 'building trades operatives', to give craftsworkers their modern title, are generally thought of as the Irish navvies of bad jokes.

Such prejudices are offensive in themselves, but they also encourage us to dismiss skilled work and skilled workers as inconsequential in comparison to the power of modern technology. It is gradually dawning on the architectural profession that the reverse is the case and that the persistent failures of contemporary building techniques should be attributed not to poor quality work, but to this misplaced trust in modern technology and disregard for the achievements of traditional technology that goes with it. The economy of the classical world was based on slavery, and manual work therefore tended to be regarded as on a par with slave labour. In *The Story of Craft*, Edward Lucie-Smith tells us that 'the institution of slavery tended to reduce the free craftsman to the level of those who were not free. In craft workshops free men and slaves worked side by side and the rate of pay for all was equal.'[6]

A basic division has long existed between those who work and those who do not: a division which was firmly embodied in the philosophy of Plato, who elevated intellectual activities and the liberal arts above all others, that is to say above practical work. The care that Plato took to separate the lofty world of the intellect from the mundane, day-to-day world of work is a reflection of the slave system of which he was a beneficiary, as is the lowly status conceded to manual labour, chiefly because it could be had so cheaply and carried the taint of slavery with it. It is not surprising therefore that in Plato we first see the architect edged out of a practical involvement in the plebeian building team and allocated a role in the realm of intellectual work. According to Plato the *arkhitekton* gave the orders to the workmen, and supervised the building process, and 'is not himself a workman, but a director of workmen and that he contributes theoretical knowledge not practical craftsmanship'.[7]

Such an attitude was readily taken up by Renaissance art theorists, even though the Renaissance did not necessarily confirm it in practice, and the same attitude has been incorporated into our current idea of what an architect should be. It would be wrong however to assume that because Plato was a Greek he knew what he was talking about when it came to building. Plato was not a practical person, and his objective was to establish a particular idea of truth – knowledge arrived at by reasoning – as the high point of human achievement. The accumulated body of practical knowledge represented by the craft tradition stood in direct opposition to Plato's abstract knowledge and so had to be demoted. I have no doubt that he was prepared to sacrifice existential truth during this campaign, for Plato was ultimately justifying slavery, a process that requires more than a little self-deception.

Historically this was a crucial contest between two ways of

understanding the world: the one contemplative, originating in the mind and therefore to be seen as noble and patrician, the other, originating as it did in work, considered menial and plebian. To Plato it was fundamentally important that the two should not be confused. Slavery freed a sector of the population from arduous toil and allowed this group to attain a supposedly higher plane of knowledge. As a consequence the central injustices of slavery were enshrined in a philosophical theory of knowledge. It was this class-based 'knowledge' that was resurrected in Renaissance Italy, and was eventually to form the foundation of science, the universities and the academic system in Western Europe. Unfortunately, in the process of elevating this particular idea of knowledge the original, empirical wisdom of the crafts was made subordinate to the abstract academic knowledge of the universities. Our understanding of the world has been unbalanced ever since.

What happened during the Renaissance was that building forms changed, whereas the content of the building crafts did not. The architectural monuments of the Renaissance were produced within a continuous tradition of complex building skills which had made the achievements of the medieval cathedral builders possible.[8] What the medieval builders had preserved and developed was a building process which survived into the twentieth century and made all the changing styles of the intervening centuries possible. Victorian architects could mix classical and Gothic motifs as fancy took them, but the basic techniques on which all this depended had been established centuries before, as had the understanding of materials, structure and climate that ensured buildings worked and withstood constant use.

There was neither 'art' nor 'architecture' in the Middle Ages. The terms 'medieval art' and 'medieval architecture' are misleading because our modern use of the words art and architecture originated well after the Middle Ages were over. We still insistently apply the term 'art' to the products of that period, but I would suggest that we will begin to understand medieval architecture and other antecedents of what we now call art only when we see these activities as something other than art, something much more akin to work.

Patrick Hughes, an art school contemporary of mine, made a three dimensional picture of a room. Papered in doll's house paper, it was constructed in reversed perspective, going in where it should have come out. Mounted on the wall and looked at from one particular position, it worked; it looked like a picture of a room – like looking into a doll's house – but the slightest movement of the head destroyed the illusion and that was precisely what was so intriguing about it. His intention was to question our acceptance of the convention of single viewpoint perspective by showing that we can be deceived, and to point out that perspective is only one convention among many, an illusion: not reality. By exploiting a visual paradox, he had managed to isolate the point at which the limits of the convention and the contradictions inherent in it became apparent. Conventions hold good only under certain circumstances and are never universally valid. When we move our viewpoint even fractionally – as, for example, when we abandon the idea of a medieval architecture – things begin to make an altogether different sense.

A significant number of medieval buildings are known to be copies of important religious monuments. The church of the Holy Sepulchre in Jerusalem was predictably copied several times. But if we compare copy and prototype, what is immediately obvious is that in the Middle Ages people were either very bad at copying buildings, or they had a strange idea of what constitutes a copy. They most certainly did not share our concept of replication. But to suggest that they were inept is so patently unacceptable that we must explore other alternatives. If we look closely at known medieval copies, what we find is that either significant dimensions were accurately recorded and reproduced, or that certain crucial configurations were noted and repeated (e.g. the specific number of columns or piers, or the roundness of the building), but these resemblances were chosen for symbolic rather than visual purposes. As a consequence, copies did not necessarily look like their prototypes, instead they embodied certain important elements of the original, becoming as it were of the same substance as the original, just as a voodoo doll becomes identical with the person it represents and – for the purposes of magic – is.

As Richard Krautheimer points out in an enlightening article on the subject, this particular idea of what constitutes a copy slowly died out from the late Middle Ages onwards:

at the same time, however, a gradual process of draining the edifice of its 'content' seems to begin. It is by no means a continuous development and is constantly interrupted by counter-movements, but it grows stronger, and reaches its peak in the late nineteenth and early twentieth centuries. Architectural patterns are then used regardless of their original significance, a Greek Temple for a Customs House ... a Gothic Cathedral for an office building ... a thermal room for a railway station ... The modern copy with all its exactness in reproducing the whole building and with its striving towards absolute faithfulness, definitely omits the elements which were important in the Middle Ages: the content and the significance of the building.[9]

The whole of modern architectural practice rests on the assumption that a building can be drawn in miniature and will be reproduced exactly in the building process. If builders produced a free interpretation of architects' drawings based on what they thought the underlying significance of the building was, planning control and building regulations would be complete non-starters and architecture as we know it would cease to exist. Yet this is precisely what happened until very recently. In *Georgian London*, John Summerson says: 'it cannot be too strongly emphasised that until about halfway through the eighteenth century there was no such thing as an "architectural profession" in the modern sense.'[10] Until then a strong element of improvisation, coupled with the exercise of deep practical skill, gave buildings a vitality and vigour which they sadly lack today.

The idea of building being carried out by a collective of skilled workers is at variance with modern practice, but is a much more accurate picture of how medieval buildings were constructed. Modern identities like designer and architect are, in effect, an impediment to any understanding of the Middle Ages. In order to appreciate this, we have to look into medieval building traditions and techniques, and at descriptions of how the whole process was accomplished, as well as at the principles which governed the ways in which buildings were copied. In other words, we have to try to understand a process rather than a series of objects. To see what it was that actually constituted a building in that era, to try to grasp what it was that was actually copied, we have to learn to see with medieval eyes, and this involves a reassessment of our own viewpoint.

If the building which was important in the Middle Ages was a symbolic building, a building of numbers and relationships between hierarchies of images; if that symbolism was revealed in the ritual use of the building; if the prayers that were said and the miraculous events that accompanied the construction of the building, along with the relics it housed, were all seen to be as important as the stones, glass and mortar; if divine intercession played as large a part in its production as the workforce, then a modern approach in terms of volumes and spaces will never unlock the mysteries of a medieval cathedral. Nineteenth-century architects designed in what they called the Gothic style, and went about Europe studying buildings, measuring and drawing, but the churches and cathedrals they designed were nothing more than reminiscences of churches and cathedrals built and used in the Middle Ages.

A Victorian building in the Gothic style bears no more than a facile surface resemblance to a real Gothic cathedral, whereas a Victorian church of cast iron and glass, built like a railway shed, with the appropriate symbolic elements and orientation, would be much more in the spirit of medieval building; for this railway shed of a cathedral would serve at one and the same time both a symbolic and a practical function, and would be constructed in contemporary materials and forms. Ironically enough, Pugin, the Victorian architect, was genuinely sensitive to this distinction when he insisted that the revival of style should depend on a revival of the feelings from which that style originally sprang.

Medieval building corresponds directly with Greek building in that it was carried out by a team of masons according to the principles and practices of their trade, which was itself growing, changing and developing. For this medieval team, working from their lodge by the cathedral site, a few significant dimensions, templates and symbolic references were enough – the rest we can take as given by the traditions of the trade. This is very difficult for us to grasp with our contemporary array of architects, offices, drawings and all the rest of the paraphernalia of an immensely divided building process. Yet we have seen that such was the nature of traditional skills that little information was needed, beyond that supplied by the trade itself, in order to construct large and elaborate monuments which would be almost impossible by today's methods.

I would suggest that the lack of evidence for the existence of individual designers of medieval buildings shows that these buildings were constructed on a far more collective basis than is generally accepted today, and that the roles required by that process were substantially different. The chief builder's job was one of coordinating the workforce, and interceding between the constructing team and the commissioning body, be it church or state, in a form of activity that was, to use a musical analogy, more akin to jazz than to orchestral music, and which placed far more emphasis on the skill and creative ability of individuals working within a group.

In all probability, the mason who organised the site and set out the templates was not regarded as anything more than chief among the masons, an elder statesman perhaps, or a site coordinator, but not an architect in any modern sense, for the medieval mason's trade included, at its higher levels of achievement, the invention and construction of palaces and cathedrals. In fact all those functions which are now ascribed to a separate, architectural profession were once part of an integrated trade.

The striking thing about the modern building process compared with that of the Middle Ages is that it is enormously divided. First there is the client, or commissioning authority, who will own the building and pay for its construction. Then there are the architects who will design the building in miniature and have control over every detail, although they will have to refer to the client for approval of the final design and will have to work within some sort of agreed brief. The architects will delegate aspects of this work to other specialists – structural engineers, surveyors and quantity surveyors – who will provide all the necessary calculations involved: stresses and strains; quantities of materials and labour; type and nature of soil; necessary foundations and so on. The architects will also call on the specialist knowledge of suppliers who can provide a whole range of components, materials, services and advice. And all these various elements will be amalgamated into a design which will, it is hoped, satisfy the requirements of the brief – within cost limits – and unify the often conflicting ideas of the specialists involved.

The design must also conform to a number of statutory bye-laws, and in particular to the building regulations which require that it be structurally sound, safe with regard to fire and accident, well insulated, and adequately lit and ventilated. Finally, the relevant planning authorities must be satisfied that the proposed building will be suitable for its location and display a certain 'architectural quality'.

At all these stages the building under consideration does not yet exist, so a very important part of the process is the production of exact descriptions of that building within an agreed convention. Scale drawings are made, along with calculations and notes, and a complete specification of works which will itemise the construction process in detail, stage by stage. These documents form the basis of all building contracts and are sent out to builders for them to prepare quotations. This is probably the first time that a builder will have anything to do with the building, for it is not common practice to consult builders about building design. Instead, they are obliged to compete with each other for contracts in a time-wasting and easily-manipulated procedure which is supposed to create a competitive market. Once a builder has been chosen, work commences, and another chain of command appears, just as extended and elaborate as the first.

According to the modern method, a building has to exist in miniature – in drawings and specifications – before it can be built, and so 'there has been a sharp antithesis between the designer of buildings, known as an architect, and their constructor, called generally a builder ... The medieval sense of mason is far less specific and could be general and almost inclusive, and it comprehended both the master who designed and gave orders and the skilled artisan who carried them into effect.'[11] It is most probable that in the Middle Ages a building was laid out full size on its site at a very early stage in the process, and that design and construction were continuous, occurring side by side on site as the building grew. In 1981, the Royal Institute of British Architects finally decided to relax its ruling about architects and builders. Until then, according to its rules, an architect was not allowed to be a builder. Incredible though it may seem, architects were thus denied any first-hand involvement in building practice and so the 'chief builder' was disbarred in this radical dichotomy between twentieth century and medieval practice: a denial of the very ethos of a building tradition with so many acknowledged monuments to its credit.

The master mason, therefore, was exactly what the modern architect is not: a skilled builder with a mastery of the complete field of building practice. Nowadays no one has the kind of overall grasp of building processes that the medieval mason had, and as a result all manner of faults are built into buildings at every stage from conception to completion. If a medieval mason could build a cathedral then, *ipso facto*, the whole elaborate business was comprehensible within the traditional skill of masonry, and therefore contained in that body of knowledge which constituted the trade of masonry, of which the skilled practitioner was quite rightly acknowledged a master.

Names – assumptions which become definitions – are confusing. We have already seen that the word architect is derived from *arkhitekton* – chief builder – and that master mason has a dual sense implying both a mastery of the skill of masonry and the organising of workers. The word mason itself was originally used in the general sense of our modern word 'builder', and the distinction between a builder in wood – carpenter – and a builder in stone – stonemason – came later. In other words all these terms refer to the same undivided process of building in which the best and most skilful workers could rise to their own level, eventually coordinating the construction of some of the most splendid works of architecture.

The modern use of the term architect has little to do with the centuries-old tradition of building which produced the Greek temples and the medieval cathedrals, yet in the West Country the word mason is still used to refer both to bricklayers and stonemasons, and retains that sense of builder it originally had. The old tradition survives in fossil fragments embedded in our language. Medieval builders were in all probability a survival of the old Roman guilds or *collegia*, and so were part of a continuous daedalic tradition preserved in Northern Italy, where

> there was in the seventh and eighth centuries a recognised organisation of building masters under the Lombard kings ... and it is all but certain that it was this organisation that provided the framework for the later congregations of masons in the various regions of medieval Europe[12]

that had its roots in the pre-classical world, and in attitudes towards manual work which differed from those of Plato and the social elite of classical Greece.

Masons travelled about from job to job, but as some buildings took centuries to finish they would often settle in the area where they were working. Skills were shared and extended by groups of masons working together, training apprentices and travelling Europe to gain experience and a familiarity with contemporary practice. They constituted their own *collegia*: a building college, not institutionalised in one place, but a living, working network extending across Europe. From this we can begin to build up a picture of an extensive body of practical knowledge and theory which was diligently preserved and developed among a close fellowship of practitioners of the art of building, a body of knowledge capable of constructing the splendours of Chartres and Canterbury cathedrals. But how could all this happen if nothing was written down, if there was no reference library of weighty tomes codifying this practice – the building regulations of the day? In a way the practice of small builders gives us a clue. A few skilled building workers could not build a block of flats on their own, but they could build a traditional house. Indeed, before the administrative and managerial side of building grew up with its proliferation of bye-laws and regulations this was the way in which most houses were built.

At the beginning of the nineteenth century, 'A man who wanted to build a house still employed a master craftsman in each trade who in turn employed journeymen and apprentices.'[13] These builders could, with the aid of a measure and a few patterns, quickly work out the details of a house or a terrace with their client. In fact, there was very little they needed to know to build a house. The site, the number of rooms and storeys, and a few other basic dimensions – factors which were accepted as part of a traditional way of building and which could all be discussed with the client without any need for drawings and specifications. The whole building process was part of a common and often local language, a vernacular understood by all. The details of the particular trades were not necessarily common knowledge, but the overall process was accessible and understood, allowing for considerable discussion and individual variation on the basis of known themes.

Patternbooks are an important key to the way in which traditional building methods worked. They were and are kept by workers in all the practical arts and trades, and are full of ideas culled from examples of work seen and admired, workshop recipes, formulas and calculations. From the eighteenth century onwards these patternbooks were augmented by the published designs and drawings which were instrumental in forming public taste. Even in the 1930s magazines were still available with sketches and plans of up-to-date styles in house building which were used extensively by builders. From an earlier period Thomas Chippendale's *The Gentleman and Cabinetmaker's Director* is a famous example of this type of reference book, which carried on the tradition of the patternbook as the personal record kept by an individual worker or by a group of masons. These patternbooks were handed down from generation to generation and treated as valuable collective property by lodges of builders, embodying as they did all kinds of specialised knowledge – an encyclopaedic volume of wisdom and ingenuity gathered together over centuries of practical activity.

Nowadays, we tend to look on builders as labourers with thick hands and thick heads, but to build well a builder must be able to draw, to set out, and to do all the necessary geometry and calculations involved in construction. In the eighteenth century builders were solely responsible for the construction of buildings and architects were really no more than connoisseurs – exterior designers perhaps – arbiters of taste who acted as go-betweens, making up for their clients' lack of taste or time, choosing reliable builders to carry out the work, and perhaps, if like William Kent they had risen from the ranks of the trades, coordinating the actual building work as it was carried out.

I can imagine the excitement with which the latest drawing or engraving of an Italian villa or palace was passed around, and the keenness that was felt to copy the style and set the fashion of the day. As Summerson says: 'To provide a row of houses with a proper Italian character might very well be merely a matter of verbal instructions to a mason or bricklayer together with the loan of an italian engraving or two ...'[14] The building method was given by the trade, and the elements used, arches and pediments, columns and pilasters, were derived either from known classical motifs or from a current patternbook.

A very old patternbook survives in the Bibliothèque National in Paris. Ascribed to Villard d'Honnecourt, it contains a wealth of detailed motifs: plans, drawings of structures such as rib vaults and rose windows, designs for statues and lifting machinery, workshop recipes, and all the assorted and ingenious ideas which were an integral part of medieval building. It has long been thought of as an architect's sketchbook, such is the low esteem given today to the practice of building, but the details are obviously assembled from a variety of sites and speak of a keen interest in the technicalities of building.

> Not only are many of the drawings highly finished to a degree most unlikely in a sketch book, but they are also accompanied by lengthy written explanations. Furthermore there are additions by later hands, at least two in addition to d'Honnecourt himself, and these imply a continuity of use for technical purposes. That the album was in fact a sort of manuscript technical encyclopaedia of the building trades is made more probable by the fact that many documentary references occur in medieval wills and other records to the existence of books of designs in the posession of master craftsmen.[15]

Our word design is closely related to the Italian *disegno* – a drawing – and gives a clue to the origins of design in the collections of drawings which workers kept for reference. The patternbook was a rich source of ideas – a craft textbook – and looked at in this light, d'Honnecourt's so called sketchbook was in fact a patternbook.

Over the years I have collected a number of joinery textbooks – a Victorian book gives me Victorian examples, a modern book modern examples – but all have one thing in common: they do not explain how to do the work. In no sense are they do-it-yourself books. They describe machinery, give sections for windows and doors, discuss wood, methods of setting out, give examples of contemporary practice where it may differ from traditional methods, and explain difficult principles such as curve-on-curve work and louvres for elliptical openings. They contain workshop recipes, notes on glues and stains, advice on safety and safety equipment, and all kinds of other useful information, but they take it for granted that I know how to chop a mortice and shoot an edge true.

Likewise the patternbook contained up-to-date and obscure information for the very reason that these things are difficult to remember. It is, therefore, a practical reference book, meant to be supplemented by workshop patterns, full-size templates for special details, devices for setting out dovetails, angles and so on, for each trade has its own distinct stock of templates and jigs which stand part way between tools and textbook. In fact, there is a whole continuum of such items which should be grouped together under the title of 'tools of the trade', because all of these jigs and patterns are just as indispensable to the successful carrying out of a job as the hand- and machine-tools of the trade: they make the work easier and more accurate.

In Japanese carpentry the tools of the trade are called the *dògu,*

which really has no equivalent in another language but means roughly the 'instruments of the Way [of carpentry]'. *Dògu* is a very old word and perhaps it has not disappeared because even though materials and tools have changed and improved, carpentry methods and the 'Way of Carpentry' have remained basically unchanged for hundreds of years. A certain pride in being an accomplished professional carpenter may also contribute to the reluctance to demote those instruments to tools.[16]

So far I have concentrated on the builders, the workers skilled with tools, templates and patternbook, but I have not yet accounted for the idea of the building and the transformation of that idea into reality. When Chartres cathedral was built, people from miles around fetched stone in every vehicle they could lay their hands on. This event was called the 'miracle' of the carts, because the necessary stone arrived at the site without any apparent planning: a significant event that augured well, and gives a clue to an important feature of medieval buildings. Medieval buildings were nothing like our modern utilitarian containers of space. One of their chief qualities was their symbolism, a fact that easily escapes us in this materialistic period, and so the most important details were those which concerned the symbolic nature of the building. This symbolism, coupled with the religious or geographical importance of the site and the relics to be housed there, would determine the final form of the building, its scale and decoration, and also its construction.

Masons could not work all of this out on their own, and the clerics would have to be consulted in the matter, but what the masons could work out was a structure to embody this symbolic building – a physical form which called on all the resources of their skills, geometry and patterns, and on that pool of ideas, precedents and references which we have come to recognise as the Romanesque and Gothic styles. People who spent their whole working lives building cathedrals and churches would inevitably consider what they were doing in some depth, refine and develop, polish and perfect it, and as a result a synthesis would be arrived at between the symbolic content and the physical form of the building. With much discussion and talk of other buildings and relics, a decision would be made in which many people participated without the modern concept of deadlines and exclusive roles – a synthesis which took its own time and much walking about the site deep in thought and discussion.

A contemporary account tells how, when William of Sens re-built Canterbury cathedral after the disastrous fire of 1174, he realised that the burnt-out choir had to be demolished, but refrained from telling the monks of this immediately, and instead busied himself with all the other details that had to be prepared before building work could begin.

> And when he found that the monks began to be somewhat comforted, he ventured to confess that the damaged pillars ... and all that they supported must be destroyed if the monks wished to have a safe and excellent building. At length they agreed ...[17]

William of Sens was engaged to supervise the rebuilding of Canterbury Cathedral because of his reputation as a mason: as a builder. He left his native France and supervised the works for five years, but met with a serious accident

> preparing with machines for the turning of the great vault, when suddenly the beams broke under his feet, and he fell to the ground, stones and timbers accompanying his fall ... he was rendered helpless alike to himself and for the work, but no other than himself was in the least injured. Against the master only was this vengeance of God or spite of the Devil directed.[18]

This is an intriguing passage because it tells us a great deal about how medieval building work was carried out. Many French and English masons had been consulted concerning the damaged building before William was chosen:

> However, amongst the other workmen there had come a certain William of Sens, a man active and ready, and as a workman most skillful both in wood and stone. Him therefore, they retained on account of his lively genius and good reputation, and dismissed the others.[19]

Why was William, alone of all the workforce, injured in the accident?
The monk Gervase, writing an on-the-spot account of the rebuilding of the cathedral, was in no doubt about who and what William of Sens was: a clever and highly skilled worker. His opinion is borne out by the fact that William met with his accident while carrying out one of the most critical operations in the whole building programme. At a crucial point in the construction of the new choir – with the massive wooden centres set in

place to carry the stones of the main vault, with all the machinery prepared, ready to lift the enormous keystones into place which would, by exerting their own gravitational mass, stabilise the structure – the accident occurred. At this moment the choir would have been scaffolded out on the inside to the top of the capitals, directly below the vault that was to be 'turned' – for curved work is built on wooden centres or turning pieces which support the stones while the mortar sets. And when the crucial operation of setting up the centres and then placing the main stones was being carried out, William of Sens was there alone on top of the scaffold, in all probability guiding a stone into position and shouting instructions down to the winch operators and the monks walking inside the huge winch wheel which raised and lowered the massive blocks of masonry.

This is why he alone was hurt. He was without doubt the most skilled worker on site, and therefore carrying out the crucial operation alone at that critical moment when the scaffold gave way. Not only was his injury justified in a way, because no doubt it was William who checked the scaffolding and approved it before risking his own life on it, but it also shows us that he had mastered the trade in a practical way which meant he was prepared to suffer the consequences of his own mistakes.

When William of Sens fell from the scaffold, he was so badly injured that he remained bedridden and had to hand over the practical supervision of the works 'to a certain ingenious and industrious monk',[20] although he continued to direct operations from his bed. This monk was doubtless a working monk as opposed to a theological scholar, and at this stage the building as a whole must have been sufficiently understandable for someone else to take over from William. He continued to take an overall interest in the building, but it was the new supervisor who would be involved with the actual business of guiding the stones into place, checking levels and heights, and getting his hands dirty. A crucial point to remember is that in this process there was no miniature building to be reproduced, for an entirely different building method was in use, and supervision meant something quite different and distinct from what it means today. A building was understood almost in its entirety as it was commenced, and the structure was implicit in the foundations. In fact one of the closely guarded secrets of masonry was the raising of elevations from plans.[21] Details could be changed, particularly where they did not affect the structure, or where there was a natural break in the process. No doubt considerable changes were made while the work was in progress – all the evidence points in this direction – but essentially the form of the building was decided in its setting out and it is in the setting out that we come to perhaps the most important aspect of all the trades as they once were, and to a certain extent still are, practised.

While writing this account, I am also making and repairing some Victorian sash windows. That is one of the ways in which I earn my living, as a joiner. I have to make one complete window to fit in above a new extension, and will eventually take out the existing frame, raise the sill height and fit a replacement with casements opening outwards, unlike the original sliding sashes. All the proportions of the original will be changed, but at the same time I must try to make my new window 'fitting' for the building, as well as a good fit in it, and the way I come to terms with this problem is by setting out the work full size on a board. In the trade this very special working drawing is called a rod, and it is the process of setting out a rod that I would like to describe because it is basic to an understanding of traditional building methods, and hence of the medieval trades.

In a joinery workshop it is often the best worker, or chargehand, who sets out the work. Sometimes individual joiners set out their own work; it is all a question of skill and experience, and the ways in which particular shops are organised. I can set out a complicated door or a curve-on-curve sash window from a few site dimensions and a sketch with any other relevant details on it; I can decide what timber to use and what sections to prepare for the various parts; all this is part of the trade 'know how'. The specific dimensions I need from the site – the actual dimensions – are marked directly on a lath or template, because measurements are easy to get wrong, in just the same way that the actual dimensions were brought back like relics from the church of the Holy Sepulchre in Jerusalem, preserved as knots in a length of cord.

Similarly, once the physical dimensions of a cathedral had been agreed, its form – vaults and ribs, pillars and arches – decided, and the patterns for its columns and capitals made, then a series of pegs would be set in the ground, squared up with a knotted line, using principles established by Pythagoras. Levels would then be established, and the symbolic geometry laid out full size on the site, in a process binding together the traditions of classical and medieval building, the geometry of Euclid and Pythagoras with the theology of the Christian mystics, and uniting the two elements of a mason's training, the practical and the spiritual in one unified practice.

After this the foundations were dug, and the remainder of the work was determined by the methods of the trades, in the sense that the building could be understood by any of the workers on the site. It was for this reason that the supervisor or coordinator of the works would have to be a practical person first and foremost. The whole operation was defined by the trades as practised: it was not contained in a set of drawings and specifications, but arose organically out of the coming together of trade methods and the building's inherent symbolic content.

What a new coordinator would have to take over was a process, rather than an object, and it was for this very reason that William of Sens could not properly supervise the remaining works from his bed. The process required a physical involvement of which he was no longer capable, and this was why he chose a less experienced worker monk as his successor. A more experienced mason, someone who could claim to be a chief builder in their own right, would not have needed William's advice and assistance, and so by bringing in a less experienced replacement William ensured his continuing involvement in the building as mentor.

But I was talking about drawing, about setting out – a central skill without which very little of what we call art and craft can take place. Nowadays we tend to look on drawing as an art activity, a mysterious and irreducible performance, but nothing could be further from the truth: we are surrounded by drawing. Drawing is one of the most fundamental ways in which we conceptualise and is central to a large number of skills. We mistakenly tend to isolate artistic drawing as something special and different, and at the same time see all other forms of drawing as mechanical and therefore uncreative. This explains much bad drawing, for people inevitably imitate the appearance of artistic drawing whilst overlooking its content: producing drawings which are bad because they have no real purpose. An engineer cannot get away with a bad drawing because technical drawing has to perform a very specific descriptive purpose. So, until recently, did artists' drawings, which were rarely signed or regarded as works of art.

Michelangelo was, if anything, ashamed of his drawings. In his thinking the 'art' stage of creative production, which he identified with the careful procedure of making studies, sketches and working drawings, was the menial and mundane side of the business, whereas true merit was for him displayed in the rapid and apparently effortless execution of a painting or sculpture. Robert Clements quotes Count Lodovico, a contemporary of Michelangelo:

> whence one may say that that art is true art which does not appear to be art; nor should one strive for any other art except to conceal art; for if that striving is discovered, this fact takes away all the credit from a man and makes him little esteemed.[22]

Clements adds:

> Since Michelangelo hoped to live up to his theory of creating without evident effort and so wished to minimise the 'Art-phase' even as a preliminary, shortly before his death he burned many of his drawings, sketches and cartoons ... so that no one might realise to what great pains he had gone and the ways he had exerted his genius to give no other appearance than that of perfection.[23]

This is an intriguing idea which reveals that Michelangelo had a significantly different understanding of what art is from our own. Ideas about art were in transition, and so were the meanings of words like art. To Michelangelo, art was synonymous with hard work, for he put an enormous amount of effort into the preparatory stages of his work. His drawings, sketches and layouts were not accomplished with ease, and yet the impression he was anxious to leave to the world was precisely the opposite. The whole issue is difficult to grasp until we realise that the word art did not have the same narrowly defined meaning it has now. If we substitute the words skill, work and labour for art, the passage quoted above begins to make sense: 'work is truly skilful which does not appear to be laboured ... the skill is to conceal labour.'

Michelangelo was actually working within the context of a tradition in which art was synonymous with skilled work and, as any skilled worker knows, the preparatory stages of any job of work are of fundamental importance and determine absolutely the quality of the finished product. But Michelangelo's work was appreciated and commissioned by a class of patrons which was already attached to the idea of genius: individuals who advertised their social status by surrounding themselves with works of 'genius'. Here we can see the very beginning of that separation of art from work with which we are now so familiar.

Drawing is central to most skilled work, but we tend to undervalue it by calling it technical drawing: drawing of a mechanical kind. My father is an engraver and die-sinker, like his father; they made rollers for embossing the paper doilies you see in cake shops and restaurants, shaping elaborate, intricate designs which take months of work to cut into steel rollers by hand. Roses and leaves, lace and cut-work, all figure as recurrent motifs, and my father would design most of these on the dinner table at home in the evenings, working from a collection of old lace and a patternbook of designs and examples he and my grandfather had made over the years. As a boy, if I was bored I was told to draw – anything, everything – the cat, the budgie ... 'Look', my father would say, 'this is how you draw a leaf. See how the ribs go. And here's how to do a rose ... Now if I hold up two mirrors to this little section of the design the reflections make up the rest of the circle.' And so my winter evenings were spent learning to draw in an environment in which drawing was taken for granted and learned by example.

I have always regarded drawing as a primary way of exploring the world, the very 'nitty-gritty' of making and doing. Similarly drawings are part of a working process and should not be regarded as precious: kept for reference perhaps, but not for posterity. When I was at school my art teacher taught me this fact very simply. He decided one day that our drawing needed improving – it was no doubt becoming too precious – and so he gave us each a pile of paper and a plaster cast to draw. Mine was the right foot of Michelangelo's David! We were told to cover every sheet with drawings in pencil, crayon, ink – anything we could think of – and that we must finish the exercise before we could move on to anything more interesting. There seemed to be an endless pile of sheets in front of me, and the task took days. I tried pencil, then pen and ink. I washed and coloured, became first bored then enthusiastic, and then bored again. Depressed, elated and just plain fed up when it all became a pointless slog. At last I finished and took my drawings triumphantly to the teacher's desk. To my horror, he simply checked to see that I had not cheated and then tossed them into the bin.

Only later did I begin to understand that lesson. While I was drawing he had criticised, praised, advised and suggested, and I had forgotten all about 'art' in my desire to complete the exercise and get on with some painting. But, to stop myself from becoming bored, I had been forced to take an interest in what I was doing, to explore and experiment, and to look very hard at that foot. All those drawings were no more than an exercise, and I a schoolboy trying to learn, but if I had started out with the intention of making 'art' then I would inevitably have failed, for art is in a way a by-product, something arrived at indirectly, a quality rather than an end product.

If we think of art as a by-product then it gives us a way of coming to grips with all manner of problems. Anyone who sets out to produce art, or architecture, or literature for that matter, is liable to fail simply by concentrating on the wrong things. They will be looking and thinking in the culturally-defined ways which our current use of the word 'art' evokes, and so will deny themselves access to authentic experience. For example: if I draw a friend sitting by a window with the intention of producing art – a beautiful drawing – I may well end up with something that looks like art and yet miss the most striking aspects of my sitter. If, on the other hand, I am surprised and excited by the effect of light streaming in through the window, across a face and a patterned chair, and concentrate on trying to render that effect, the result may well be art. Look hard at some of the most famous drawings and you cannot fail to see how much effort went into them, how much concentration, how much of what Michelangelo recognised as work and tried so hard to disguise.

What my art teacher had achieved was the Zen trick of jerking the mind out of its routines. The art I had produced was made without the intention of making art, and the value was in the realisation, the making real, of what I had seen, not in the end product.

Making a window has two distinct, but not separate, stages, the one conceptual, if you like, when the window is described exactly, and the other practical, when that particular window and no other is made. The conceptual part of the process is as much a part of the trade of joinery as is the craft of the productive part. The setting out is a rehearsal for the making, and a good joiner combines the two. In reality each part informs the other and the art is a by-product of the constant interplay between these two components of skill. In joinery the first stage, the setting out, is often done by a setter out, with the mechanical part of the job left to the joiner, but to my mind that cuts out all the art from the beginning. When the setting out is discussed, as is often the case with more complicated jobs, the process becomes entirely different: a synthesis of two slightly divergent approaches which allows a greater variety of factors to be considered and in which each participant can learn from the other. It has long been the proud boast of skilled workers that they are always ready to learn from someone else, but unfortunately the modern goals of productivity and profit encourage a division of labour for the sake of efficiency, and result in a reduction of skill which removes more subtle considerations – the art – from the process.

Back to my window. First I take a board which is long enough to get the full height of the window and some surrounding details on to it, then I set out the hole in the wall where the window is to fit. Measurements taken on site on another rod or lath are transferred to my board, and from these I can mark out the brickwork reveals of the building – exactly where the window must fit. From the very start I am considering the relationship between the window and the building which will eventually contain it. A mistake at this point could easily mean that my window might foul the brickwork when opened, or that it might turn out to be impossible to clean. Similarly, when medieval masons set out a window, I have no doubt that their first consideration was the relationship between that particular window and the building in which it was to fit.[24] Since my window has to fit in reveals – that is to say, that it has to fit behind the outer skin of bricks which will shelter it from the weather – the next consideration will have to be how I am going to fill up the space behind these reveals.

I decide to make a box frame, rather like the original window, and so I draw this on my rod – four-and-a-half inches deep – plus the thickness of the plaster to fetch it up flush to the internal face of the wall so that the joint can be neatly covered with an architrave. Next I must decide how far into the opening the frame has to project if the casements are to open and close without binding on the brickwork. At the same time I must allow a rebate for the casements to close into – one that will keep the weather out – and to accommodate for this the front lining of my box will need to be longer than the back. Those parts of the frame the casements close into will also have to be thick enough to allow for the rebate, and so I thicken them by half an inch, the traditional depth of such a rebate.

All this time I am thinking in brick and timber sizes. Timber comes from the timber yard in specific dimensions which are reduced by planing and, not wanting to waste time, energy or wood, I must design my window in terms of available wood sizes. This is all further complicated by the fact that the house was built in feet and inches and timber now comes in metric sizes. If I want to see a true match between the old and the new, then I must work in the same units: a subtle difference at first sight that can result in a very obvious awkwardness if ignored, so I have to translate backwards and forwards from metric to imperial. I decide to make the casements ex 50 x 50mm softwood (which would once have been two inches square), this will finish at 44mm, or just under an inch-and-three-quarters. If I am careful enough, I can finish at a full inch-and-three-quarters, bumping my dimensions up from metric to imperial to make the windows look right. I know that the rebate will have to be a half-inch by one-and-three-quarters, 12 x 44mm in metric, so having allowed clearances for closing and opening the casements I can now draw in the rebate.

Where the front and back linings meet the rebated face of the box, I decide to run a quirk bead, a traditional round bead worked on the edge of the wood, which will conceal the joint and match the remaining windows in the house. On I work, fitting the window to the building and then the casements to the window frame, constantly thinking about proportions and how the wood is likely to work. I make an allowance for fitting the casements and choose a moulding to run around them, a delicate ovolo, out of the cutters I have. I decide on the depth of the bottom rail, very important in terms of proportion and balance, and think about how the catch and bolts will fit, and how the two casements should meet as there is no central mullion.

I know the glazing rebate will be 9 x 12mm, and that the rebate to the meeting styles will be 12mm by half their thickness, 22mm. I draw this on the rod, and then decide to run a quirk bead down the meeting styles to balance the joint, which is of necessity off centre. Because I am working with the real and final dimensions, I can offer my cutters up to the drawing to see what these beads and mouldings will look like, and so am dealing with real quantities all the time. Finally, I mark in all the check grooves and throats that will stop capillary action, and form drips on the underside of sills to ensure that my window will keep the rain out. Some patient checking, when I go over all these decisions again, and the job is finished.

I have designed the window, not in miniature or in the abstract, where bricks and walls are square and flat, but exactly to size, taking into account the actual building into which it will fit, the materials I will make it from and how they will change when they are worked on, as well as what timber is available of a suitable quality and price. When I make the window, I will offer up pieces of wood to my rod, marking off dimensions and checking sections and joints, all those subtle pieces of information which are never contained in a scale drawing, even a full size architect's detail. My drawing is derived from the real building, and the measurements on it are real, it is not dimensioned and I never take a measurement off in either inches or millimeters but always by marking directly from the rod on to the actual piece of timber I shall machine. Further, my drawing is based on the traditional working methods of a trade which developed them over centuries; it is real in a sense that the architect's drawing can never be.

When I come to making the window, I shall be concerned with the wood itself, with working, shaping, jointing, fitting and, because I have solved all the problems of how the window will look and work in the setting out, I am now free to concentrate on the making. Without any distractions, I will be able to choose my wood carefully for its purpose. But that is another job, and before moving on I would like to look a little more closely at this setting out process.

The crucial point to notice is that apart from a few given dimensions, which are derived from the building itself, the whole procedure, all the information I needed to design and lay out my window, came from experience, from within that body of knowledge which *is* the trade of joinery. That rod could have been drawn by someone else, or the window designed in miniature by an architect, but then the process would have been divided, and not, as we have seen, complete and integrated. Indeed I would go so far as to say that joinery is a complete process; anything less is not joinery at all, but a shallow parody of a traditional way of mediating between ourselves and the natural world.

We can say exactly the same of medieval building and traditional Japanese house construction and, I suspect, of virtually every traditional and vernacular building process; from this we can draw two conclusions. First, it is our own categories, like art and architecture, that fail to match the reality of what has existed throughout long periods of history. Secondly, this failure to match idea with reality has hindered our understanding of other periods to such an extent that we are left with little on which to base a critical reassessment of our own period. So certain are we of our own cultural superiority that we are incapable of recognising quite simple facts which could help us expand our understanding of the world through a recognition of the essentially creative function of work.

3
The Pig

Having argued for the existence of a skill-based, practical understanding of the world – an era of domestic and localised production prior to the division of labour into handwork and brainwork – I try, in this chapter, to show how vestiges of that culture still persist in some rural areas of Britain.

We kept a pig in Lincolnshire. A great gobbling, snuffling, snorting grunter of a pig. Although his masculinity was little more than a memory, we called him Robert, and he lived at the back of the house. We built him a big pen out of old doors and corrugated iron, with a shelter in one corner covered with straw bales to keep him warm. He was very clean, not like the pigs we have all been told about, and pissed and shat in one corner of his run. The only time he wallowed in shit was when we had visitors and then, as if driven by some irresistible inner compulsion, he would roll in the muck corner and present himself in a glorious haze of pig smell. The kids loved Robert. Zim would go and talk to him when he felt miserable, and Kenny from across the common used to climb in his pen and have a friendly wrestle whenever he came visiting. In the summer Robert got very sunburnt and we were terrified that he might die of the dreaded 'purples', but he survived. In the autumn, when the ground turned muddy and soft with the rain, he dug great holes and pits and rolled around in the mud. We grew very fond of Robert, and he grew very fat.

Our neighbours at the other end of Love Lane were extremely interested in Robert, especially when Fran went to see them to find out how to salt him down. Mr and Mrs Horrey were retired farmers and had lived in that part of Lincolnshire all their lives. They had never, they told us, spent a night out of their own bed in all their married life, and had retired to Commonside where Mrs Horrey had been born and brought up. She used to play the piano in the now empty and decaying chapel just across the field, but that was before the tractors and huge fields, when trees touched over Love Lane and the common was busy and populated.

Built on a promontory of higher land marking the edge of the marshes, where the Romans had harvested salt long before the Fens were drained, our house had been the old smithy and meeting place, where news was exchanged and slow conversations followed their own pace while the smith worked and the horses waited patiently, snorting white breath on still, cold fen mornings. The new smithy was on the main road two miles away, but the smith's son was wary of taking over from his ageing father. He made more money driving a tractor. Soon there would be no smith at Wrangle. A tradition that went back to Weland Smith and Daedalus was hanging on the edge of extinction.

In the three years since we had arrived, the farmhouse opposite the chapel had been pulled down to make way for the new breed of monster tractors, and in the winter, when the fields were ploughed, odd patches of pink brick rubble would drag up to the surface, marking the site of a cottage or barn. In the summer, lines of a different green in the cornfields traced the pattern of old ditches filled in and hedges grubbed up years ago. A silent testimony. The earth itself and a few old people remembering.

One day at the level crossing on the way up to New Leake, waiting for the Skegness train to hoot past full of holidaymakers from Sheffield and Nottingham, the old man who opened and shut the gates with an arthritic limp told me of the tree-lined roads, wild flowers, hedges and banks which were there when, as a boy, he walked to school up the drove. Hard to reconcile with the bleak modern landscape where machines plough and spray to the very edge of the road and hardly a tree can be seen.

From our kitchen window we could see acre after monotonous acre of field, brown in winter, green in spring, a uniform yellow-brown in autumn, and in the middle of those hundreds and hundreds of acres one solitary ash growing in a ditch, left only because it did not hamper the machines, or perhaps because someone could not bring themselves to root out the very last tree in all that desert. Beyond the tree was a clear view to the wood at Friskney three miles away, bristling up from the flat fields like a stubbly mole on an old woman's chin.

Although the Fen landscape was so changed, stripped of all variety and ploughed into one huge roofless factory, the people were not, especially the older Commonsiders. The youngsters had their motor-bikes and pop-music, but the older generation still lived at a slower rhythm, and talked of days before the big machines came. Days when Mr Horrey's father would go off to reap for a week or more with his scythe and whetstone, sleeping under the hedge through the short, hot August nights, and Art' Horrey, not yet a young man – what the East Anglians call an old boy – had to carry out cider and food to the field. In so many respects the fens are still as remote as parts of rural Wales, yet modern technology stalks the fields. Small planes spray by the hundred acres, and still, amid all this, Ray Bee, Mr Horrey's nephew, walks his few acres of wheat, roguing wild oats by hand.

When their son was married the Horreys fattened a pig for a wedding present. To them, a fat pig hanging in the shed as bacon and ham is true security, a perfect start to married life, food for the winter and a future to face with confidence. Their son and daughter-in-law however, being more modern in outlook, had no interest in fat pigs. They would rather have a young porker ready jointed in the freezer than what they thought of as 'mouldy old fat bacon' hanging in the shed.

Mr Horrey still ate fat bacon – no lean, just the fat – with tomatoes for his breakfast. They were hurt, the Horreys. Their way of life and a carefully-preserved set of values had been rejected, just as the trees and hedges had been grubbed up. And they felt a small but cutting personal slight. So when Fran knocked at their door, notebook in hand, to find out how to salt down our pig they were overjoyed. Later they told us how they had laughed at the idea that anyone could write it down in a little book and reckon they knew how to do it, but they willingly lent us their salting tub, and Fran went off with her shopping list to buy salt and other essentials.

We were holier-than-thou with our friends, who simply had their pigs butchered for the freezer. We were going to process the pig ourselves. Robert had been loved and cared for and, although we were taking him to the butcher to be slaughtered, we were going to do all the rest properly – no alienation for us. The pig's death would be justified, and so on. How naive we were, and how right of the Horreys to laugh at us and our notebooks.

Coming back from the butchers, we felt like traitors. The butcher had poked and shouted at our poor pig, and Robert had refused to leave the van until we coaxed him out. Later in the day, Fran went down to collect the intestines which she was going to clean and use for sausage skins, and came back with a great slimy, smelly bag full of them. But she set to and scraped them as she had been told, putting the fresh cleaned intestines in salt water. They were now all white and transparent, a bowl full of condoms ... round one to us.

That evening we went down to the butcher's on the main road, a little late really as they reckoned to close at five. It was dark. 'Oh, its OK', I shouted to Fran above the noise of the engine, 'they haven't cleared the window yet.' There was meat everywhere. In the window, on the slab, on the counter. Gradually the scale of what lay before us sank in. All that meat, all 239 pounds of dead flesh, was ours, and we had to salt it down, make sausages, ham, bacon, lard, brawn and haslet out of it before it went off!

We piled the meat up in wire baskets which the butcher lent us and packed it into the back of our faithful old Moggey van. When we got back home, we carried the baskets into the kitchen and sat looking at our meat mountain. We had already decided that half of the pig was going into the freezer for pork – thank goodness – and so were able to pack some of it into bags which we labelled according to what was in them – 'Spare Ribs: 3lb. 2oz.' – and started to fill up the freezer. At least that gave us some way of coming to terms with what we had taken on. When that was done there was still an enormous quantity of meat left, but the weather was cold and so, covering what remained with tea-towels, we went to bed. The next day, I was going to work and Fran was going to sort the pig out; at least that was the theory. What actually happened was quite different.

Fran went down the lane to the Horreys to ask for a little help in identifying all the different cuts of meat, and I decided to stay behind for a while to see what happened. The truth was that we were both overwhelmed by the scale of the whole operation and didn't know where to start. The Horreys, of course, were all ready, only waiting to be asked, but not prepared to arrive uninvited. They fetched big knives and saws, a huge black iron pot for rendering the lard, basins and plates, and a big old Spong mincer with a sausage-making attachment. Mr Horrey had taken the precaution of sharpening the cutters in the mincer the night before – just in case!

I never got to work that day. In fact it took all four of us the entire morning to get the pig 'put away' as the Horreys said. Art Horrey was painfully crippled with arthritis in both hips, but he spent all morning on his feet, cutting and sawing, filleting the meat for sausages, preparing the bacon joints and trimming the hams. There was a strict sequence of events and a specific division of labour. Mr and Mrs Horrey scrubbed their hands like two surgeons at the sink, and set to. Mr Horrey showed me his part of the job and Mrs Horrey showed Fran hers. The meat had to be boned, trimmed and sorted for whatever purpose it was to serve. Special pieces were set aside for wrapping the haslets in, others for sausage meat. The bacon joints were neatly cut into recognisable shapes, the flitches carefully filleted, and the ham bone cut back flush to the meat. The Horreys called the bacon flitch a 'flick', and every piece had its own local dialect name, most of which have been forgotten. They took great care to speak plainly to us, without too much dialect, but even so the phrasing and the rhythm of their speech always sounded strange.

Fran and Mrs Horrey diced up all the off-cuts of meat and fat, and soon filled a large basin with neat little cubes ready for the sausage making. The best lard, 'caul lard', was also chopped up into cubes and rendered down in the large pot, which had been set to warm on the Raeburn. It had to be melted very slowly and the small cubes stirred regularly. The second best lard was set aside for separate rendering in the oven. Suddenly it was mid-day and we were only just starting the sausages.

First the meat and fat were minced together with a bag of sage leaves which Mrs Horrey had picked fresh for the purpose that morning, probably before we got up. A small handful of fat, a small handful of lean, and four or five sage leaves were pressed into the mincer. The ritual was repeated until all the meat was used up. Next, the minced meat was mixed with a little brown bread to bind it, and seasoned well until, raw though it was, it tasted good. Then back into the mincer which now had a funnel on the front with sausage skins rolled on to it like stockings.

We took it in turn to crank and feed the mincer, and out came the sausagemeat into the skins. Mr Horrey showed Fran how to link them, and suddenly there were basins full of them, just like an old-fashioned butcher shop; and sausage meat over for the haslets.

When Fran had visited the Horreys with her notebook they had asked wickedly, 'And how will you get the meat into the skins?'

'Oh I suppose I'll just poke it in', said Fran hopefully.

After she had gone, they roared with laughter. Now at last we heard the full story and they laughed again.

Salting the bacon and ham was the last task, the one that had taxed my imagination the most, and yet it was the easiest. We simply dumped the meat – two hams, a shoulder, two forelegs and a flick – into the massive salting tub, which looked like a lidless coffin, rubbed a little saltpetre around the ham bone and patted salt over the exposed meat until it was just covered in a thin layer. Not buried, as I had imagined, in a sort of garden fete lucky-dip tub, but neatly patted all over with salt.

'Is that really it?' I asked.

'Oh yes', they chorused, 'that's it!'

It had taken the four of us about five hours to process half our pig, which by local tradition was a small one, and we had not even killed it ourselves. How long would it take to get a really big fat pig 'put away' I wondered. A very long, hard day, and plenty of help from the neighbours ...

The Horreys were pleased. We were the only people to kill a pig on the common that year, in the traditional way that is, and they had passed on some of their knowledge to a younger generation. We were happy to have done it, particularly Fran, who was the driving force behind it all, and to have got to know our shy neighbours so well in the process.

We had learned a great deal: not simply how to preserve a pig in the local, traditional manner, but also how that tradition had survived and how fragile it was, how it was intimately bound up with a local culture, and how close to extinction that culture was. Mr and Mrs Horrey had passed on a real inheritance, not to their children, but to us, the outsiders. We have moved now, and as the older inhabitants of the Common die out so do the old skills. Bert, who had helped his wife Barbara run the youth club since their courting days, remembered his apprenticeship, making salting tubs and milking stools. He started telling me once how to make a salting tub, but even though I am a joiner by trade I could not follow him because I had nothing to refer to, no picture in my head. I had never seen a salting tub before the Horreys fetched theirs out of the shed.

Old Mr Ellis the woodturner in Boston still made washing dollies, though they were destined for the antique trade now, and even had the wooden valves for waterpumps hanging on his wall, clacks I think they were called. He could talk all day if there was anyone to listen to him, marvellous stories of buying standing trees in Revesby and Shire woods, cutting them and fetching them out with horse, cart, and just an old boy to help. Stories of terrible accidents and injuries. But most of all he talked of how things were done. We have lost sight of the self-sufficient age he was born into, when most things were made where they were needed, fashioned by hand from available materials. A time when capability was all, and real knowledge was knowing how. He would stand amongst his piles of squared timber blanks – blanks for warming pan handles, blanks for chair legs – talking of all manner of things until you backed out of the workshop. Nothing could stop him once he had started. He must have been eighty when I last saw him and was still working then. When he dies, so much will die with him that it terrifies me to think of it. Our university libraries are stacked high with books, but I often wonder just how much knowledge they contain. After all, there cannot be many people left who can make a water pump from a tree. No book will ever tell us how to do that – not properly![1]

I have met many old men like Mr Ellis, who are so clever and yet so little valued by the world at large. My father, who has been an engraver and die-sinker all his life, is one of these men, and probably gave me an early respect for skill. Tommy Atkins the woodturner from Swineshead, with his irrepressible grin and arthritic joints, can still make a fool of any self-styled artist-woodturner. Tommy has spent his life turning bowls and banisters, and I don't think he could produce a bad piece of work if he tried, but he has no idea of what his skill is worth and will doubtless die, as he has lived, in cheerful poverty. Over the years I have come to love and admire these unassuming, gentle people: all so generous with themselves and their knowledge, living very much for the doing of what they do so well.

On Wrangle Common it was traditional to make 'pig fries' out of all those parts of the pig which could not be preserved, and plates of these pig fries were taken around to the neighbours. Everyone joined in the celebrations, for killing a pig was a social event, and one more family was secure in the knowledge that there was meat hanging in the larder and in the shed, perhaps enough for a year or more.

We talked a lot about the pig, Fran and I, and especially about the work involved, all the skill we had been so ignorant of, how arrogant we were to have raised and slaughtered this huge animal convinced that, armed with a couple of books on self-sufficiency, we could salt it down and make our sausages, or that one of us could while the other went off and did a day's work! At first the division of labour which the Horreys had been so strict about conflicted with our ideas of equality. Such things were a bad idea generally we thought, but, faced with the enormousness of the whole process and the efficiency with which the Horreys carried it out, we could not brush it aside as part of the old sexist role-playing which would have to make way for a more modern egalitarianism.

Fran put her finger on it when she said that the context in which it all made sense was when two people lived together. There was simply too much to do to the pig. One person alone could not manage it, and any arbitrary division of labour would mean that a couple might or might not know how to deal with their pig. Not a good basis for survival in the inhospitable Fens. The sexual division of labour here meant that each couple shared all the knowledge necessary for survival, for preserving their food against times of shortage. Within the convention of marriage, there was in this instance an equality of knowledge. Each part was indispensable, and preserved within an oral tradition of skills for survival which were passed on by example, by helping with the task and by talking, as old Mr Ellis did, about how things are done.

Certainly the Horreys gave equal importance to their separate tasks, and worked as a close team. Perhaps, having failed to appreciate the scale of our task, we would now have to revise our simplistic ideas about the division of labour along gender lines. We had been blind to the size of the job because, having learned to learn from books, our first thought was to refer to our self-sufficiency manuals. Since it took us only half-an-hour or so to read about it, we had dismissed it as a simple task. From then on, we took our manuals with a pinch of salt!

I learned to make pastry standing on a stool in the kitchen while my mother baked – doing it with her – and I can still make good pastry. Recipe books tell you the quantities, what to do and how hot the oven should be, but they never tell you *how* to do it, what pastry dough should feel like. My mother filled that gap in the cookery books for me, and now I read them for pleasure, but practical learning has to come out of doing: traditions like this have to be seen and experienced to grasp how deep they are and how much knowledge is involved. Just as the cookery book can never replace the experience of making pastry with someone who understands it, so reading about a traditional skill can never replace the experience of doing it, talking about it, and watching it done well.

I think it is significant that the division of labour into narrowly defined routines, which is the basis of modern factory production, has its origins in the late middle ages, and was clearly established in the sweatshops of the seventeenth and eighteenth centuries, well before the steam powered machines of the Industrial Revolution began to take over from hand work. That division and specialisation of labour was based on the values of a rising merchant class which placed profit first. The traditional skills look back to an earlier culture with different, less worldly values. Very little of the value systems inherent in those skills have survived mechanisation, not because this is impossible – I don't think it is – but because modern production continues to operate on the assumption that profit is all.

We talk about a feeling for wood or stone, which the machine does not have, a flair for cooking, the green fingers of the gardener and so on, all ideas which suggest something far removed from the subject-object relationships of our autocratic technologies. We dispense drugs and fertilisers by pushing buttons, and become increasingly distanced from the materials and techniques we use. But a physical sensitivity to the materials of a trade or craft is central to skill itself, distinguishing the traditional, sympathetic arts from dispassionate modern manufacturing processes, and it is this very sensitivity, a sensitivity which has taken generations to develop, that we are on the verge of losing.

By reviving this traditional use of the word art we can recognise that art and skill are, or were, identical. Cookery is an art, we still call it that, so is fishing, and from this point of view all the sensitive, symbiotic, traditional skills are arts. The joiner is an artist in wood. We still use expressions like this, and the ideas lie dormant in our language. Nor is this sort of art a strange, inscrutable activity, but the very way in which skills are used and practised, with art and artistry. Indeed, until very recently it would have been perfectly correct to describe as arts all those skills learned by apprenticeship and by practice.

As a definition, this usage is much closer to the original meaning of the word art. People who make things well are artists, and vice versa, and it is this doing and making things well, with care and concern for how and why they are made, that brings real quality into everyday life. As a definition, it accounts for both the 'fine' and the 'useful' arts equally well, for both are ways of doing things well, and therefore of bringing quality into everyday life, a quality which takes us beyond material wealth, and gives us a truer way of measuring value than a market economy does.

Unfortunately, the institutions which surround art in our society all seem to be intent on distancing it from the simple everyday origins that might make it more accessible and understandable. Art is no longer a quality experienced by the maker and the user; instead, vested in objects, it has become a saleable commodity and, while artists are not specifically to blame for this development, they have been a party to it. As a consequence, the quality that was once part of everyday life has been separated, institutionalised and now hangs on a wall behind a security system.

The division of labour the Horreys practised was not alienating at all, it was art in this traditional sense. They both worked together at a task which placed them firmly in the world of real things – animals, food, survival – where a pig's death had some meaning, and the carcass was treated with some reverence. In our aggressively 'modern' society it is not just the trades, traditionally a man's preserve, which have been debased, but woman's work too. The whole field of cooking, the preserving and preparing of food, now occupies at best a stall at the village fête, or worse still a supermarket cold shelf, and the art of midwifery is considered as little more than a superstition. These traditional skills, along with other complex arts and trades, are now on the wrong side of a dividing line determined by class and gender. And in this crucial sense the male dominated, middle-class and essentially elitist professions have supplanted the practical, egalitarian, working-class arts.

We lose these traditional arts and skills at our peril, not because they are part of our history and culture – that alone would be bad enough – but because being skilful in a traditional sense is irreplaceable. Having a feeling and respect for materials and resources, and an understanding of the processes involved in making products that last a lifetime is central to a whole set of values and an outlook on life which is near extinction. As we lose touch with the spirit of the traditional arts, we also lose touch with the values that went with them and, ceasing to care, accept shoddy substitutes for a reality we have all but forgotten.

In the Fens, a sexual division of labour still exists which bears the traces of a cooperative life that ensured survival in a harsh world, and it is difficult to say with any certainty that the division was essentially unequal. The skills both sexes practised, nurtured and passed on to their children were mutually dependent and overlapping, and without the essential female and male combination survival was uncertain, if not impossible.

The inroads that mass production and consumerism have made into this originally self-reliant interdependence are of course enormous. When Fran was working at the local factory and the half-shaft of our old van started knocking, she asked around for the nearest scrap yard, drove off and dismantled one from another van in her lunch hour – a demonstration of self-reliance that became a legend around the factory. The young girls at the youth club would pose in their high heels while the boys showed off on their motor-bikes, yet the old world was never that far away. By the time those same girls were twenty, they would be joining the gangs of bulb and potato pickers, backs bent double in the field for eight or ten hours a day – work that would defeat many a smug young city lad. Contemporary gender stereotypes are essentially urban, as are reactions against them. It is only in the remoter pockets of rural life that we can still find evidence of a rich tradition of skilled manual work, and the few remaining traces of a valid division of those skills between the sexes.

I doubt if anyone killed a pig in the traditional way on Wrangle Common this year, or last year, but I bought some 'Lincolnshire' sausages at the supermarket the other day and, although I enjoyed them, they still confirmed what the Horreys said when we made our first bangers: 'Once you've tasted these you'll never want a shop one again!' They were right.

4
Assumptions

In this chapter I look at the way in which the separation between hand and brain becomes yet another unquestioned assumption, shaping not only the way we think about the world, but our actual perception of it. Art, I suggest, is essentially an innovative activity and a very effective vehicle for challenging assumptions that all too often confine us within a narrow and rigid interpretation of the world.

Behind our tendency to conform, to behave and think in similar ways, is the need to have a common agreement about the nature of the world we live in. A baby's earliest learning is overwhelmingly concerned with acquiring a series of assumptions about the world: assumptions which become the world for that child, and assure it that it inhabits the same world as the other people around it.

In this sense, culture can be described as an interpretation of the world specific to a particular group, religion, race or people. Languages fall into the same category of systems of social agreement governing ways of accounting for the world, and ways of describing it. We are conscious of how different people from other parts of the world are, and are either intrigued and often charmed by these differences, or deeply suspicious and intolerant. Foreigners are made the butt of jokes everywhere in a ritual through which we caricature differences to reinforce the idea that our own culture is sensible, normal or superior.

This is not surprising since we think and communicate through the medium of languages which embody specific and very different cultural concepts: languages which circumscribe experience in very definite ways. In the same way that languages may be described as agreements about the world, scientific theories and religious beliefs are culturally determined agreements rather than revealed truths, just as madness is not so much a mental failure as the refusal or inability to match a personal construction of the world with society's norm.

Our accounts of the world may be conservative or revolutionary; they may conceal as much if not more of the world than they illuminate, and are at best selective in terms of what we accept as information, and what we reject as nonsense. Our senses provide us with more than enough information, and so, as we go about our daily business, we have to be selective, deciding what is important to us and what is not. These decisions are ultimately enshrined in our mental processes and, unseen, become the very medium of experience: a cultural programming which often masks information that could be useful to us.

Perception is the key. I tried to explain this to Ivan, my ten-year-old son, one night when we were walking with the dog along Wrangle Bank. Past the old chapel, where Mrs Horrey used to play the piano, empty and neglected now, with ivy growing through the roof and the door swinging open – a black hole in the darkness. Sometimes it scared me and I had to run past it with the dog close by. Other times, like that night, it was simply there. Perhaps it was the strong moonlight, perhaps because Ivan was with me, but that night I was not scared. We saw three satellites in twenty minutes or so, wobbling across the sky, and shooting stars. In the Fens the sky dominates the landscape. On a clear night it surrounds you like a calm sea. Remembering the time when we watched the moon through Ivan's telescope and how, as we turned almost imperceptibly to follow it, we found ourselves locked momentarily into the planetary ballet.

That night Ivan and I were talking about computers making mistakes, mistakes that seem ridiculous to us because human beings operate in such a radically different way from computers. To us an electricity bill for £10,000 is absurd, to a computer it isn't. A computer is a machine of extraordinary calculating power and yet is profoundly simple in its 'mental processes'. It can make the most absurd mistakes. I tried to explain how this is all to do with different ways of thinking. Computers think in straight lines – yes/no, on/off – they obey instructions and are utterly dependent on them. A dog, however, reacts directly to sensory information. One flicker on the horizon and our lurcher is all a-tremble, ears pricked and eyes wide, deciding whether that movement is a hare or a bird. Human beings react above all to change, constantly comparing things with how they expect them to be.

I walk down the same street every day, but hardly ever see it. Often enough I cannot even recall walking down it unless something memorable happens; normally I can be home without realising it. What I do have, however, is a picture in my head which I hold up to the world, a picture called 'my street', or 'my mum', or 'Wrangle Bank'. As long as the world conforms to that picture, as long as it fits the pattern, I fail to notice it. But as soon as something changes, I know all about it and, like the dog, am suddenly alert. In the dark, images are ill-defined and distorted, nothing really fits the pattern, the world is no longer certain and I am easily scared.

Not that I immediately see what is different. I start with a feeling that something is not as it should be, that something no longer makes sense, no longer fits the pattern. From this feeling of unease, I gradually piece together what it is that is unexpected. To me the outrageous telephone bill is so odd that after the first wave of fear has passed I recognise it as a preposterous error. What impresses me is the magnitude of the error and the implications of it. In my panic, I reach for the telephone to protest about it, but to the machine the bill is just an error, one of a predictable percentage of errors, a bored keyboard operator, a momentary hiccough in the electrical supply, a minute variation in temperature, a decimal point in the wrong place. The magnitude is immaterial.

Computers don't think like us at all. They are much better at calculating, but unlikely to differentiate between errors. Knowing none of the middle ground in which we operate, only yes/no alternatives – positive and negative, correct and incorrect – computers make far fewer mathematical errors than we do, but human beings tend to sift their major mistakes because they look and feel wrong. In other words, we have an idea of what the answer should be. Were the bill only a few pence out, I would never notice, a few pounds lower than it should be and I would probably turn off my critical faculties with a sigh of relief because it was so small. Computers make gross errors without noticing them because they lack the filtering process so important to us, but this sifting function is not always a help, it can also become a blockage, a way of avoiding the truth, as responsible for what I don't see as it is for what I do.

An animal like a dog lives in a very different world from mine. Lots of smells and not much colour, a world of much greater texture I suppose, and one in which time is almost tangible, a tantalising gradient of smells. I can never perceive as our dog does, and so will never know that world at first hand, but I can be sure that it exists, and that the worlds we inhabit, the dog, Ivan and I, are very different: separate yet co-existent realities.

In my world I name things. I hold up my filters, noticing only what fails to fit my preconceptions. As long as I can hold back that classifying, naming urge, I can see the world in a different light, but often, as I concentrate on not concentrating, the old blinkers snap back into place. By playing games that involve looking in categories I can trick my brain into reversing the process. I am very interested in Victorian and Georgian building techniques, in all of traditional building practice in fact, and as I walk along the road I concentrate on certain details, like joggles for instance – the little decorative horns that appear on some sash windows – or rubbed brickarches, or the old coal-hole covers that were often decorated with elaborate patterns and builder's names. If I do this, the sifting process begins to work in my favour and suddenly I notice a wealth of detail which had previously been buried under the blanket ideas of 'house' and 'street'.

Artistic perception is often talked about but rarely accounted for. Shrouded in mystery, it is used almost as a justification for the status of art and artists, but to me it is above all the very simple ability to see freshly, to preserve a momentary experience before the sifting processes of conventional thought cut us off from contact with the world around us. Far from being a miraculous talent, it is something common to us all, part of a lost childhood, and a skill we need to rediscover. The idea that art and creativity are to do with making contact with the real world, with the source of our perceptions, is not new. Many artists have been acutely conscious of the fact that creativity is dependent on our keeping in close touch with that source, constantly reevaluating sense experience and redefining our relationship with nature and the dominant ideas of the culture we live in. But this feeling about the value and relevance of creativity has been losing ground to the idea that style is all. Originality often means little more than novelty, and art has delved into an obscurity which has itself been elevated to the status of art.

The same confidence trick that fills our galleries with vacuous rubbish also denies working people anything but a menial role in life. Skilled workers have been demoted from artist to artisan by a trick of language, and from artisan to machine-minder by the demands of production and profit which increasingly shape social relations. It is easy to point to the loss of quality in our buildings and environment which is a direct result of the impatient imperative of productivity, and it is also easy to point to other tricks of language which compound this state of affairs. But it is harder to see how these changes affect the quality of life in the negative way they do. This requires a reassessment of the value judgements that seep into our thinking, along with words like professional, words which reinforce the social divide separating artist and artisan.

Professionalism is fraught with contradictions. On the one hand it establishes a class distinction between those who play sport for the love of it and those who play it for money; on the other hand it suggests a class distinction operating in the opposite direction when applied to work. The despised professional of the sportsfield becomes the respected professional of the office. A significant shift of meaning from gentlemen and players to professionals and tradesmen. The professionals were often workers in the trades who aspired to being gentlemen – groups of people professing themselves to be solicitors, architects, accountants, estate agents. Emphasis has moved away from the act of doing, of practising a calling, to the fact of belonging to a select group. In this way the professions have effectively become the closed shops which so many professionals abhor on the factory floor. Of course, professional bodies try to maintain standards by setting exams and overseeing training, but they also close ranks to protect their members against criticism which is often justified, resisting change and monopolising the exercise of important skills, just as the trade guilds did some 500 years ago with the practical skills.

This rift has done particular damage to the building industry. Not only is it extremely wasteful of resources and skills but, in elevating one set of skills above the rest, we have lost the art of producing good buildings to such an extent that often all we are left with is good-looking buildings which do not fulfil their functions. The feeling of mutual respect between designer and maker, the sense of team effort and joint achievement that made these two roles virtually inseparable until well into the nineteenth century, has been replaced with the idea that a technology manipulated by a design elite can solve all problems at a distance.

In my pocket dictionary, technology is defined as the 'systematic knowledge of industrial arts', yet the idea of technology as something new denies the validity of traditional technologies. Bricklaying is without a doubt an industrial art; apprenticeship is a way of acquiring this system of knowledge through practice. The skilled bricklayer, with a systematic knowledge of the industrial art of bricklaying, is without doubt a technologist in these terms, but the bricklayer is also an artist practising an important craft without which our civilisation would not exist. In the bricklayer's humble trade, all these important concepts come together: art, craft, trade, technology – words which account for ways in which we work on and shape the world around us – active practical concepts that are threatened by the idea that technology has to be modern to be relevant. Some modern technologies may seem to be superior to traditional techniques, but this can never be more than a value judgement. It should be open to reassessment and revision as circumstances change. Traditional techniques are increasingly recognised as effective by a Western science that cannot understand them in its own terms.

It would be folly to discard something because it seems of little use at this particular moment. Our traditional technologies have stood the test of time, mistakes have been understood and problems solved and, although there is always room for real progress, to sacrifice skills which had their origins in the Middle Ages and before would be short-sighted. Not only do our new technologies regularly go wrong but, more ominously, they affect the world on such a large scale that their failures (or the mere possibility of failure in, say, atomic reactors or computer-controlled weapons systems) are potentially disastrous.

Modern industrial technology is by now so firmly established, so dominant and so certain of itself, that to question it seems presumptuous. Yet, at the extremes of scientific experimentation and investigation, certainty breaks down and the future looks far less secure than it does in the mainstream of consumerism.

To recognise reality as uncertain, and with that the multitude of possible, alternative constructs of the world, is of course in line with most Eastern philosophies and religions, which assert that the world is illusory: a collective illusion constructed and held together by our collective belief in it. The same can be said of the West for, propelled by its own internal momentum, our collective world illusion is self-sustaining and constantly reconstructed in a present which replicates past assumptions.

In certain Eastern philosophies, to recognise reality as illusion is to free ourselves from the hold that the material world has on us. A creative approach to reality can tell us much more than this; it can suggest that the world does not have to be as it appears to be, that it could be very different and that, far from being helpless in the face of fate, we can and do shape and construct the world ourselves. The Dadaists and Surrealists took a revolutionary approach to the social conventions that make up 'reality'. Dada has now been accommodated as art history and tamed in the process, but when the Dadaists originated their ideas, they had hoped to make artistic experience itself a means of breaking down conventional reality – to make a revolutionary project of art which would change the material world by changing our perception of it.

As fashion and marketing become global, so the significance of cultural diversity is diminished until the mysterious orient becomes no more than a package tour away, something else to be consumed rather than experienced. Whereas we might once have subjected ourselves to the magic and strangeness of other cultures, these cultures are now little more than the objects of our tourism. We photograph them to prove we have been there, stay in hotels which replicate our lifestyles, and protect us from the shock of being exposed to any values other than our own. Wrapped in cultural cling-film we, as tourists, are invulnerable to the adventure of travel because we have divested the rest of the world of its ability to challenge the validity of our own way of life.

It is intriguing to realise that the original tourists were members of the English upper classes who sought out the classical remains of Italy. The Grand Tour of the eighteenth century was in fact a grand consumption of culture, an orgy of 'art' which in theory completed the education of a social elite. Inevitably, once art and culture had been abstracted and separated out from daily life, they became commodities to be consumed. In the eighteenth century, the consumption of culture conferred status in the way that a Rolls-Royce does today, but this consumption of art and culture marked the beginning of a change in attitudes. Western culture seemed to rise above others, which in turn became part of its empire, up for grabs and on display, like trophies, in our museums.

Such assumptions permeate our thinking. The first tourists, even though they were perhaps humbled by the classical world, still assumed a superiority over it. They owned it, and by extension made it part of their status. Classical sculpture and ruined temples in the garden, menageries of exotic beasts, black slaves, beautiful mistresses, all are effectively the same: possessions, objects – power expressed as status. But once enshrined as cultural concepts, such ideas come to dominate our expectations of the world just as our interpretations of the world become social determinants.

In order to belong, we have to conform to established patterns of thought and behaviour. The need for an agreement about the nature of the world easily becomes the insistent demand that we accept certain conventions as reality itself – group-think – and our institutions thrive on this type of collective non-thinking. Army, public school, church, university, professions: all demand agreement, resist controversy, frequently subject people to elaborate initiation rituals, and ruthlessly subordinate individuality to the group's version of reality. Not a *folie à deux*, but a collective madness where, in the land of the blind, it is the sighted who are handicapped.

The acknowledged great post-Renaissance artists like Goya, Blake and Rembrandt were innovative not in terms of style or technique, even though their works may be clearly marked with an individual style, but precisely because they broke through the constraints of traditions and conventions of seeing which dominated the particular societies in which they lived. We still respond to the clarity of their vision for the very reason that it does not fit within accepted canons of art and beauty. Blake showed us the chaos beneath the veneer of order. Rembrandt painted old age as ugly in conventional terms, but showed us something more about it, which transcends the fear and withdrawal old age often inspires in us. Goya depicted not the glory of war, but its horrors.

Rembrandt was a professional artist in the sense that he made his living by painting. But he also managed to make a vocation out of his livelihood. In his later years this same vocation threatened his livelihood, for as his vision grew increasingly unfashionable he persisted in pursuing it at the expense of his career. More interested in preserving and protecting his perception of the world than in promoting his social status, Rembrandt slipped into disfavour.

What happened to Rembrandt is deeply ironic and reveals a central hypocrisy in our attitude towards art and artists, for by protecting a clarity of vision the artist is almost inevitably obliged to risk social rejection. Starvation in a garret or suicide have become part of the myth of artistic self-sacrifice. Both are acceptable in exchange for posthumous fame, for a secular sainthood, but the transition from rejection to acceptance is so total, and the money values involved so immense, that the artist's vision no longer exists in any context where it might pose a threat to the social values it challenges. In the Middle Ages, Lazarus sat at the rich man's gate for ever, carved on the front of the church, an inescapable image set at the very hub of village life, and the message was clear. Now the starving peasants who inspired Van Gogh are framed in gold in a museum where today's tourists ogle at the fabulous wealth these paintings represent.

Perhaps it is a mistake to try to reassess our assumptions about the world through the medium of art. Perhaps 'art' is too far divorced from daily life and too easily institutionalised, too easily perverted into a way of absorbing and neutralising penetrating vision. Perhaps art galleries, museums and art history are too successful in obscuring and defusing the meaning of art. Perhaps the transformation of radical vision into ultimate consumer object which art galleries achieve is so complete that any struggle against twentieth-century values will have to take place elsewhere. Somewhere where it is less easily recognised and contained.

5
It's not Normal

In this chapter, I try to suggest that refusing to conform is more than just another way of reacting against a world which is not necessarily of our choosing. I examine ways in which non-conformity can be a liberating and positive act of choice, and look at the role that creativity plays in shaping our perception and understanding of the world. In a changing world, our ability to adapt and grow, to develop alternative strategies and avoid the determinism and stagnation inherent in a narrow and conventional interpretation of what life has to offer, is an essential tool for survival. Creativity, mysticism, eccentricity and revolution are all routes to an alternative view of the world, with their own claims to truth and discovery.

The woman behind the counter of the village shop wore a permanently sanctimonious expression on her face. Not an uplifted look, but an expression of unadulterated self-righteousness: a perfect confidence in her own view of the world, passing silent moral judgement on her customers as they shuffled their way around the rows of tins and socks and sanitary towels. At first I thought this censure was reserved for us, for the newcomers alone. Only later did I discover that I was wrong; the shop was the village court where she sat, both judge and jury, at her cash register, the bench.

As we left the shop she leant across the counter to confide in her lone customer:

'Did you see that?'

'Yes I did! ... He was wearing earrings ...'

'And she was wearing boots!' They exchanged meaningful looks, then chanted in concert: 'It's not normal!'

No doubt they realised they were overheard. It is just possible they might not have noticed the other customer in the shop but he was one of the locals, and passing judgement was part of their public duty. Anyone who dissented was suspect as far as they were concerned.

Ray had lived in the village all his life, working on a local farm and concealing the fact that he was different – not normal – an outsider in his private life and a misfit in public. Constantly feeling the cutting edge of a social conformism which alienated him absolutely from the rest of the village, Ray savoured his other identity – his homosexuality – his non-conformity, and with it that feeling of otherness which had led him to his own, independent set of values and attitudes. Thrown constantly into relief by the rigid social behaviour of the rest of the locals, Ray's identity was defined by this distinction. It was in this sense sufficient for him. He had never moved, run off to London or abroad to escape the narrow world of the village. Instead, he lived an internal life which opposed the values and morals of the village with a constancy and consistency which gave him a role in life, an identity and a reason for being.

The words 'not normal', whispered across the counter, rang in Ray's ears, and he decided to introduce himself to us at the earliest opportunity. We took an instant liking to him, and he soon came to treat our house as a haven from normality, where he could stop off, relax and be his other, intimate self. Talk, play jazz records, smoke Russian cigarettes and gossip about the neighbourhood. Scandal, to Ray, was a way of pulling the mask of respectability off all those locals who so steadfastly clung to it, and whose censure forced him to wear a different mask. In our house Ray was normal, and so were we. Together we defined a space in which abnormality was normal and dissent an affirmation of other ways of being.

We often referred to the incident at the village shop; it gave us a lever to prise away at the question of what normality really is. Surrounded as we were by enforced conformity, this question was important to us. We were all productive members of society, earning our own livings, and doing our bit for the community – Fran and I, for example, helped out at the local youth club. In other words there was no disputing the fact that we were all useful and contributing members of society, yet who we were, and the way we thought and felt, was somehow threatening and had to be censured. The feeling of censure, that forbidding conformity looked for by the world at large, was so strong and in a way such a threat to us that we censored ourselves, modifying our behaviour and hiding our identity to make everyday life possible. From the village's point of view, we were always outrageous, but there is no doubt that we felt constrained in our public lives.

I had known that feeling before, particularly as an adolescent when the demands of family and school pressed heavily on my growing sense of identity. As I became aware of a world outside family and school, films and books played an important role in introducing me to new ideas that had the power to reduce the world I felt trapped in to nothing more than one among many ways of experiencing life. As a result, I began to feel not simply different, but pleased and grateful that I was so.

Not conforming gave me an identity, but it also gave me a critical approach to the world. I was a dissident at an early age. Wars and injustice were not necessary, any more than the petty authority and tyranny of school discipline and the pat morality of church and adults in general. These realisations, together with an instinctive distrust of the aspirations that school and parents sought to encourage in me, made me doubt and question. A sense of the deep-seated insanity, the absurdities and pettiness lurking behind the mundanity of daily life, all pushed me into seeking a precious if precarious personal sanity in a sceptical attitude towards convention. I took refuge in the art room at school, which gave me an escape route to a world of alternative ideas I needed to preserve my own identity.

I took to art like a duck to water. I had been encouraged to draw from an early age, and found art not just engrossing, but a justification for the way I felt about the world. I was different – not normal – an artist, I thought! At least that was how I gave some substance to a new found sense of my identity. Our art master was a real human being compared with the other teachers. He talked to us endlessly about films, books and the theatre; his previous career as a make-up artist in the West End had given him a fund of anecdotes which broadened our horizons immensely.

Normality, for me, became synonymous with all the dull, boring, uncreative people and activities I sought to escape. It was creativity that made the world a dynamic and interesting place to live in, and imagination became the most powerful of all weapons, protecting me from what I regarded as the stultifying conformity of most of my contemporaries.

I can now see that agreed conventions are necessary for all social animals, and serve to hold groups together so that everyone can participate or at least understand what is going on. These conventions underlie the feelings of morality and justice which can, and should, give rise to a cooperative, collective society. Without a common world to live in we would all be isolated – autistic – locked in the competition prescribed for us by a narrow view of evolution. The truth is that we are not in constant competition. We cooperate instinctively, and a certain conformity of behaviour and feeling is without doubt an evolutionary advantage. But rigid conformity is also an evolutionary dead end, for if we cannot change and develop we are certainly doomed. Creativity, the ability and urge to change the pattern, must always struggle with conformity: knowing people like Ray was a constant reminder of this.

A normality which is also creative and positive is quite possible on a small scale, but on the larger scale of school/village/society, normality seems to work in the opposite direction, stifling dissent, innovation and creativity. Nor is this narrowing conformity restricted to conservative social groupings; it happens among radicals just as readily, stifling the ability to question and challenge assumptions which we so desperately need if we are to remain a viable species. Our ability to survive depends directly on our ability to change and rethink our assumptions.

Authority is a key problem. Small social groups are often self-organising and egalitarian, but in larger groups authority easily becomes repressive. Experience and group consensus can supply an authority which exacts and depends on mutual respect, yet allows individuals to flourish. In this form, authority becomes a moral expression of the group as a whole, but once handed down as received wisdom, it becomes repressive. Suppression of the outsider and a blanket insistence on conformity crush the humanising, inventive and creative elements in society.

In Boston, the nearby town, there was one pub where the outsiders all drank. Rockers, dropouts, anarchists and gays all congregated there because as separate little cliques they could never have taken over a pub in the same way. In a small market town they had to pool resources to create a space in which to be themselves, a space where 'not normal' was the rule.

The constant pressure to conform drives many people away from the country, away from the villages and suburbs into the big towns and cities, adding to the ghetto quality of life there, and sucking the rest of the country dry of its potential for change and development. Instead of spreading through society as a benign and leavening influence, this abnormal element is ostracised in the cities by the oppressiveness of conventionality. In city ghettos groups set up their own conventions, often just as stultifying, and so our world becomes progressively less diverse. Variety, diversity and non-conformity are edged out of the mainstream of life, just as the trees and hedges have been grubbed up from the Lincolnshire landscape to make way for the tractors of progress.

In my early teens I went through that period of rebellion which is common to most of us as I began to find myself in an environment not of my choosing. History and chance, not choice, had placed me in my family, in the suburbs of London, and I had made no conscious decision about these crucial events. Suddenly everything became questionable. The concrete world of the suburbs was a desert in which I could find little to excite me, and my parents and their attitudes were part of a conspiracy which stifled energy and enthusiasm. I argued at home, and found my house, my family and the streets claustrophobic. But, just when I felt hopelessly overwhelmed by the oppressive atmosphere of what had, until then, been a happy childhood, I discovered an escape route.

I took to climbing out of my bedroom window at night and, with a bag or rucksack to look the part, walking the half a mile or so down to the dual carriageway to thumb a lift to Oxford. The moment I reached the road my mood changed (it still does when I travel on my own). Trapped feelings dropped away. I had no idea who would pick me up, or where I was going, and my naivete let me in for some hair-raising experiences, but the risks were acceptable because my life became deliciously precarious and unpredictable.

At some time during the night, I had to turn round and head back home to normality and the next day at school. At that moment the sense of freedom vanished, even though I still felt charged by the experience. In those days however, I had no choice but to go back home, climb in through the bedroom window and pretend to my parents that nothing had happened. But what those secret escapades did was allow me to discover myself as a person in my own right: different and unique.

I remember one November night very clearly. There was a bright moon, with just a few clouds passing slowly. I had walked up to the dual carriageway and stood, as I usually did, under an old oak tree. The oak stood on its own and had spread unhindered like those carefully-placed trees on large estates. That night, instead of getting on with the business of thumbing a lift and starting the adventure, I looked up into the tree and was gradually drawn into the wonder of the just-bare branches swaying in the breeze, the changing patterns of light as the clouds drifted by. I was looking at something mysterious and marvellous which absorbed all my attention. I was mesmerised by the living silhouette. Tree against sky gave way to a sea of changing pattern. Yet within this pattern there was growth and life. The outstretched twigs, the space in and around them, the intermingling of solid and air, the contrast of light and dark ... the moon plunged behind a cloud, the night air felt chill, and there I was standing by the road. In the distance a policeman pedalled towards me on his bike. I ducked under a wire fence and slipped off across the waste ground until he had passed.

Creative activity is rooted in forms of experience which can only be described as unconventional. In our developed society, art and ritual are no longer integral to everyday life. The tree no longer harbours a goddess, and the woodsprites have fled before the tractor and the chainsaw. Our lives have become so dominated by material posessions, and our dealings with the raw facts of nature so estranged by the machinery of modern industry, that we have to find mystery away from the natural world. Magic and mystery become the province of art and it is the artist who deals with the mystery of the tree, trying to *re*present it to the rest of us by drawing on a special form of experience which is no longer normal. Yet this form of experience is a crucial ability to reinterpret the world around us, to grow, change and redefine ourselves and our environment. It is a special and specific adaptation which our species has developed as a way of coming to terms with a changing world; a means of reassessing constantly how we feel about the world and how we come to know and understand it.

The artist looks with the eyes of a child. In this sense artistic perception is a form of regression in which childhood perception and experience are carried into adult life, enabling us to make creative advances, and so evolve. It appears to me, however, that the same form of experience is at the root of both creativity and the desire for cultural and social change which is such a constant theme in modern history. In the modern world, these abilities, which I suspect are common to us all, are normally eradicated by cultural influences – the discipline of family, school and work – and all those other pressures which encourage socialised role-playing rather than creative individuality.

In *Reason and Violence* (Laing and Cooper), a particular form of childhood experience is described: 'A child experiences himself [sic], sometimes in a stupefying moment of revelation, as existing a certain identity. He is himself and no other ... but his destiny is in his own hands and nowhere else.' They call such experiences: 'germinal realisations from which philosophical totalisations develop',[1] moments which start us thinking outside the framework of convention. Such experiences suggest an essential and intimate self which exists before and outside social roles and acquired behavioural and perceptual patterns, prompting artists to assert an individuality at variance with the conventional norm.

Here is a mode of experience which lies at the root of creative activity, and both artistic expression and paralysing self doubt arise from this ability to question conventional experience. If the germinal experience is repeated often enough, and reinforced sufficiently to hold back the corrosive effects of socialised experience, then the artist may approach madness, but at least is convinced of the validity of a personal vision. If the experience is tenuous, it is easily contradicted by the pressures of convention, and self doubt creeps in. At this vulnerable moment of doubt, the accepted role of artist is wheeled in to control creativity by giving or withholding acceptance. The acknowledged artist is drawn back into the fold of acceptability, restraining what Jean Genet has called 'the development from poetic genius to revolutionary enterprise'.

In his introduction to *Soledad Brother: The Prison Letters of George Jackson*, Genet says:

> If we accept this idea, that the revolutionary enterprise of a man or of a people originates in their poetic genius, or, more precisely, that this enterprise is the inevitable conclusion of poetic genius, we must reject nothing of what makes poetic exaltation possible. If certain details of this work seem immoral to you, it is because the work as a whole denies your morality, because poetry contains both the possibility of a revolutionary morality and what appears to contradict it.
>
> Finally, every young American black who writes is trying to find himself [sic] and test himself and sometimes, at the very centre of his being, in his own heart, discovers a white man he must annihilate.[2]

What Genet refers to as poetic genius is, I believe, both that which inspires art – the drive to explore and create – and creative activity itself. Creativity in this sense is not necessarily confined to making objects –

although the materialistic society we live in only recognises art as somehow embodied in specific objects or performances, texts or scores – but must inevitably turn its attention to the world as a whole. When this happens, creativity becomes identical with the possibility of change. The world as given ceases to be absolute; it becomes contingent, and the individual escapes from the prison of determinism.

So Genet talks of young American blacks trying to find themselves and discovering at the centre of their being a white value system they must annihilate. Artistic consciousness gives us the capacity to objectify the identity society has forced upon us, and makes us aware of the conditions which have shaped that identity. It was this awareness of the possibility of a self-determined identity that allowed George Jackson to experience his oppression in its terrifying completeness, and that enabled him to begin to transcend it by building a secure identity to refute the values of the society which had imprisoned him. It was the similarities between his contest with a society that invalidated him as a person and Genet's own struggle against a buttressed value system and morality that made Genet – the homosexual thief – so sensitive to Jackson's achievement and its implications.

Somewhere behind books and paintings and poetry lie experiences which can be equated with my confrontation with the tree, or Jackson's confrontation with himself. And behind all our artists and poets there lies a vision of the world which generates in them the will to become something of their own choosing. The institutions of art are concerned in the main with either acknowledging and containing that experience, or with rejecting it as invalid; with conferring success and failure on people who depend on them for recognition. Validity is given only to a small minority of artists, most of whom conform at some level to obtain that recognition. The rest, and their experiences, are rejected by a self-appointed art establishment and an investment-conscious art market.

Very subtle mechanisms conspire to render ineffectual the devastating vision of a print by Kollwitz or Goya by forcing it to fight for our attention in the dehumanised arena of the art gallery which, like television, reduces everything to a bland sameness. Extraordinary experience is contained in a world of 'shush' and 'do not touch', a world of intellectual posturing where most spectators are so unsure of their own ability to judge or appreciate that they turn to what they can understand without effort – sea-horses and green ladies. In the galleries of the world, the naked vision of the artist is obscured beneath layers of not-expecting-to-understand and trying-to-pretend-comprehension, behind faked orgasms and intellectual one-upmanship. What better way to censor any attack on accepted value systems than to place it on public view, so that anyone who might respond is intimidated before entering the gallery, and to enmesh artists in a web of self-deceit which compromises their output from the start?

So artists end up trying to please a system which is intent both on exploiting and on absorbing their extraordinariness. If such elaborate devices exist to alienate people from the messages of art, art must pose a serious threat to the status quo. To see why we will have to look more closely at the nature of artistic perception itself.

As I see it, one of the primary functions of art is to extend experience, to discover significance in the most ordinary things, revealing them as marvellous and extraordinary, beautiful and horrifying, naked and terrible. In a world where nothing is finally absolute, nothing is true or real, and everything is dependent on how we perceive it, artists give us access to their own ways of seeing the world. We can judge how successful they are by how convincing their worlds are, whether they can engage and hold our attention, whether they can, for a moment or two, allow us to see with their eyes and catch a glimpse of a reality through which we can escape the limitations of our own particular experience. As André Breton said: 'It is impossible for me to consider a picture as anything but a window, in which my first interest is to know what it looks out on.'[3]

There is a startling colour photograph of the *Herren Hausen* in Hanover taken by David Hockney. I first saw it as a postcard – in fact, I have never seen it in any other form. Trees and grass in strong light and shade on a bright summer day. The pattern is so regular, strong and abstract that for a long time I took it for a painting, assuming that Hockney had made his own adjustments to achieve the effect he wanted. Only when I looked at it closely did I realise that the detail was inconsistent with a Hockney painting and recognised it as a photograph. The magic of the picture was that David Hockney had managed to see both the scene and the abstract pattern so clearly that he could photograph the two together and draw our attention to the inherent tension between object and pattern. It was not a scene changed into some ideal arrangement of his fancy, but an actuality that existed for anyone who had eyes to see. It is this ability to see the interaction of colours and shapes in mundane situations, to sense the upsurge of growth in the form of a plant, to see the colour in shadows, to see property as theft, to respond directly and immediately to sense-data and ideas, to associate freely and imaginatively, to experience the world in an extensive way, which is the real hall-mark of artistic perception.

In his book, *The Ghost in the Machine*,[4] Arthur Koestler proposed a view of evolution via regression – *reculer pour mieux sauter* – describing childhood as a more flexible and not necessarily inferior or incomplete state relative to adulthood. He stressed the close links between childhood play, curiosity and creativity, as the source of evolutionary change and development. I think that if we are prepared to look beyond the sensory aspects of creativity we can recognise this evolutionary function equally well in social and cultural terms. By retaining a youthful flexibility, we can acquire the ability to examine more than sensory experience with freshness: we can look sharply and critically at social and cultural custom and so introduce essential change into the system.

Throughout the last ten years or so, Maurice Claydon has been a reference point and an inspiration to me. Like so many of those wonderful people who give their life a personal significance outside conventionality, Maurice is, by most accounts, mad. Like Ray, he is by no stretch of the imagination normal but, unlike Ray, Maurice's abnormality is not an extramural affair. In his particular search for self-expression he has reversed all the common conventions of eccentricity. The textbook English eccentric is wealthy; indeed that special eccentricity considered so typically English has always been fostered by wealth and privilege. Maurice is poor, and always has been: a bad start for a budding eccentric.

Born an epileptic, his fits were treated by the doctors of the day with strong drugs – phenobarbitone among others – and at one point lobotomy was considered as a remedy. Gradually, over the years, the drugs took their toll, eroding his nerve-endings and leaving him partially crippled and unable to work at any conventional job. A side-effect of his condition, and of the treatments prescribed by his doctors, was to shift his perception, his consciousness, a few degrees out of phase with 'normality'. As a consequence, for years Maurice inhabited a world which vied with conventional reality. Coming to terms with the relativity of these two realities – recognising that the world can never be a fixed and unchanging substance – gave him a profound if unarticulated insight into the impermanence and uncertainties of life.

It was only in the 1960s and 1970s, when people began to experiment with drug consciousness, that the seemingly unshakeable and immutable fact of the world around us, the world as we perceive it, began to be doubted on any scale. Most of us take perception for granted, accepting what is no more than a conglomeration of assumptions and commonsense rules of thumb as real, given and unchangeable fact. Not Maurice. He knew those feelings were no trick of the imagination, to be dismissed as an aberration, but an insight into another world, a rent in the fabric of normality which he passed through as easily as if it were a door or a side turning off the street; a thoroughly accessible reality which most of us only glimpse and dismiss as fantasy.

Maurice has lived in Oxford Road, Cambridge, all his life. His father was a seafarer of some sort, but I never discovered much about him, except what I could imagine from odd facts and the remnants of a disused heating system he installed based on some nautical principle of hydraulic engineering – great hefty pipes passing through walls and along the insides of cupboards. A dark-browed, Victorian man with a puritanical streak, great knotty forearms and dirty fingernails, I concluded. I never heard Maurice talk of his mother.

An early career as a petty criminal gradually developed its own romantic overtones, and thoughts of freedom were followed swiftly by the realisation that money and freedom are intimately connected. Eccentricity is not so much the exclusive vice of the rich as the expression of a common urge which few of us can afford to indulge. Maurice was no doubt charged with that desire to choose freely, to absorb himself in the minutiae of whatever interested him, without being forced to bend to the demands the world of economic necessity made on him. His criminality was a rejection of conventional roles which were unacceptable to his sense of himself, and homosexuality, especially in the late 1940s, added a further dimension to his rejection of normality.

The way out of this pecuniary dilemma was obvious, and Maurice took it. Unfortunately the bank robbery went absurdly wrong. Maurice was arrested a few days later. In the Scrubs he spent as much time as possible in the woodwork shop. The experience gained there, combined with a period working for a small Essex builder, supplied him with the skills on which he later built his own personal escape route from the non-future that society had prescribed for him. Like all true originals – Jean Genet, Facteur Cheval – Maurice Claydon challenged the authority of convention at the point where it most successfully denies us an identity of our own choosing by victimising and pouring scorn on those it labels misfits.

I first got to know Maurice when I worked with him re-roofing part of the windmill at Histon. That was really my introduction to house carpentry, and to Maurice as more than an interesting friend who talked deep into the night about all manner of subjects. Working alongside someone gives you a very different idea of what they are like, you see them in action, a whole person. But Maurice was always a wonderful talker, and as we worked I played the role of humble apprentice while Maurice talked. His hands and feet were too weak for him to have worked safely on a building site, but with someone to help – foot a ladder, steady a rafter and so on – the job moved along well.

He intrigued me with a romance of wood and carpentry. We found an old coin, a George III penny, under one of the rafters, and he explained that in the days when the windmill was built, or last renovated, builders would lodge a coin or keepsake somewhere as a mute testimony to their presence, a lucky token. We kept the penny and left a half-crown in its place in honour of the tradition.

Although Maurice had no academic training at all, and was not adept at gleaning information from books and libraries, he had a feeling for his subject – for the trade – that allowed him to fill the gaps in his knowledge with intuition. In a sense, he had again avoided the necessity of work, making more than a pleasure of it. In his hands work became an adventure, a voyage of discovery, but the years in jail had also taught him the parsimony and self-control essential to anyone determined to survive in the face of adversity.

He fed himself and the kids on a tiny budget. Even the dog's bones from the butcher fed the family first – the dog had second pick. A piece of scrag-end of neck rolled around some stuffing was a joint for Sunday. This capacity for survival meant that his disability pension provided for the family's needs. Work was no longer a compulsion, but Maurice chose to work when the state said he was incapable of it, and he chose to work for pleasure and interest.

Not black economy work, done for the money, but work undertaken for its own sake, the sun on your back and blood pumping through muscles, for the deep pleasure of an interesting job well done and a fine building put back in good order. This was almost payment enough. Add the complexity of favours owed and exchanged which are built up around the activities we choose to undertake for friends and neighbours, and Maurice had tapped a rich vein of pleasure by refusing to be useless, as society said he was.

The truth is that Maurice thought more than he worked, but then in a sense thinking and working are intimately connected, and although he had made some sort of philosophical breakthrough, he had not yet taken his ideas to their logical conclusion. Achieving this involved the house.

Somehow or other Maurice had inherited the family house, or rather a share in it and the right to live there. The house, which was all he had, and all he was ever likely to have, became central to his personal quest for freedom. Inspired and supported by Anne – who lives with him and has encouraged and cajoled him through a long and seemingly never-ending commitment – Maurice turned the rebuilding of the house into a major project. Fate and medical ineptitude may have conspired to deny him the ability to work in any conventionally acceptable way, but Maurice turned all that on its head, and found, in choosing to work, a real freedom which denied the constraints of work as we know it. By defining his own terms and refusing everyday logic, he discovered a valid activity outside or, more correctly, despite the barriers fate had thrown up around him. Instead of giving up and giving in, Maurice made the world acknowledge him by refusing to accept that it had cast him aside. In that refusal he discovered a new dimension, with its own geometry, running parallel to our everyday world.

I suppose one of the things that pushed him in this direction was the knowledge that the house was all he would ever really own. With no money, only free time and a developing skill at his disposal, he set about total renovation of the house. Instead of repairing and modernising it – thus sentencing it to the fate that will befall every other house in Oxford Road as the cowboy builders take their toll – Maurice decided on a more radical but sympathetic solution. He would re-design the house and rebuild it as he thought it ought to be, learning from the process of dismantling and reviving, not an architecture of appearance but a tradition of building. So Maurice entered into a relationship with this house which turned out to be long and obsessive.

This new courtship opened up other worlds. He had learned to survive on site, as most of us do in the building trades – how to get by, how to make a decent bonus or complete a second fix in time – in short how to reduce the quality of his work to an acceptable minimum and churn it out in quantity. But now he was free of all such constraints and could choose how the work was to be done. This marked the beginning of a consuming interest, a passion for traditional building methods. Maurice structured his obsession as a quest, an attempt to understand traditional building methods not in theory but in practice – by doing. Turning convention on its head yet again, he set out to rediscover the complexity of traditional skills.

There was so much to be learned. Not by reading books, although Maurice read voraciously, but by taking the past apart, by rediscovering the forgotten details of an earlier practice. Bricks had to be salvaged, so Maurice scoured the demolition yards of Cambridge and the local villages. Timber came from skips and building yards, old joists seasoned over decades and boards from abandoned warehouse floors. All his joinery was made from scratch out of hard-won, cadged and stolen materials. Douglas fir for the doors and windows, redwood for the carpentry, all carefully de-nailed and checked for rot and worm.

Having established that particular mouldings and other details of workmanship give buildings of different periods their own special feel and style, Maurice decided against simply choosing some moulding planes from his growing collection. He was committed to understanding the whole process from beginning to end and, as the decorative details were an essential part of that whole, his mouldings had to be designed from scratch. He made his own planes for the purpose, which was no easy operation because, to ensure an even, clean cut, the cutting iron in a moulding plane is often set at a complex angle. In practice the actual profile of the iron is not the same as the moulding it cuts, and a complicated piece of geometrical projection is required to work out the true shape of the iron from the proposed cross-section of the moulding.

Maurice faced up to this baptism of fire with enthusiasm. It led him into a whole new world of geometry – the very geometry that sustained the medieval cathedrals – and in exploring it he began to understand and appreciate a tradition dating back to the Middle Ages and beyond. More than a tradition, a complete culture carried across Europe by groups of itinerant practitioners: the medieval masons.

Building for love came alive under Maurice's hands, and although his damaged nerve ends robbed him of the certainty that is the hallmark of traditional craftsmanship – that deftness of touch and sureness of action in which hand, tool and brain function in complete harmony – his work still carried with it a force and conviction that is totally lacking in our modern parody of traditional work.

Bricks and bonding (how the bricks fit together) was another area he explored. Special bricks from the demolition yards, bonding details noted on walks through town and carefully recorded, all were gradually incorporated into this personal shrine to the past. None of this was done with the pedantry of archaeological reconstruction, but with a joy and exuberance which gave it an immediacy museums can never capture. He moved from one problem to another, giving each element of the building a sense of individuality. Each challenge was met and resolved, not necessarily with complete success, but always with a sense of intrigue and adventure.

Window posts were wreathed in carved ivy and vines, decorative panels appeared on doors and shelf brackets, and the whole house gradually took on a unique character. Within all this activity there was an inescapable sense of exploration, of a journey which I suppose will be completed with the same mixture of relief and regret that the intrepid voyagers of the sixteenth century must have felt when they finally sighted their native soil.

All this was no vain, eccentric self-indulgence on Maurice's part, but a process of discovery and understanding. Spurred on by Anne he became an inspiration to a number of people, myself and his children included. Rachel became a typesetter working for a local press, Reuben, a romantic like his father, became a competent but unworldly plasterer, and Seth, always the boy scout of the family, applied his own personal twist by becoming a meticulous and successful worker. A painter and decorator who refuses to tolerate a patch of rotten wood, or paint over a loose undercoat, Seth has taken pride-in-a-job-well-done to his own extreme.

Choosing and freedom are intimately connected, and lack of choice is the real poverty in many people's lives. We work to free ourselves from the persistent demands of survival, but in working we never escape the constraints of economic reality. We find ourselves trapped in a present of no choice. Maurice escaped. Instead of the soulless routines of everyday life he discovered a world full of rich pleasure and interest. However, as each of us is drawn into the cycle of production and consumption, we are offered roles increasingly divorced from the possibility of choosing either for ourselves or for other people. Maurice managed to reverse this process. Denied his social role as a building trades operative, he reinvented an older form of activity over which he could exercise his own control.

The nature and importance of Maurice's choice lies at the heart of what I would call art: a sympathetic, practical, creative involvement with the material world. An artist by virtue of his insistent refusal to accept an allotted place on the slag heap of modern society, Maurice consistently affirms that principle, and so joins forces with all the outsiders and visionaries of history.

'Art' lies in wait for people like Maurice. It offers a role to the outsider and non-conformist, and with it the possibilitiy of being accepted and acknowledged. But just as it acknowledges the outsider, 'art' also ensnares and puts the extraordinary on show in the world's galleries and museums, where the powerful can experience the thrill of a danger safely under control, bought and sold as a commodity.

6

The Work of Art

All art – including what are claimed to be the highest achievements in art – is dependent on skill, training, method, tradition and other qualities which characterise manual work. By linking creative activity to the humble traditions of work, we do not demean it; on the contrary we actually give it greater relevance. Significantly, the artistic achievements of the Renaissance were deeply rooted in medieval working methods and in traditions still evident in craft and trade practices.

William Morris argues most of these points at length in his writings and lectures on art and work but here I concentrate on those moments in history when artists tried to prise themselves free, first from the artisan class to which they belonged in the Middle Ages, and later from the suspicion that their 'work' might be in any real sense manual.

In Paris an elegant building and extensive grounds are dedicated to the work of one sculptor: Rodin. The main rooms of the *Musée Rodin* are furnished with full-height panelling, decorated with delicate, sensitive oak wreaths and garlands. A masterpiece of skilful work, regular and repetitive, yet subtle and varied, all achieved with a truly remarkable degree of observation and feeling. The panelling is painted white, so the evidence of the carver's touch is hidden. To modern eyes, it might just as well be a plastic moulding stuck on to the surface, for the quality of the work is virtually invisible, part of the styling and decoration of the interior. Yet the carver's skill in handling tools and material, expressed as a feeling for form and a sensitive response to the natural world, is every bit the equal of Rodin's more obvious art.

I have no idea who carved these garlands. They do not appear in any catalogue, nor is there any plaque on the wall to tell me. Indeed I wonder if Rodin, who lived and worked there, had any idea who made his house so beautiful. He probably knew the architect, but the artisans were almost certainly unknown. Rodin's art and his personal status as an artist are so far removed from the world of work in which the woodcarver's achievements exist that we have no way of acknowledging the similarities. Rodin's social status was of course a reflection of the status of art, just as the woodcarver's was a reflection of the status of work, for in Rodin's day craftwork was valued well below that of the artist, with the result that we still dismiss much that might give us pleasure. To the American tourists, with their thirst for authentic culture, these woodcarvings are invisible.

By the nineteenth century, artistic status had ceased to depend on skill and ability as it did in the Renaissance, and the value placed on work was directly related to the social status of the worker. Intellectual work was valued more highly than manual work and the professions therefore commanded higher wages than the trades. But art became problematic, being an essentially manual activity. Sculpture, for example, is very physical, and is carried out in a workshop but, to justify the value it has acquired as art, it has somehow to avoid any suggestion that it might be a form of manual labour.

The concept of labour value can of course be extended to account for differentials between the trades and professions by reference to factors like training and education but, given the almost inevitable fact that the woodcarver responsible for the *Musée Rodin*'s garlands was paid a very humble wage for that work, any rational attempt to justify the enormous variations in pay and status that different types of skilled work attracted could not explain why we overlook things like those woodcarvings. This paradox is the key to a vexed issue. How is it that art, which is bought and sold as a commodity, can command market prices bearing little or no relation to the quantity of labour necessary for its production? When craftwork, which is in many respects similar, is subject to market pricing which so directly reflects the quantity of labour involved that handicrafts vanished rapidly as machines came to perform a similar task more quickly?

The level of skill required to produce the carvings in the *Musée Rodin* is such that we can distinguish them from the machine-made object only with great difficulty. Fine, repetitive carving must be done to a rhythm, and this gives it a precision and crispness which can leave the cut wood full of lively expression and vitality, in which variations are subtle and have to be looked for. Under a coat of paint the differences go unnoticed, and these carvings drop out of the world of remarkable objects of 'art'. I noticed them only when they were being prepared for redecoration, even though I had visited the museum several times before. Yet when they were produced they represented an appreciable quantity of skilled work and had a significant value consequently transferred to the building, which we instantly recognise as elegant because of the costliness of its decoration. They were no doubt painted and perhaps gilded. Now we might be tempted to strip off the paint to show that they were done by hand and are valuable because of the rarity of such skills. I assume they were to be repainted to retain the authenticity of the building as an art gallery.

To me the contradictions involved are very revealing, giving some insight into the confusions surrounding the values we attach to different types of skilled work. What we have done in effect is to create, in the idea of art, an aristocratic form of work. We have replicated the class divisions of society in divisions within the nature and value of work, which reflect the social status of the workers. But by tradition aristocrats do not work and so the aristocrat of work has become somehow a form of not-work, but art. Were art to remain skilled work, we might begin to ask questions about the level of skill involved, which in turn might undermine the class divisions and the inequality of rewards.

In a famous court case of 1878 the painter Whistler sued Ruskin, the Victorian critic, for accusing him of having asked 'two hundred guineas for flinging a pot of paint in the public's face'. The painting in question (*Nocturne in Black and Gold*), was one of a series of evocative, atmospheric paintings produced with reference not to detail but to overall effect. As a result, they displayed none of the minute detailing in vogue at the time, and can be seen as a protest against the predominance of subject in Victorian painting.

The burden of the questioning to which Whistler was subjected was how he could possibly ask 200 guineas, at that time a working wage for a number of years, for two days' work. Whistler replied, rather lamely, that he asked the money not for two days' work but for the knowledge of a lifetime. The curiosity of the case lies in the fact that the argument centred on the time taken to produce the paintings – the labour value involved – and that work was seen as having a value which could be calculated by the day. Had Whistler had the sense to claim that his asking price was based on the potential value of the paintings as investments, he might have had more success, for this idea was well understood by the Victorian art-buying public. But arguing on the basis of labour value got him into deep water.

Even high-grade work representing a large quantity of social labour – the argument a professional would have used to justify high fees – could not be worth 100 guineas a day. Whistler's claim that he was asking payment for a lifetime's experience was no way out of the trap either, for it still suggested that the value of a painting could be measured in terms of the effort involved. Although this answer could be true in a limited way, it carried little conviction, as is evident from the token damages of one farthing awarded to Whistler. At 100 guineas a day, he could afford, in theory at least, to pay for a court case or two, although the truth is that the costs of the case virtually ruined him.

Had Whistler's claim been true, by his own argument he would have been paid many times over for this knowledge, since each picture he sold carried a similar premium, whereas a skilled craftsman who could make the same claim to a lifetime's experience and knowledge was paid only for the hours as worked. There is no doubt that the special cachet Whistler was laying claim to as a justification for the prices he charged was 'art' or genius, and the mystique that surrounded it.

During the Renaissance, artists were contracted for a given quantity of work which was measured almost as building work is today, by the square metre and metre run. And although they were paid in relation to their skill, and to a certain extent how fashionable they were, the work was still seen as labour and valued accordingly. What the Renaissance artists traded in was skilled labour, not genius, and this is made very clear in contracts of employment which have survived from that period.

There is evidence from household inventories that, during the Renaissance, paintings by such great artists as Giotto were not valued very highly when compared with goldsmiths' work because of the value of the precious materials used. This suggests that the labour value of artistic work was relatively low compared with the rarity value of the materials and is confirmed in contracts which allow specifically for the extra cost of expensive pigments like lapis lazuli. What we would now refer to as art was valued no more highly than craft; indeed the two words were almost synonymous in their meaning, for artists were not merely looked on as artisans, they *were* artisans.

In *Patrons and Artists in the Italian Renaissance*, D. S. Chambers makes this point quite forcibly:

> Those who had the right social background, acquired some humanist values and useful introductions might well obtain more than artisan status ... On the other hand not all artists necessarily sought to become rich and ascend the social ladder; though Mantegna aspired to rise, buying himself a title from emperor Frederic III ... Donatello (according to Vespasio) refused Cosimo de Medici's offer of smart clothes and (according to Vasari) kept his money in a basket which was frequently rifled.[1]

He also tells us that Mantegna, with all his new-found social status, received an annual salary of 180 florins, while the highest paid lecturer at the Florentine Studio was paid 120; a good income for a lawyer in the same period was 350 florins. The social mobility Mantegna enjoyed carried him in effect from the artisanal to the professional class, a change in social rank that was achieved during the Renaissance. Before that time the majority of artists were simply specialised workers, although the more important of them were solid middle-class burghers. Nor is Michelangelo's claim to have been paid 3,000 florins for the ceiling in the Sistine Chapel out of proportion once account is taken of the four years it took to complete, especially if that sum included materials, scaffolding, overheads and models. If we make a conventional allowance of 50 per cent for overheads and materials and 50 per cent for labour, which is how most skilled work averages out, Michelangelo would have received about 325 florins per annum for his labour, precisely in line with that of a decent lawyer, and nothing like the 100 guineas a day Whistler was asking.

In other words, the great artists of the Renaissance ranged in social status and financial reward from artisan through to the equivalent of the professional middle classes. Within that range, the value of skilled work was the major factor governing remuneration. Any premium placed on the work of the most prominent of Renaissance artists was over and above a basic recognition of the value of skilled work, and reflected competition for their services.

But how did art cease to be work? How did the workshop of the Renaissance, with its artists and apprentices, with its enormous variety of skills and techniques and its place in Italian city life, become the introspective studio from which nineteenth-century artists were so keen to escape?

Leonardo da Vinci and Michelangelo were both apprenticed as boys, and in the artist's studio of the day status went on merit alone. Indeed, one of the great strengths of the medieval workshop tradition was that artistic merit was not confused with middle-class sensibility as it was in the nineteenth century, but was founded in real practical skills. As a consequence, social position was no prerequisite for a career in the arts, and it is important to recognise that this was the case until very recently. Henry Moore, for example, is very much an exception to the middle-class domination of the English art scene from the late eighteenth century onwards.

By the nineteenth century, the majority of artists came from the ranks of the middle classes and were educated in the academies which were springing up all over Europe. They competed with each other in the rarified market place of academy shows, salons and tasteful gatherings of the period, and the values of the art-buying public were formed by self-appointed arbiters of taste. Inevitably this hermetic system of artist, critic and public became a self-justifying merry-go-round. Artists produced 'art' which the critics and connoisseurs duly recognised as such, the public admired and the collectors bought. The system held together because the effective separation of art and work allowed the commodity bought and sold to become an abstract entity – 'art' – with its own branch of philosophy called aesthetics. In its journalistic mode aesthetics became the art criticism which justified the social elevation of art in general and some artists in particular, while relegating those skills which were no longer considered special to the world of work. Thus the practice of some arts ceased to be 'art': joinery and cookery, for example, became menial skills in a mundane world which art had quit for loftier and more abstract planes.

Art ceased to be the practice of skill and, by implication, works of art were assumed to contain some secret ingredient over and above skill. This devaluing of skill became a perfect justification for the supplanting of hand manufacture with machine manufacture, and ultimately a way of separating out the idea of work – labour – as a commodity to be bought and sold. As skills passed from human hands into the 'hands' of machines, work became the human element in a dehumanised process of production organised and controlled directly by and for the interests of profit. Work became an alienating activity in which the worker, unlike the skilled craftsworker, had no control over any aspect of the process of production; art was associated with the production of culture, that is to say with the reaffirming of middle- and upper-class values and sensibility. Culture, as a concept, was defined as the ability to appreciate art, literature and style: the circular justification of a social hierarchy.

As a consequence popular culture was ignored and eventually eradicated. Not by neglect, but through the destruction of traditional communities and the growth of cities, the common people were impoverished to the point where the only culture they could sustain was popular song. Later an extensive culture grew up around a growing class-consciousness and the working-class organisations which arose out of that consciousness. But prior to this, the damage done to popular culture in this country alone was enormous. So art, which was once an homogeneous and skilful activity, defining a mode of production of goods, services, and the social relations that surrounded them, was divided into the separate fields of art and work. Skill ceased to carry its previous social significance and began to lose its central place in everyday life, while work became burdensome toil. Art on the other hand became the property of the rich.

When the French Academy of Painting and Sculpture was founded under the patronage of Louis XIV he said to the members of his new artistic elite: 'I entrust to you the most precious thing on earth – my fame.' John Berger says of this remark:

[it] offers us a clue about the nature of academicism in the arts. Academies were and are formed as instruments of the State. Their function is to direct art according to state policy: not arbitrarily by *Diktat*, but by codifying a system of artistic rules which ensure the continuation of a traditional, homogeneous art reflecting the State ideology ... it is intrinsic to all academic systems that theory is isolated from practice. Everything begins and ends with the rules ... when art is an activity of artisans, the rules are intrinsic to the *practice* of working from prototypes ... By contrast the Academy centralises all artistic activity and regularises all standards and judgements. The humbler activities which remain outside its control are dismissed as primitive or 'folk' art.[2]

The academies in France, England, and later in Russia, placed art firmly in the service of the state. They not only drew a line between what was and was not considered art, but also set about organising the several accepted arts into a hierarchy, with the greatest art directly under state patronage and serving to glorify the state and its ideology. What the academies did, in effect, was to draw a line between fine art and the lesser arts and crafts. The fine arts were also differentiated from the other, so called *liberal arts* and sciences which had all originated in the practice and exercise of skill. Under the influence of self-appointed arbiters of taste like Reynolds and Burlington, the high point of 'art' came to be seen as embodied in the work of the great artists of the Renaissance – Raphael, Michelangelo, Leonardo – and culture became an acquired taste gained on a Grand Tour of the culture spots of the classical world.

In a short period of time, the works of the Italian Renaissance gained a rarity value that became synonymous with the value placed on genius, and artists came to be seen as the source of qualities which were somehow embodied in works of art. In this way art and work were finally separated out as ideas, genius being associated with art, and work with manual labour.

Whistler was asking 200 guineas for his genius, not his skill. And by the late nineteenth century the idea that genius could be embodied in the work of certain rare individuals had gained a currency it has never really lost. In *The Story of Art*, E. H. Gombrich says of Michelangelo: 'It is very difficult for any *ordinary mortal* to imagine how it could be possible for one *human being* [my emphasis] to achieve what Michelangelo achieved in four lonely years of work on the scaffoldings of the papal chapel.'[3] To my mind, the most important point about artistic achievement is that it is entirely and essentially human. If contemporary society produces nothing to parallel the achievements of the Renaissance we must ask ourselves why and stop pretending that Renaissance artists were gods, the like of which will never be seen again. Ironically, artists themselves began to challenge the assumptions which had bolstered the academies. It may have been this self-same belief in their own genius – a genius which was, by the nineteenth century, synonymous with artist – that gave them the self-confidence and sense of their own superiority finally to challenge the edifice of academic art and its blatant double standards.

The powers of academic censorship are enormous and largely unacknowledged. Art history conspires to ignore anything that does not fall within the conventional criteria of art, concerning itself almost exclusively with the art of elite groups within a narrow definition of civilisation. The history of European art is, in the main, the history of

Court art, Imperial art and Church art, and it is only in this last category, Church art, that such a view even begins to concern itself with objects which were familiar to more than a minute sector of the population, let alone with what might be called 'popular' art. It is as if there was no creative stirring among the great mass of people, as if their lives were totally devoid of significance and interest.

This may be the only answer the available evidence suggests, but we come to this conclusion because the processes involved both in identifying and preserving art are in themselves highly selective. What we are left with is the tip of an iceberg of human creative activity, which represents the cultural pretensions of a very narrow sector of society.

There are constant complaints in the West about Russian censorship, and yet censorship of one kind or another has been practised in the West for centuries. To survive as part of our heritage, works of art have had to pass through a series of cultural sieves – iconoclasm; the dissolution of the monasteries; Victorian prudery; Nazism in Europe; McCarthyism in America and so on – as well as the more insidious selective processes of changing taste and fashion. What has survived these vicissitudes is not necessarily representative of the creative genius of people as a whole.

The ways in which art has been preserved have always been highly selective, but there has been a persistent tendency to regard survival as somehow on a par with natural selection – standing the test of time – when many of the factors involved can hardly be described as favouring the survival of the best of art. Ruskin, in his role as executor of Turner's will, 'testified that a parcel of sketchbooks containing "grossly obscene drawings" was burnt at the behest of the National Gallery Trustees in his presence in December 1858'[4] – presumably because they considered the subjects lewd and unfit to leave to posterity as part of Turner's *oeuvre*, while other Victorians added fig-leaves and veils to works they considered indiscreet, destroying and concealing a whole heritage of honest nakedness and replacing it with a dubious if tasteful pornography. The iconoclasts, with zealous wrath, took hammer and axe to any object they considered idolatrous. But beyond mere human whim and prejudice, the material structure of many works plays a large part in determining their survival, and there is no doubt that blues and jazz are recognised as impressive forms only because of the invention of sound recording. Nor should we forget that many of the classics of early jazz were originally issued as 'race' recordings for consumption by an emerging black market the record business hoped to exploit rather than champion. It was only much later that black music (arguably North America's most significant cultural achievement) was recognised as an art form in its own right.

Buildings and sculpture stand a fair chance of surviving, especially if they are owned and protected by powerful groups in society, but frescoes, being part of the more fragile fabric of buildings, are susceptible to climatic conditions and especially to building alterations and changes in taste. Canvases are in a way more durable, but can easily be stolen or damaged, and so the rarity value that time has given to certain objects contributes more than a little to our awe.

Fabric, clothes, tapestries and furnishings survive only under very favourable conditions, and festivals and pageants – individual events – survive only in occasional records or by word of mouth, unless they establish themselves as traditional festivals. We know that Rubens was not only a court painter, but was responsible, as many court artists were, for festivals, carnivals and entertainments. His famous cycle of paintings depicting the triumphant arrival of Marie de Medici in France still hangs in the Louvre, but of his festival designs only the merest fragments survive, which can never provide us with an adequate basis for assessment of his work in this field.

So much of art, of creative activity, is ephemeral by its very nature and intention, and there is no doubt that, due to material factors, our art 'heritage', and consequently our understanding of the history of human invention and creativity, is severely restricted. Although the medieval period was resplendent with courtly and civic pageantry, few descriptive records survive and so the history of medieval art is grossly unbalanced in favour of tangible and overwhelmingly religious art. Secular art was subjected to so many physical assaults, especially as temporal power changed hands frequently and possessions were either destroyed by the ravages of time and war or carried off as trophies. Just as important in this context, personal possessions were probably used more continuously than religious objects, and were not collected as they are today unless they were made of precious materials which could be salvaged if money were needed in a hurry.

Religious manuscripts on the other hand were carefully guarded in monastic libraries and treated as semi-authentic relics containing the very word of God. Yet the survival of even religious art through periods like the dissolution of the monasteries and the Reformation seems almost miraculous. Such important manuscripts as the Book of Kells were preserved and discovered in bizarre ways, by act of God almost rather than mere chance. If we compare the descriptions of the magnificent books and relics brought from Rome to the Northumbrian monasteries of Monkweremouth and Jarrow in what are called the Dark Ages with the scanty evidence that remains, it is clear that even among religious objects survival is arbitrary.

Recent periods of history provide us with more complete evidence and a truer picture of the dominant culture, but none the less any culture not protected by power and wealth is far less likely to survive in record and fact. The survival of art is threatened by natural causes; by moral, political and religious prejudice; and by changing tastes and fashions. It would be wrong to claim that history gives us either a fair or an accurate picture of past cultures. Not only is the surviving evidence far from complete, but in various subtle ways art is frequently recognised as such only if it conforms to often dubious criteria which ensure that much of what we should regard as art is not included in art history.

In any period, the exercise of power makes it possible for elites to provide themselves with material possessions and preserve those at the expense of any genuinely popular culture. It would be ridiculous to suggest that, because there is little surviving evidence, there was never any popular art, or that the often disenfranchised, disinherited and impoverished masses of any society are incapable of self-expression. We have only to look at the vast store of folk music, traditional dances, rituals and customs, let alone the traditional skills and arts that have survived via oral and mimetic tradition to see that the opposite must be the case. Yet in almost every period the popular arts have been dismissed as unimportant, disregarded as less than art, and considered unworthy of preservation.

The word art, in its original sense, meant skill or the practice of skills, a sense it still has today when we talk of, say, the art of wheelwrighting. Technology, derived from the Greek equivalent *tekhne* – the how of doing things – has taken over some of the original meaning of the word art; in fact the two words, art and technology, are closely related. But the idea of technology has already been distanced from this original, practical sense – the exercise of skill – and is increasingly perceived as a form of power. So the very process of shaping the raw materials of the world into artefacts for use, which was at one and the same time art, technology and magic, has ceased to be a sympathetic, symbiotic and intimate relationship based on human skill – an art – and has instead become a dangerously abstracted, distanced and exploitative power relationship. The traditional arts were always much more than mere practical skill; they were extensive bodies of knowledge drawn from experience and handed down directly from one person to another, complex philosophies and ways of knowing the world. To master an art implied the acquisition of skill, both in theory and in practice, and a sensitive appreciation of the qualities of natural materials: not the acquisition of power in a modern sense.

The Italian artist was originally an artisan, a skilled worker and member of a trade guild or *arte*.[5] Artists were raised in the rigorous and often restrictive background of the medieval craft workshop, and the apprenticeship training was governed by the regulations of the guild which acted as the guardian of trade skills. The guilds controlled production methods within the various arts, stipulating standards, conditions of work and the organisation of the workshops, maintaining and regulating monopolies and other concessions in each particular trade. This workshop tradition, for which the trade guilds were responsible, constituted an ancient but vigorous and developing body of knowledge, practised, nurtured and handed on, often through the medium of the extended family. Artisanal production was based very much on the extended family, and apprentices were often treated as part of the family unit.

Trade guilds and organisations have a history almost as extensive as civilisation itself. They were recorded in the fourteenth century BC,[6] and there can be little doubt that guild organisation was crucial to the survival of the orally and practically transmitted skills which made civilisation possible. The original function of the guilds was not to monopolise production but to ensure the survival of vitally important skills, which in their turn ensured the survival of the community, at a time when the range of skills cementing communities together included essential activities like the preparing and preserving of food, the tending of the sick and the raising of crops.

The orally and practically transmitted skills, and the tools and processes that went with them, were developed on an empirical basis over very long periods, and for this reason became highly sophisticated. The loss of any particular skill or technique, silk-weaving for example, could take years or even centuries to replace. Tools, too, developed along different principles in different parts of the world. Japanese saws, for example, cut on the upstroke rather than the down, being pulled through the wood on the cutting stroke. A finer blade can therefore be used which suits the intricacy and subtlety of Japanese carpentry so closely that it is difficult to say whether the trade developed from the tools or vice versa. Thus a multitude of techniques was developed and guarded jealously as trade secrets; to be admitted to a guild was to be admitted to a special body of monopolistic knowledge.

The idea that classical learning was revived during the Renaissance is only partially true. On the one hand, Renaissance artists and scholars based their idea of classical art on limited and often dubious examples – late Roman copies of Greek works, for example. On the other hand, the skills and technologies of the classical and pre-classical world had been preserved and amplified by the craft tradition of the Middle Ages, and the Renaissance was dependent on this workshop tradition, which formed a continuous link with the past. In a very real sense the trades are our oldest branch of learning, yet have no place in an academic tradition which is a recent phenomenon.

The universities do not teach the trades; they are the subject of polytechnic day-release classes, and the crafts are taught in art schools. As a consequence, we have become accustomed to the idea that learning comes from books and so tend to disregard practical skills as a way of knowing and understanding the world. The massed knowledge of years of experiment, the insights of countless unknown individuals who made the development of whole civilisations possible – houses; cloth; the preservation and preparation of food; irrigation; sewage disposal – all the substance of human existence is the product of skilled work. It is these extensive skills which are now invested in machine production: every lathe owes its existence to the individuals who cut the first lead screws by hand little more than a century ago. The practical skills may seem mundane because they are not obviously based on scientific method, but early forms of medicine knew of a huge variety of remedial effects achieved by using herbal and manipulative techniques which are only now being understood by the scientific method. These traditional skills did not spring out of thin air; they contain a wide-ranging and precise knowledge of materials and processes without which civilisation could not exist.

In the trade and craft traditions, specialised knowledge and skills were held by acknowledged practitioners of the individual arts. Nor were these skills restricted to men in the way we now imagine. Joseph and Frances Giles tell us that:

> Women work outside the home at an astonishing variety of crafts and professions. They may be teachers, midwives, laundresses, lacemakers, seamstresses, and even members of normally male trades and occupations – weavers, fullers, barbers, carpenters, saddlers, tilers and many others. Wives commonly work at their husbands' crafts, and when a man dies his widow carries on the trade. Daughters not infrequently learn their father's craft along with their brothers.[7]

In an idealised form this was very much like our concept of the university as a repository of knowledge. The trade guilds were of course never completely ideal in their activities, but neither are the universities. Self-interest, jealousy, competition and all the other human foibles, infiltrate all our institutions. But in a real sense the practical arts and the trade guilds that preserved them constitute a tradition of learning which is several thousand years old, older than the universities and older than classical learning. I believe that the Renaissance marked a turning point, not from darkness and superstition, but when abstract knowledge began to assume an ascendancy over skill and the practical arts. Our irrelevant, impractical 'art' and unchecked modern technology are consequences of this triumph of abstract knowledge over practical skill.

Ironically, during the same transition, the trade guilds became increasingly secretive and specialised, dividing up manufacturing processes between several guilds whose practices were so codified as to exclude experiment. The probable reason for this was that only by such means could the guilds resist the increasing industrialisation of manufacture and maintain the control of handwork within the organisations of handworkers, rather as modern trade unions resist change with restrictive practices. It is a mistake to assume that industrialisation came with the Industrial Revolution and did not exist before it. The industrialisation made possible by the discovery of a new source of energy – steam – was applied at first to already existing mechanical processes. Water power and wind power had been exploited for centuries before the Industrial Revolution, and highly developed machines existed in what should rightly be called the textile industry of the fourteenth century. But it was steam power that finally facilitated mechanisation on a large scale and encouraged centralisation of production in factories, contributing fatally to the breakdown of the artisanal workshop tradition and its skills.

Nowadays, when we consider people like Leonardo da Vinci, we are struck by the enormous diversity of their interests and activities and the originality of their thought, but we forget that they were not constrained by our narrow ideas of art. The artists of the Renaissance were practical people, trained in a tradition of high quality skills. They were practical by definition. Not one of the three greatest architects of the Renaissance, Bramante, Raphael and Michelangelo, was an architect by training, claims Nikolaus Pevsner,[8] missing the point. Nor were Brunelleschi the goldsmith, nor even Giotto the painter, who was appointed Master Mason to the Cathedral and City of Florence in 1334. We have difficulty understanding the Middle Ages and the Renaissance because we are continually reinterpreting the facts in the light of present-day concepts and roles. As soon as we stop thinking in terms like painter, sculptor and architect, we can begin to see how the workshop training these artists received as apprentices gave them a genuinely practical understanding of the world on which they built through their own research, unhindered by the assumptions which trap modern artists and architects within a labyrinth of abstractions.

The art historian, E. H. Gombrich, tells us that Leonardo da Vinci:

> would be introduced into the technical secrets of foundry work and other metalwork, he would learn to prepare pictures and statues carefully by making studies from the nude and from draped models. He would learn to study plants and curious animals for inclusion in his pictures, and he would receive a thorough grounding in the optics of perspective and the use of colours.[9]

In other words, all this was part and parcel of a medieval workshop education which, rather than being restrictive, provided a broad and thorough grounding in all the practical and intellectual skills of an art education which, in my opinion, was far superior to any that has existed since.

The practical and empirical tradition learned in the workshop was the foundation on which the achievement of artists like Michelangelo and

Leonardo was built, and the more detached art became from this practical base, the more effete and mannered it became. Giotto was capable of taking on the role of Master Mason to the City of Florence for two reasons. First, his own trade – mural painting – was directly involved in the construction and decoration of buildings. Giotto would therefore have been well acquainted with the processes involved and accepted by the other builders of the city as an equal in skill and experience. Secondly, building work in the medieval tradition proceeded logically from a few given dimensions and a series of collective decisions made by the builders themselves. Giotto would be required to coordinate rather than to design and instruct. He would have been working with highly-skilled builders, whose level of competence was far above present-day standards, and relatively unfettered by modern divisions of intellectual and manual labour. Between them they could and did build cathedrals and palaces which still stand as monuments to their consummate collective skill.

In England, the tradition of the master builders survived into this century via Nash, Cubitt and the Victorian house builders, to expire finally with the advent of the modern speculative builder. This was the tradition in which Giotto worked, but he was also a forerunner of those Renaissance artists who tried to break out of the tradition and establish themselves as individuals of talent and genius. 'Fine Art' arose from these attempts to improve the status of the practical arts and escape from the restrictions of the trade guilds, but as artists broke with convention they quickly found themselves working under the patronage and protection of rich merchants and nobles to whom they finally owed allegiance.

In Pursuit of Reality

Art has always played a central role in shaping the way we think about and come to understand ourselves and the world around us. It reflects the concerns and interests of the time, place and social groups that give rise to it. Like a mirror, it gives us back ourselves, shaping our perception and understanding.

In the past, art history concerned itself almost entirely and obsessively with style, rather than the broader cultural issues which deepen our understanding of art. In this chapter – as in the previous one – I am concerned with challenging some commonly-held assumptions which have shaped the way we think about art and art history. Consequently, I have drawn my examples from the most popular introductions to the subject. My intention is not to denigrate the authors, who have inspired enormous interest in art, but to suggest that they should be read as a way into a subject open to widely divergent interpretations: not as received wisdom. My concern is also to reclaim art history as a springboard for the practice of art, by trying to give some insight into the motivation of artists.

Art history has always been a problem for me. I have studied it and taught it, but remain wary of its tendency to concern itself almost exclusively with styles, objects and internal, artistic values, instead of coming to grips with artists as people, and with the social context in which different artistic styles and movements occurred. I have always been intrigued by artists as people, but what I wanted from books about art was some access to their feelings as a way of penetrating what art must have been about for them. I suppose that art historians feel they should describe objects as much as possible, because their medium – words – is so completely non-visual. But focusing on the objects, on the works of art, as opposed to the people and above all the times that formed them, for me fails to give any access to artists as whole human beings living in a real world. This is even true of monographs which rarely manage to place artists in an understandable relationship with the world around them.

There is also a tendency implicit in the idea of stylistic development, and *avant-gardes*, to see history as a series of events leading up to the present – a tendency to view time and human activity as a linear process through which past events are understood in the light of the present day, rather than vice versa. Consequently art history, with its emphasis on interpretation, often tells us more about the period when it was written than about the period it describes. Much depends on how facts are linked together and where divisions are made between movements and events: arbitrary decisions which can reflect the prejudices of the writer rather than the actuality of the subject. Something as basic to our interpretation of subsequent events as the origins of the modern movement in the arts can be considered by one historian, E. H. Gombrich, to be found at the end of the eighteenth century,[1] and by another, Nikolaus Pevsner, 100 years later in the break between the Impressionists and the Post-Impressionists.[2]

On the one hand, we are presented with modern art beginning with a departure from representation, and on the other modern art which develops out of a series of challenges to academic convention. If we follow Pevsner and start modern art off at the end of the nineteenth century, its origins are to be found in a conflict between the representation of surface as practised by the Impressionists, and the reinterpretation of visual experience by the Post-Impressionists. If we locate modern art 100 years earlier, with Blake and Hogarth, the conflicts centre around bitter objections to the academic system – around internal debates among artists. In both interpretations there is no reference to external influences or causes, and the reasons for artistic change appear to depend on stylistic development alone.

Gombrich allows that the French Revolution must have shaken up many 'assumptions that had been taken for granted for hundreds, if not thousands of years', but he immediately qualifies this admission by identifying the accompanying changes in art as concerned with 'the artist's attitude to what is called "style" '.[3] Thus, by focusing on disputes within the academic tradition itself, we are left to conclude that the chief causes of artistic change originate in the practice of art and, by implication, that art is a separate activity divorced from everyday life and driven by its own rules and dynamic.

I see every reason for artists to respond to social change in a very direct way which can produce real changes in content – in subject matter – but I can also see them acting as agents of social change in ways which can challenge ideas about the value and purpose of art itself. Artists are not immune to social issues and, in my experience, one of their primary concerns is to formulate a genuine response to these issues.

Of course it would be rash to dismiss all of conventional art history out of hand. Pevsner is right in one sense and Gombrich is right in another, but neither is wholly correct. Interpretations need to be superimposed, overlaid and seen within the cultural framework which gave rise to them if they are to be truly informative and not mere opinion. But there is little doubt that a conventional view of art history tends to exclude social and political events from any influential role in the processes of change, as if culture exists alongside, yet independent of social events: as if art follows its own rules and can be separated from the mainstream of history. I would argue strongly that this is not the case at all. As a creative person, I am keenly conscious of the social tensions that inform not just the way I think about the world but, equally important, my perception of it.

If instead we try drawing a line around 1850, starting the modern movement with the Realists on the Continent and the Pre-Raphaelites in England, it is possible to see events in a different light. The backdrop to the enormous artistic changes taking place is not so much a sudden trauma, the 1848 revolution, though this no doubt exerted a powerful influence on the rest of the century, but the growing confidence of the Industrial Revolution and the society it produced, which was about to display its wares proudly in the great exhibitions of England and Europe. The challenge to artistic tradition becomes an absolute confrontation over subject matter reflecting social, political and philosophical changes in the world at large and, as a result, a challenge to those social assumptions on which the academic tradition was based.

The Industrial Revolution was far more advanced in England than on the Continent, especially in its effects on the countryside and social life. Perhaps escape into a romantic medievalism was the only course open to the Pre-Raphaelites, allowing them, as it did, to compare Victorian England with a very different epoch in a way which would reveal something of the sordidness of life in the mid-nineteenth century. The solid peasant basis of the French rural economy on the other hand provided an ample and contemporary reality for Millet and Courbet to draw on. Each situation gave rise to a different artistic interpretation, but in both cases an objection to the reality of a burgeoning industrial revolution provided the driving force for a revolt against convention. Both groups provoked uproar in artistic circles, both were attacked for their rejection of academic practice, and both were seen to take a stand against the mainstream of artistic fashion.

These artists were rejecting not just artistic but social values as well. In their bohemian and unconventional behaviour they were challenging accepted standards of personal and public morality, and asserting what they saw as the freedom implicit in creativity to explore both feeling and morality through a subjective response to their social environment. This social rebellion drove artists to explore sections of society and ways of life which had not previously been considered suitable subject matter for art, except as a cosy and bogus genre art surviving today as wide-eyed, sad urchins. It also led to experimentation with opium and other drugs which gave imaginative access to experiences outside the realm of normality. Artistic and social rebellion went hand in hand, holding out a promise for new kinds of culture, new attitudes to art and work, and new forms of social organisation looked for by growing sectors of nineteenth-century society.

Drawing lines between historical events is always a dubious activity, but recognising the growing reaction against industrial society in all its manifestations which surfaced in the middle of the nineteenth century makes subsequent developments in art more comprehensible. The personal vision of artists like Blake and Goya was formed in opposition to the values of a society of which they were highly critical. The precise skill of such artists lies in their ability to present that personal vision with sufficient clarity and force to allow us, for a moment, to glimpse the world through their eyes. So we can see the artist as dissident and the artist as propagandist for a new world emerging as parallel themes, linking the late eighteenth century to the early twentieth century and spanning two moments of revolutionary change.

By the end of the eighteenth century artists were becoming increasingly dissociated from the mainstream of social life. Ideas about the social and cultural role of the artist, which had their origins in the Renaissance and conceived of the artist as genius and free imaginative spirit, became common currency, together with other Renaissance attitudes which saw art as an activity distinct and separate from work. Such ideas thrived in a climate where the academies were largely responsible for fostering a rigid differentiation between artist and artisan.

At the same time, the realm of the imagination was seen as a source of deeper truths, giving access to a poetic reality beneath the surface of everyday events which could be explored only through artistic sensibility. There was a continuum between private and public worlds which our modern use of the word 'Romantic' does not acknowledge.

Rather than being the flight from reality which we now associate with romanticism, the concern of many artists in the early nineteenth century was to express a reaction to the shape the new industrial society was taking. It was a theme uniting political and artistic innovation in the quest for a qualitatively better life within a new social order, and it was to become a major driving force behind social and artistic innovation well into the next century.

It is no coincidence that Courbet, who coined the term Realism, should believe that the purpose of art lay in presenting the truth as uncompromisingly as possible to 'shock the bourgeois out of his complacency'.[4] This combination of artistic integrity and forthright opposition to bourgeois taste and values surfaces again and again in the stated intentions of artists. Some 60 years later, it found complete expression in the intentions and activities of Dada as the Dadaists mounted a ferocious attack on well-entrenched bourgeois morality. Hans Richter, Dada historian, says: ' To outrage public opinion was a basic principle of Dada', and quotes another Dadaist, Marcel Janco: 'We had lost the hope that art would one day achieve its just place in our society. We were beside ourselves with rage and grief at the suffering and humiliation of mankind.'[5] Richter identifies this primary objective of Dada more clearly when he tells us:

> Our provocations, demonstrations and defiances were only a means of arousing the bourgeoisie to rage, and through that rage to a shamefaced self-awareness. It is understandable that art historians, professionally trained to distinguish the formal characteristics of particular stylistic periods, have been unable to cope with the contradiction and complexities of Dada. They were prepared to measure the length breadth and depth of Dada, but found it hard to do justice to its actual content.[6]

I agree with Richter here, for it seems to me that art history, because of its obsession with style and period, with the measuring and describing of objects, has successfully isolated art as an hermetic subject developing under its own inner momentum with little or no reference to the world at large. This is simply not borne out by the facts as we know them. The Dadaists stated quite explicitly that their art was a reaction to world events. Hans Arp said: 'Revolted by the butchery of the 1914 World War ... We were seeking an art based on fundamentals, to cure the madness of the age.'[7]

Picasso painted *Guernica* inspired by a real and horrific event which because of his painting will not be easily forgotten; some 130 years earlier Goya, another Spanish artist, produced a series of etchings called *The Disasters of War* as a comment on the atrocities of the Franco-Spanish War; and in Britain the Artists International Association was formed in reaction to world events in the 1930s. We can see, therefore, that art and artists are not set apart from the real world, but an art history which has its origins in the cataloguing of collections of objects in the galleries and museums of the West, in the counting of private wealth, will inevitably reflect the attitudes which give rise to such institutions and collections. It will have the greatest difficulty in acknowledging the influence of external factors in the development of art, and can hardly be expected to recognise that the philosophy it underwrites stands in direct opposition to what many artists think and feel, supporting as it does a value system artists were rejecting well over a century ago.

I am not an art historian and cannot aim here at a comprehensive account of the origins and development of modern art, but I do discern among the many and sometimes mutually-opposed strands a current of thinking and practice which promised new attitudes to work and art. I see these ideas emerging from a very broad critique of the industrial society that was growing up in nineteenth-century Europe, and that was by no means restricted to the arts. William Morris, who straddled so many areas of creative and political thought, was harbinger and prophet for these tendencies. Morris valued work and art equally, and campaigned for their integration in new forms of creative labour which he hoped would provide the foundations for a more humane society.

Over the course of the next century artists, architects and social thinkers grappled with the questions Morris raised in his writings and lectures. What is the significance and relevance of art, and what role does it have in the shaping and functioning of society? What is the function of work, and how can it be humanised and reclaimed in a period of industrialisation, mechanisation and factory production? I am convinced that it was a cultural, moral and political revolt among nineteenth-century artists which formed the springboard for modern art. William Morris leaves us in no doubt as to the motivation behind his rejection of the heroes of what he saw as a bogus classicism and institutionalised academic art, and his desire for new forms of social organisation within which an authentic art might flourish.

> Both my historical studies and my practical conflict with the philistinism of modern society have forced on me the conviction that art cannot have a real life and growth under the present system of commercialism and profit-mongering.[8]

He saw in the Middle Ages a different organisation of work, and different values surrounding it, which he looked to as a potential cure for the sickness of his own age and a palliative against it. Similarly in the early twentieth century the Bauhaus, first of the truly modern art schools, was founded on a desire for different values in art and society which would combine to give concrete form to a world of social justice. Walter Gropius, its founder, also looked back to the Middle Ages for inspiration: 'Let us create a new guild of craftsmen, without the class distinctions which raise an arrogant barrier between craftsman and artist.'[9] In the building of the medieval cathedrals Gropius saw precedents for a unity of the arts and crafts within an architectural whole which he believed capable of shaping a humane modern world, very much as Morris did nearly half a century earlier.

Over a long period of history, art had been in the service of the wealthier orders of society, but as artists began to break away from the academies and wealthy patrons who had supported them, they also began to take sides in what was becoming an intense struggle over the shape of society itself. This challenge was not confined to Western Europe. In Russia a group of artists cut themselves loose from the Petersburg Academy in 1863. Calling themselves the Wanderers, they claimed that art should be subordinate to reality, and set up travelling exhibitions to take their work away from the salon society of the cities into communities intimately in touch with both nature and tradition.

Chernishevskii of the Wanderers claimed that 'Reality is more beautiful than its representation in art', interpreting, as Camilla Gray points out, 'the current idea that art should be an active force in the cause of social reform, by laying an emphasis on the subject-matter of their works.'[10] The Wanderers, like the French Realists, directed their attention towards the common people – the peasants of Russia – rediscovering an Eastern cultural tradition, just as the Pre-Raphaelites, Morris and later Gropius found inspiration in the medieval tradition of craft skills and cooperation.

This turning to the real world as a source of subject matter was not restricted to fine art alone; it became an important theme for nineteenth-century novelists like Dickens and Tolstoy. From one end of Europe to the other, a pursuit of reality was engaged, at first in an idealised form and later with a deepening perception of both the natural world and the social realities which would eventually inspire the diversity of modern art and politics.

Courbet's rejection of compromise and his radical approach to subject matter are central to any understanding of the deep questioning of both artistic and social values which developed over the latter years of the nineteenth century. The Realists turned the conventions of art on their heads, painting ordinary people, who until then had provided the subject matter for lowly, often humorous, genre paintings, in as heroic a fashion as the great figures of classical mythology had previously been portrayed. Millet's monumental paintings of peasants are just that, peasants painted as Poussin painted the gods. To bourgeois society this reversal of the accepted hierarchy constituted an assault on propriety and a direct challenge to the social order itself.

Many of the isms which spread so much confusion through the history of modern art are no more than names given to groups of artists by an often uncomprehending public; names coined on the spur of the moment by journalists and critics, or artists talking tongue-in-cheek. Looking back over the complexity of artistic exploration which occurred around the turn of the century, we can see how equally uncomprehending it is to insist on a particular, sequential development of artistic styles. If, instead, we look on this as part of a continuous reassessment of the cultural panorama of the Industrial Revolution engaged in by philosophers and political thinkers as well as by artists and novelists, it becomes clear that these movements were motivated by much more than a narrow concern with aesthetic problems. They were not an internal artistic debate, but part of widespread and growing social discontent which was evident on the streets and in the cafés where these artists lived, worked and discussed political as well as artistic issues.

The definitions of art were stretched, and suddenly 'primitives' like Rousseau the customs official and later Cheval the postman, came to be considered artists. Unlike the other artists we have been talking of, these so-called primitives had nothing to do with the academic system. By comparison, their work presented a new, authentic vision, haunting in its completeness and utterly true to itself. In such works 'real' artists could now recognise an intuitive grasp of ideas they had struggled with and an alternative tradition of popular culture. A traditional, national, non-bourgeois culture was to form an important focus for much Russian art – particularly evident in the work of Chagall – and artists throughout Europe and Russia were increasingly influenced by forms of art which did not come from the mainstream of Western culture.

Japanese prints, African masks, Middle-eastern textiles, Russian icons, folk art and other non-Western traditions are often cited as chance influences on twentieth-century art, but the extent to which artists went out of their way to seek alternative sources of inspiration is generally overlooked. The move towards abstraction typical of early twentieth-century art was not an introspective development, but was born of a growing awareness of the validity of non-Western cultures and traditions. In tribal and particularly nomadic cultures, abstraction is often used to condense narrative and mythology into a form of symbolism applied to utensils and other everyday objects as more than decoration. Abstraction in art has a history every bit as long as representation itself, and the swing away from representation that we call modern art should be more correctly seen as the redressing of a fundamental imbalance between representation and abstraction which began somewhere around the end of the Middle Ages and was specific to Western art.

Artists like Picasso and Braque rejected both the idea of single viewpoint perspective common to practically all post-Renaissance art and the idea of the picture as a frozen moment of time. Instead, they found in popular and non-Western art, in medieval and African works, examples of other long-established traditions not tied to the same notions of verisimilitude. So many artists went through a Cubist phase that it is obvious Cubism was integral to a larger search for meaning, and indeed different artists used Cubism as means to very different ends. In Europe, Mondrian saw it as a stepping stone to abstraction, initially deriving abstract form from real life, and later returning to the idea of representational abstraction in works like *Broadway Boogie-Woogie*. In Russia, artists like Malevich moved towards a mystic and meditative abstraction, grasping at infinity, whereas other Russians like Tatlin were – in their abstract researches – developing a growing concern for a very different idea of what constituted reality. Tatlin's constructive art was, as he saw it, a real art made of real things from which all illusion in the form of representation had been excluded.

Ultimately, Tatlin and and his compatriot Rodchenko embraced factory production and industrial design for social use, seeing the artist's role as one of shaping a new world by designing and making products: real objects with real uses. Naum Gabo, a contemporary of Tatlin and Malevich, moved in a different direction. In his 'Realist Manifesto', which was pasted on the walls and hoardings of Moscow in 1920 he declared:

> *We renounce* the thousand-year-old delusion in art that held the static rhythms as the only elements of the plastic and pictorial arts,
> *We affirm* in these arts a new element, the kinetic rhythms, as the basic forms of our perception of real time.[11]

All these artists experimented with Cubism as part of their formal investigations, yet arrived at very different conclusions as to the nature and purpose of art. Rather than being separate little groups, as art history tends to see them, artists of this epoch constituted a unity in diversity. They took a very close interest in what their contemporaries across Europe were doing, showing none of the insularity which the separation of distinct styles and movements implies. In Hans Richter's book on Dada, there is a picture of George Grosz and John Heartfield in Berlin in 1920, holding a large poster proclaiming: 'Art is Dead – Long Live Tatlin's New Machine Art': an expression of the desire to break with tradition and the past which all three artists had in common. The movements and isms of art were never as separate as they appear on our bookshelves: art history would isolate these three into neat little categories, but the practice of art united them.[12]

So far I have tried to show how artists as a body resisted the growing dislocation between art and everyday life which came with the Industrial Revolution by rejecting the social and artistic forms industrialism gave rise to. But there was another side to this artistic revolt which manifested itself as a rejection of the conventional art market. Now that late nineteenth- and early twentieth-century works command astronomical prices, it is difficult to appreciate the personal risk the artists who actually produced these works took by antagonising the potential source of their own patronage – the art-buying middle classes. Similarly, it is easy to ignore the role played by private means and private patronage in giving to artists the independence they needed to persist in their experiments regardless of society's approval. Because of this change in the artist's role from producer of desirable objects to producer of often offensive objects and behaviour, art ceased to be the solid trade or profession it formerly was, and became a marginal and risky activity.

The buying, selling and producing of objects is so central to the whole business of art that we inevitably concentrate our attention on the objects and on artists as individuals, expecting the history of art to consist of a sequence of important works by important individuals. The value, of artworks is finally established in the auction rooms of art dealers, and reflects the importance accorded to artists whose status and worth is firmly fixed only after their deaths. Historical significance and rarity are two of the most crucial factors governing prices in an art market concerned with valuing art in terms of money alone, and so a second-rate Rembrandt is more valuable than a gallery full of brilliant works by lesser-known figures. Consequently, when we look at works of art, we tend to invest them with magical qualities to complement their fabulous monetary value. We store them in museums and galleries behind ropes and signs which say 'Do Not Touch', and these same galleries become churches of art in which such objects of veneration have become too valuable to be exposed to any danger. Not wishing to denigrate the role of museums and galleries as storehouses of cultural history, I must still object to the fact that when we visit art galleries we are all too frequently confronted with a series of objects divorced from any significant context, related only to each other in categories of period, style and, ultimately, monetary worth. Isolated, sad objects which can give us very little understanding of either the time or the social context in which they originated.

Today the contradictions surrounding the relationship between artists and the public are even more pronounced. Institutions of art have so little idea of their purpose that the Tate Gallery in London can, in all seriousness, exhibit barely arranged bricks, while the *Musée d'Art Moderne* in Paris puts tinned artist's shit on display with an equal naivete. The artist's intention may well be to say something meaningful about our ideas of art and the uses to which we put it, but a gallery is not an appropriate forum for this discussion. Only the converted are preached to while the rest of humanity finds the whole debate incomprehensible, irrelevant and often risible. Artists are all too easily drawn into this absurdity, having to produce objects to sell unless they have private means, and looking to the galleries to validate their endeavours by exhibiting them. They acquiesce in the charade and even when they try to express their scorn for the system by canning their own excrement, they demonstrate only the remarkable resilience of the art market and their own continuing dependence on it. The dilemma facing aesthetics, on the other hand, is to account for something supposedly inherent in works of art that can possibly justify the absurd values the art market gives to them.

Over a few hundred years these values have changed dramatically. Becoming an artist is like entering a lottery where the few lucky ones collect fabulous sums of money while the many end up empty-handed. This has not always been the case. As far as I can ascertain, an established Renaissance painter with a workshop, assistants and apprentices could expect a similar remuneration to someone working now in the crafts or trades and running their own workshop. There is little doubt that these were the conditions under which the great works of Giotto and other early Renaissance artists were produced. However, as soon as we move out of the secure arena of what is perceived primarily as work, we require a special theory of art to guide and instruct us. In *Art and Its Objects*, published as recently as 1968,[13] Richard Wollheim presents us with just that – endless philosophising over the 'logical or ontological status of works of art' – but expends barely a word on the context of art, on where and how it is made, or on the artist's relationship with society and the world at large. It appears that all art exists in a complete vacuum, where no outside references are permitted to sully the hushed gallery atmosphere.

By contrast, one of the marvellous features of medieval art is that it can still be experienced in context, in religious buildings and books which, although damaged by time and changed by circumstance, still convey some of the original intent which inspired them. If we start to look at the *work* of artists as a way of shaping the world in which we and other very different civilisations live, and as a way of changing our perception of that world, it becomes all the more difficult to imagine how art can be possessed when it should really be more of a process and less a collection of things. The process that began in the middle of the nineteenth century was concerned with the definition of a new reality. Modern art gave us new ways to experience the world around us, and made us realise that the world does not have to be as it appears – that appearances are always deceptive. All this cannot be bought and sold; it is a form of awareness which has permeated our consciousness, and the achievement of art has been the unfolding of that awareness. Styles and isms were never separate and sequential developments, but always part of this growing, changing, evolving consciousness.

I would argue that the true function of art is to shape, define, form and inform the ways in which we create our environment day by day. We are the only species who can be said to have reversed the process of adaptation by obliging our environment to conform to our demands and apparent needs. But if our demands on the environment start to outstrip or pervert our real needs, the creative adaptation of the world – the structuring of reality – becomes destructive, both of the world and of ourselves. Unfortunately this destructive process is well advanced, and the separation of art from work has produced a deep-seated alienation, not just in our workforce, but in our artists as well.

Two world wars in this century effectively halted the momentum of artistic demand for a revolution in art and life, leaving artists with no recourse other than to revive academicism under the guise of respectable modern art. In the 1960s and the 1970s a resurgence of energy began to appear in anti-art happenings and events, and in political demands for a revolution in everyday life: a joint attempt to restore an element of ritual and celebration to a uniformly bland life, and to point out the absurdity and violence of that life. Nor is it surprising that such forms of spontaneous art as the powerful posters of the Atelier Populaire, street theatre, and imaginative graffiti and slogans surfaced among the events of May 1968 in Paris, and spread across Europe and America to inspire a generation of artists who turned their backs on the conventional art world. Suddenly, again, there seemed to be the possibility of uniting a spontaneous art with the shaping of a new society in which people could give valid expression to their longstanding frustration in the face of an alienating culture.

In retrospect, it was perhaps a short-lived tilt against the growing confidence of technological materialism and the consumer society, but it was nevertheless an expression of what has been an unrecognised current in artistic endeavour for over 100 years, one that appears in William Morris's writings and lectures, and is reiterated by the Dadaists and Surrealists, telling us that art cannot thrive until the social order changes in such a way that art can again assume a major role in shaping and informing everyday life. Until then, artists will either remain outsiders or become, as did Morris and the Situationists of the late 1960s, social revolutionaries trying to create conditions in which art can flourish once more.

8

From Utopia to Ronan Point

In this chapter I take issue with what is becoming an entrenched attitude towards 'modernism'. Instead of being progressive and enlightening as it would claim to be, this anti-modernism is, I think, smug and deeply reactionary. We should learn lessons from the past, not look to it for scapegoats for the present.

After the heady, revolutionary, early years of the twentieth century, artists found a renewed social purpose in art, and set about using the experiments of cubism and abstraction, and the formal language that they had shaped, as a basis for building a new, rational world with people at its centre. In Russia and Europe, architects saw the possibility of a socialist Utopia, but they did not reckon with the consequences of the abandonment of traditional building practice which this rational architecture seemed to demand. Nor did they realise that, by creating a recognisable 'style' of modern architecture, their progressive, socialist idealism could be subverted to the dubious cause of consumerism.

The real problem of modernism in architecture is the abandonment of skill which comes with mechanisation and automation; a problem not restricted to architecture and building. If, however, we persist in making the architects of the modern movement the scapegoats for everything that is at fault with our cities, we are unlikely to confront, before it is too late, the difficult and crucial contradictions inherent in our attitudes towards technology which are the root cause of these problems.

I brushed the last shavings off my bench and arranged the tools in their proper order: planes under the bench, stone and oilcan in the well – at the back – and in front of them rule, marking knife, tape, square and bevel, two pencils – one hard, one soft – and my favourite red-handled chisel: the Swedish one. I filled out a time sheet and clipped it to my board along with the drawings for some recent jobs, cutting lists, and other notes I kept for reference. Finally I swept the floor, leaned the broom against the shavings bin and, the ritual tidying that marked a job completed, walked down to Bill's little office.

Bill the foreman glanced up from his lists. Sitting on his high stool with a knitted mitten on one hand he looked for all the world like a character straight out of Dickens. It was autumn, with a hint of frost on the morning

7

air, and Bill, who was still recovering from a nasty stroke, was troubled with poor circulation.

'Have you finished those frames then?' he asked, his voice rising and falling with a fenland inflection that made a question of every sentence. I nodded.

'Well, you'd better make a start on these doors then', he said. 'I should think you can make fifteen pair.'

'The balcony doors!' I exclaimed to myself. I had been almost praying for that job. Previously I had made some sashes, about 50, for the same site – interesting and tricky things they were, not at all straightforward – and I knew that the doors would be similar: a bit of a challenge and something to break the boredom of churning out council house door frames day after day. What a soul destroying job that was! One and a half hours each if you were to make your bonus, from rough timber to finished item. Complete with waterbar, drips and grooves. No mouldings, not even a bevel to break the monotony. Nothing pretty, nothing inspiring, just work like mad if you want to make that bonus and pay the bills. But the balcony doors ... that was different! Prestige estate, fancy joinery, no expense spared.

Bill pulled the rod out of a pile leaning against the wall, disturbing the layer of fine dust that gets everywhere in a woodworking shop no matter how good the extraction system. We walked through the peppery cloud, out the back door and down stairs. Bill's office was a virtual corridor between workshop and back stairs, leading to the machineshop and timber store. He took me down now to show me what to use.

There was a large pile of 50 x 150 mm redwood in the racks, bought in specially.

'We couldn't get any two-be-five', explained Bill.

'It's not very good, is it?' I said, checking the wood over. 'Look at all that heart!'

'Well ... pull out enough for your fifteen pair and see what it looks like planed up', said Bill.

I pulled the timber out of the rack, disappointed now. They could never bring themselves to buy decent timber. I grumbled to myself as Bill shuffled off back to the warm, and could see at a glance that this would never make good doors. There was heart right through the middle of some pieces – they would split, sooner rather than later – or the heart was close to the surface, and would spoil the face with shakes and pith by the time it was planed up. Other pieces were already beginning to warp and twist, almost imperceptibly, but enough to suggest what was going to happen to them. By the time I had planed that out they would be undersize and still moving! Hopeless!

What I would have bought, given the chance, was good quality two-by-eleven or two-by-twelve Kara Sea redwood, shipped out of Siberia in the summer months when the ice has melted, and stamped E**I in red on the end of each plank. Slow grown timber without serious knots – a little more expensive and a bit resiny, but worth it. I would have cut any pithy heart out of the middle when I split the boards in half, and still have finished up with two pieces a full five inches wide. But more important still, by reassembling the two halves as one door I would have ended up with matching stiles. Not only would that look good, and these doors were to be stained, but the doors would have been balanced in tension, with internal stresses equalised. The result of that exercise would have been good traditional quarter-cut door stock, and stable, long-lasting doors.

Making a door is not at all as simple as it seems at first sight. Redwood is temperamental stuff, and difficult to obtain in good quality. As the northern forests are depleted, trees are cut down before they mature, and so the wider boards tend to be cut through the middle of trees to make up the desired width. Such boards are inherently unstable, whilst the faster growth and faster seasoning which are now the norm make the timber even less reliable and less durable. Wider softwood boards or planks, two inches thick and upwards are traditionally called deals. The name has gradually transferred itself to the timber, and in timber yards you will often be asked if you want red or white deal. A better quality deal will cost a little more, and the boards really have to be seen in the yard before they are bought, but this is one area where the builder can shave costs and save money. A little phoning around, a good price, and timber bought unseen can keep the quote down and win the contract.

By tradition, a door is made from a deal of the appropriate width, which is then ripped into two to produce the matching sides of the door, the stiles. With care, a skilled joiner can place rebates and mouldings in such a way as to remove or minimise any last defects in the timber – an edge knot here, the remains of some heart shakes there – and produce a pair of first class stiles from a plank which originally looked suspect. Cut as they should be, with the grain laying in the right direction, those stiles will remain stable and serviceable for 50 or 100 years and, framed up properly, will make a door that will warp only if it is seriously abused.

That is the joiner's art: a feel for materials combined with a traditional skill. Methods which have taken centuries to develop, which accommodate the nature of the materials, stabilise and neutralise internal stresses and tensions, and produce a sound durable piece of work with deceptive ease. Done carefully, there is remarkably little waste in the process and a good door is the almost inevitable result. But the timber has to be right in the first place: fitting for the job at hand. Still relatively new to the firm, I couldn't make much of a fuss without jeopardising my job, and so I got on with facing up the timber. There is a very fine dividing line between what can and cannot be done with materials like timber, and it is impossible to know that line without understanding and respecting both tradition and materials. Once you overstep that line everything starts to go wrong, but tradition, if understood and acknowledged, safeguards against mistakes. People have learned by the long process of trial and error just how materials should be worked – what can and cannot be done – and we abandon these principles at our peril. But we joiners had no say in the matter, we just had to make what was on the drawings with the materials provided. The unfortunate truth is that an architect cannot be expected to know as much about making doors as a skilled joiner, for architects have no real contact with the tradition that tells the joiner how a door should be made. But as architects and designers specify and describe everything more completely, there is little room left for the tradition to survive. Soon no one will know these things, and we shall all be the poorer for it.

Over the last 40 years the tradition of quality in joinery work has been seriously undermined. The architect does not necessarily produce a satisfactory design, and is tempted to depart from tradition in search of originality, while the joiner is alienated completely from all the important decisions about how things are made but is the only person who knows – or did know – how to make them well. The builder is obsessed with profit and under constant pressure over prices, the architect is obsessed with appearance, judged finally in the pages of the architectural glossies and not on the ground; and the building worker watches the clock and worries about the bonus. It is the end product – the door or building – and consequently the process of building that suffers.

An architect once asked me to build some fitted cupboards into an old house. The drawing looked very modern – rectilinear shapes with thin frames stained in contrasting colours – the sort of bold bright abstract style I like. I told him I thought it was a very striking design, but would not work. He was taken aback. I suggested some modifications in the spirit of the design that would have made it work: they might even have improved it. But he was adamant. His design was precious – not to be changed – and would work because he said so. There was no point in arguing, so I took him up to the room and held a plumb rule against the wall. It was one and a half inches out from top to bottom. I laid a straight-edge on the floor, which rose in the middle, probably above a partition wall below. I measured the diagonals of the room – a key indicator and the traditional way to test for square – nearly three inches out. His wall to wall, floor to ceiling design would never work and that was obvious to me as soon as I saw the drawings. I had no need to examine the room because I knew from experience that a Victorian terrace would have moved a little in nearly 100 years, especially in London's clay soil.

One of the chief reasons why Georgian and Victorian housing has survived so well is because it was built to accommodate some movement, some settlement. Lime mortar was the traditional building material until the beginning of this century, when cement was introduced. Unlike cement mortar, a sand and lime mix never really sets. It can be reconstituted by adding a little water, and will not resist the inevitable movement of a building over a number of years. In effect, the mortar keeps the bricks apart, while gravity holds the building up. Cement mortar has very different properties. It sets hard and sticks the bricks together. As the building inevitably settles, enormous stresses build up in the walls and, if the mix is too strong, the bricks themselves can split. Even if they don't, the mortar joints break as the building moves, and water can penetrate through the resulting cracks. Lime mortar on the other hand will allow the bricks to move a little and will heal itself afterwards. Lime mortar takes so long to cure that when Soissons cathedral was damaged during the 1914–18 war, it was discovered that the mortar between stones deep in the walls was still green – 700 years later![1]

In London, the clay soil goes through cycles of expansion and contraction depending on annual rainfall, seasonal changes and longer-term weather cycles determined by sunspot activity which can cause serious disturbance to foundations and buildings. In the Lincolnshire Fens I have seen houses built on concrete rafts which have cracked in two with their backs broken by the shifting soil, while much older lime-built houses lurch drunkenly along the drainsides but remain intact.

I tried to explain to the architect that even a new house will never be truly square unless the builders have gone to extraordinary lengths to make it so. Little errors occur, and a real measure of skill is how well we can overcome the inaccuracies of previous work and the errors of designers and managers. I had my way in the end, but it is still of very serious concern to me that the professions have assumed such arrogance. Another architect once told me in all seriousness that he thought there couldn't be much to bricklaying and that plastering must be the easiest trade of all. This set me thinking. My own experience of the 'them and us' divide between architects and skilled building workers has left me with such deep resentments that it would have been all too easy to dismiss this as further proof of professional arrogance, but I respected this architect and so had to try to understand.

Obviously he could see that plumbing and electrics, for example, are not altogether straightforward for there is plenty of theory and physics involved in those two trades. He could see a substantial technical side to them, but failed to recognise the extent of the manipulative skills involved – the know-how. As I thought about this, it became clearer to me that without any direct experience, any real acquaintance with the complexity of practical skills, it is impossible to appreciate them. As architects have little or no genuine education in the actual practice of the building trades, they cannot be expected to grasp the significance of practical skills.

This has not always been the case. One of the most striking examples of an alternative approach to architectural education was evident at the Bauhaus – the famous radical German art school of the 1920s – which brought together ideas which had motivated the arts and crafts movement with those current in the VKhUTEMAS, the art and technical college of post-revolutionary Moscow. At the Bauhaus the students underwent a practical education in one of the crafts or trades. Each subject was taught by two tutors, a designer or artist and a skilled practitioner, and this combination of the practical and theoretical, the concrete and the imaginative, balanced and informed teaching in each subject with remarkable results. The dynamic tension inherent in this approach stimulated originality amongst both staff and students which went way beyond the confines of a traditional academic training. Gropius, the founder of the Bauhaus, regarded architecture as the most important and challenging of the arts, and for this reason argued that students should achieve a practical understanding of one of the crafts before being allowed to move on to the study of architecture. He took as a model the schools of medieval builders with their universality of knowledge and capability, recognising that their achievements had been built on a solid foundation of practical skill.

Without such a keen awareness of the significance of practical skill, my architect friend was in no way equipped to judge the building trades he so regularly commissioned and directed. The hierarchy of the trades he referred to might perhaps have reflected the theoretical content of each discipline, but in terms of manipulative skill it was all wrong. Plastering is a very difficult skill to acquire and requires constant practice. Like playing a musical instrument it can appear effortless in the hands of an expert, but such a facility is easily lost without practice. Having plastered the Sistine ceiling himself, Michelangelo knew all about this, but my architect was blind to manipulative skill, and the blindness he suffered from was cultural. He was not unaware of skill, in fact he had a profound if rather vague admiration for it, but no real understanding of it.

This ignorance is unfortunately built into the way architects are trained and is part of the low regard we, as a society, have for practical skill. In this country architects have no craft training whatsoever. Because of this separation of mental and physical work a profound ignorance of the content of crafts and trades has grown up which threatens to undermine our understanding of work as a creative process.

Older workers often display an astonishing practical ability, and yet are almost apologetic about their skill, while professionals exude a studied air of self-confidence that lends credibility to their every opinion. The confidence with which erroneous ideas about bricklaying or plastering are aired can give them a weightiness which is rarely justified, and the moment such pronouncements are taken seriously the trades themselves suffer. Traditional building skills are no longer protected by the trade guilds, but depend for their continued existence on the architects who commission them. Unfortunately, few architects recognise the importance of this and even fewer make efforts to fulfil their newfound role as guardians of traditional building skills.

A new technology is all too often welcomed in place of older skills because it side-steps those awkward people who insist on making their own decisions about how a job should be carried out. Modern technology apparently removes the problematic human element from building and should therefore produce better and cheaper building. That's how the theory has it, but the trouble is that the products of this technology, the buildings themselves, patently don't work. Flat roofs leak, high-rise buildings collapse and are hated by their occupants, concrete spalls off reinforcing bars and cavity wall-ties corrode to such an extent that there is a growing industry devoted solely to correcting the faults built into modern buildings. Recent reports seriously question modern building systems, suggesting that during the 1940s, 1950s and 1960s, rather than solving the post-war housing shortage local authorities were building the slum cities of the future. Central government provided substantial financial inducements to authorities that embarked on system-building programmes, and resulted in a de-skilling of the building trades which made a large scale revival of traditional techniques unlikely, if not impossible.

The root cause of all these problems lies in the fact that skill has been devalued and edged out of modern consciousness. At the same time changes have occurred in the ways in which we see and think about the world. In particular, we have lost sight of what used to be called art, of a whole philosophy of doing things well. We can see this happening when we look at a ballet dancer for instance. Words like grace, poise, sensitivity, feeling and technique fall from our tongues, but when we look at a rough and ready bricklayer a completely different set of ideas springs to mind. We immediately see a menial, clumsy, uneducated, insensitive, less-than-human being. But to lay bricks well requires considerable skill and technique, as well as a theoretical understanding of the art. The bricklayer must have a good eye, be neat, dextrous and nimble; in short he too must have all the skills of bodily coordination that are so easily recognisable in the ballet dancer.

To build a complicated structure the bricklayer must have a grasp of the whole as complete as any dancer's understanding of a particular ballet. Look carefully at some good example of the bricklayer's art – some Victorian alms houses perhaps – with their coloured string courses, rubbed arches, reveals in special bricks, their sills and sailing courses. These were not built by ignorant clumsy oafs. The workers who constructed these buildings drew on a vast repository of skill and knowledge which they combined with a feeling for the intimate details of how each brick relates to the next and for the totality of the building as a whole.

It was impossible to turn up on site one morning and simply build such buildings. So many factors had to be taken into account and kept in mind. Much of the work had to be set out in the workshop or on site: special bricks and coloured bricks all needed stacking out ready to hand; brick arches were 'rubbed' to exact sizes and fitted dry in the workshop on the centering which eventually supported them *in situ* while the mortar went off; formwork and joinery had to be organised with care and exactitude. Nor would the building rise from the ground mechanically, course by course. The corners had to be raised first and lined in, courses counted, piers bonded, and the walls filled in with careful attention to any decorative patterning. All the bonding details had to be correct from the start and anticipate each opening in the wall – each window and door – and for this allowances were made in the initial setting out of the bond. Just like someone knitting a Fair Isle jumper, the bricklayer, in laying the first course must always have a mental picture of the entire building or at least the section under construction, and understand how it will grow on top of that first course of bricks.

The final building is implicit in this first course. Once the bricklayer has begun this plastic symphony there is no turning back: it must be completed as a continuous process, and any mistakes have to be corrected as the work proceeds. A good bricklayer, like a good knitter, makes the work seem effortless, in a way that would have made Michelangelo profoundly jealous. But this is only part of the enjoyment of the work. There is also that constant display of physical economy and dexterity that makes the artist seem at one with the materials and tools of the trade, in a very intimate and sympathetic cooperation with the physical nature of the work, in which human beings shape elements of the material world into a new and previously non-existent reality.

Many words apply equally well to artist and artisan, to bricklayer and ballet dancer, but this should not be so surprising, for they both produce a work of art as part of a performance. We accept the validity of a dancer executing a difficult passage with faultless grace and artistry, but fail to see, in the equivalent discipline of the bricklayer, anything other than a low-grade skill. Yet both are exponents of important and consequential arts, without which this world would be a meaner place. Why this inability to recognise the true value of practical skill, and why the distinction between art and work which sentences so many people to a life of menial toil?

In the late nineteenth and early twentieth centuries, it was still possible to recognise the depth of understanding about the natural world embedded in traditional skills and transmitted via the medium of apprenticeship: a practical way of learning through intimacy and familiarity. When Morris, and later Gropius, talked of these skills, they were referring to a living and continuous tradition that stretched back to the origins of civilisation itself. And although that tradition had been eroded and depleted, it was none the less evident in a way that it is no longer. Here at the fag-end of the century we can only hint and conjecture, trying to discern the outlines of a former age, like archaeologists poring over aerial photographs.

Traditional skills were taken for granted and exploited well into the twentieth century, and in many respects made the post war consumer revolution possible, in the same way that the medieval workshop system made the Renaissance possible. Unfortunately, the real value of skill, the deep and sympathetic understanding of materials and processes which is an integral part of it and learned through apprenticeship, has never been fully understood. As a consequence skill has been debased, in particular by people who see the need to organise production in disciplined ways, which they perceive as progressive and 'modern'. So progress is equated with a mechanistic view of the world, which is certainly capable of production in quantity but at the expense of a whole range of qualities which give significance and meaning to important aspects of life and work.

It may be possible to harness the skill and experience of traditionally-trained workers, and exploit this through, for example, computer-operated paint-spraying equipment, aping the behaviour of an original, skilled operative whose precise movements are memorised and converted into a programme to drive automated machinery. But while machines can mimic a set of actions, they cannot learn the sensitivity and thoroughness fundamental to skilled work. In fact, they cannot be said to learn at all, except in the narrowest of terms. Trade skills are a mystery to our automated machines, precisely because the inventors and programmers have no experience and no understanding of skilled work. They do not see the need for a symbiotic relationship between machine and operator, and so look to eradicate the remaining element of uncertainty in the system – the human element. If skills are not practised and taught, they will atrophy. And when they do who will be left to instruct the machine?

Complete automation of production is not the only future that computer-controlled machinery offers us. Production based on smaller machines programmed by individual operators to perform a diversity of intricate operations is conceivable. This would make small-batch production not just feasible but cost effective in a way it cannot be at present, opening up the possibility of an endless variety of customised products. We would then be able to escape the inevitable standardisation of products which accompanies line production and return to something much closer to workshop-based craft production, in which individual skills would be highly developed and apprenticeship training again viable. We stand very much on an edge at the moment, at the beginning of a new industrial revolution that will change our world as radically as the last. We still have a choice about the direction in which revolutionary changes in the nature of production will take us. Large-scale automated production will require such massive organisation of finance and resources that we as individuals will feel increasingly inconsequential and alienated, except in our ability to consume. Small-scale automated production, on the other hand, offers us the possibility of a human-scale, decentralised society capable of providing for itself at more than subsistence level, in a diverse, creative and challenging future in which old dreams of merging country and city, field and factory could become reality.

The original conception of the Bauhaus as an experiment in which artist and artisan would unite in a 'Guild of craftsmen without class distinction', redesigning and redefining every element of the manufactured environment, from fabrics and typography to architecture and town planning, backfired on the idealists who instigated it. Instead of liberating people from toil and producing a harmonious world full of appropriate and useful objects, the closely-defined design task and the standardisation and detailed definition of manufactured objects became the very backbone of the production lines of modern industry and the alienating, highly-disciplined work which had already evolved around them.

The intention of the new art schools, the Bauhaus in Weimar and the VKhUTEMAS in Moscow, was born of a desire to reassess the objectives of production, to reconcile spontaneity and standardisation, and to reunite the world of art with the world of work. By reviving the medieval tradition of craftwork alongside modern technological processes, and by giving to art a new and constructive social purpose, the VKhUTEMAS and the Bauhaus tried to prepare the ground for a transformation of European culture, which was swept aside by the rise of fascism in the 1930s. Contemporary disillusionment with the reality of consumer society – vast blocks of empty offices and desolate flats, deficient systems of industrial building, shoddy products hiding behind glossy exteriors and elaborate packaging – the marketing of fantasy – has brought with it a nostalgia for traditional products and a largely unwarranted criticism of 'modernism'. Modernism has become a convenient scapegoat for the excesses of capitalism. But to brush aside the modern movement of the 1920s and 1930s as one huge self-opinionated mistake is another strategy for avoiding the real issues. Laying the blame for consumerism on individuals rather than on the structure of society paves the way for a renewed endorsement of the present, in which technology is inevitably presented as progressive and as such appears to need no other justification.

It is all too easy to attack Gropius *et al.* The God-like status which he and other founders of the modern movement in art and architecture have acquired was bound to bring a reaction sooner or later, but it is a mistake to overlook the extent to which experiments like the Bauhaus and the VKhUTEMAS tried to come to terms with fundamental problems concerning the relationship between art and society, which we are even further away from solving some 50 years later.

So many different political and artistic experiments of the early twentieth century demonstrated imaginative if partial solutions to the problem of propelling society in a creative rather than a materialist direction. These experiments have often shown a real historical consciousness, looking to the past for models of a future society. So modernism itself should not be mistaken for a blind advocacy of progress, but as a preparedness to use new techniques and technologies where appropriate to progress towards a new society. Progress in this sense is radically different from the progress represented by 'modern' technology. It is not progress measured in terms of greater material wealth produced with less physical toil, but social progress as the evolution of an egalitarian and participatory society in which techniques and technologies enable people to express and fulfil themselves individually and collectively. This was the vision that inspired the work of so many artists of the 1920s and 1930s, and which led Gropius to talk of his guild of craftsmen without class distinction.

The fact that Western affluence is built on Third World poverty, and that in Europe and America increasing numbers of people live in poverty, reveals the extent to which modern technology and industrial production have failed to provide material sufficiency for the majority of people. The reduction of human labour in modern industrial processes is creating not leisure for all but massive unemployment, and in the West a growing sector of the population is not only poor but looked on as useless because it is not involved in material production. As a consequence, the wastage of human potential grows alongside the material waste implicit in consumerism, and our consumption of raw materials grows daily with no real benefit to humanity.

This shift to consumerism was facilitated by the creative experiments of the early twentieth century which were diverted from their original objectives in a direction determined by economic and political factors. Even the most far-sighted and idealistic of those experimenters inadvertently played their part in initiating changes they would probably no longer condone. The Russian architect Lubetkin, who was born in 1902, participated in the intensive and heady discussions on new art and architecture which were a feature of post-revolutionary Russia. Little finance being available for building, much architectural activity was restricted to the speculative discussion of possible forms and purposes for buildings of the future. Forms that would house people and, like Tatlin's monumental tower celebrating the Third International, symbolise and celebrate that future.

Lubetkin came to England in the early 1930s after a peripatetic 'journeyman' period in Europe when, like Villard d'Honnecourt, he visited major centres of architectural practice. In England he founded Tekton, an architectural collective dedicated to confronting the complacency of the profession. Experienced in building materials and techniques, he adopted a positive and innovative attitude towards building and architecture as a social force, arguing with conviction that architecture should be more than mere self-display and that individualism had to become a thing of the past. He said recently:

> After the war I went to Auschwitz, and there was a road as white as the paper you are writing on. White with the bones of people. That shows how unimportant biography is. One should be interested in architecture, not in architects.[2]

On a collective basis, Tekton developed a form of discussed, accessible design, concerned with socially useful projects.[3] They described and accounted for their buildings not as special, sacrosanct works of art, but as ideas open for discussion, as vehicles for involving people in decisions about their physical environment. Sunlight and ventilation, electrical fittings, circulation and a flexible use of space, all were presented in the form of drawings which invited participation and discussion: proposing alternative solutions, explaining why choices had been made, and opening up the process of design to public debate. The intention was to develop a form of architectural practice which would be a complete break from the past – democratic rather than dictatorial – and committed to confronting the social need for buildings which provided essential facilities for people living not as isolated individuals, but as integrated communities. The Finsbury Health Centre in North London (1935–8) is a fine example of this approach. An intimate, relaxed building which escapes all the alienating institutionalism of so many hospitals, it is human in scale, light and airy, and above all flexible enough to meet the changing needs of a local community.

In their concern to investigate new building techniques and exploit the potential freedom of construction these techniques made possible, the designers of Tekton developed innovatory procedures like the movable shuttering system used in High Point flats at Highgate. This technique, which presaged much of modern *in situ* concrete construction, allowed floors and walls to be cast as one, giving enormous flexibility to the design and freeing the internal space of structural clutter so that movement would not be restricted by the form of the building. Their intention was to design habitable spaces which would retain this flexibility throughout their useful life: a breakthrough that should have involved builder and designer in a new and exciting collaboration, with the potential of extending the quality of life in regenerated towns and cities. Unfortunately these new techniques were set aside by the advent of the Second World War, only to be revived and exploited immediately afterwards as a way of dispensing with expensive, skilled building labour which was in short supply as a direct result of years of warfare and the neglect of the apprenticeship system.

System-building, despite obviously indequate design and development and high prime cost, was ushered in as a way to cope with the aftermath of war. But instead of giving us the cities of Lubetkin's vision, system-building was directly responsible for the horrendous estates which are now breeding grounds for despair and drug addiction. At the same time the strength and autonomy of the skilled trades unions, which had demonstrated an alternative approach to the rebuilding of our cities in the achievements of the building guilds in the 1930s, was broken. Apprenticeship began to fall into disrepute, and a de-skilled and alienated workforce is now all that remains of the proud lineage of the medieval builders which architects like Lubetkin and Gropius admired so much. In his book *Tenants Take Over*, Colin Ward gives a graphic account of the considerable and little publicised achievements of the building guilds, which were a form of cooperative firmly rooted in the building trades unions.

The Addison Housing Act of 1911 made it possible for housing to be built with little capital, payment being made as the work proceeded. The building unions in Manchester saw the possibilities this offered and, influenced by S.G. Hobson, a wellknown guild socialist propagandist, formed a Building Guild. Meanwhile in London, Malcolm Sparkes persuaded the operatives to form the London Guild of Builders. The movement spread and in no time at all there were 140 Guilds which joined forces in 1921 as the National Building Guild. For legal purposes only the Guild was registered as a limited company, which undertook centrally the work of finance, insurance and supply, while the making of the contracts was in the hands of Regional Councils, elected by the local guild committees and by the craft organisations of the region (including professional organisations of clerks, architects and engineers). Capital was borrowed at a fixed rate of interest, and full trade union rates paid during the currency of the contract 'in sickness and in health, in good weather and bad' – something unheard of in those days.

Surpluses were to be used for improvements and development, not distributed to individuals. In cases when a job worked out cheaper than was expected, the saving on the contract price was handed back to the local authority employing the guild ...

The London Guild landed a £500,000 contract at Walthamstow, and the Manchester Guild had contracts worth £1,428,918. By April 1922, from less than a year's actual work they had received £849,771 in cash and had spent £30,283 on plant.

The Guilds attracted the best men, and there was genuine workers' control. The independent investigator, Ernest Selly, after examining the contracts on each site, concluded that:

1. The Guilds have proved they are organised on business-like lines and are able to carry out building operations in a workmanlike manner

2. The quality of work produced is distinctly above the average

3. The weight of evidence goes to show that the output per man on Guild contracts is as good as that obtained by the best private contractors, and certainly higher than most.

Ten years after they were built, the estates of Manchester built by the Guilds were shown to have cost the local authority least in maintenance and repair work.[4]

No wonder the banks and master builders' associations joined forces to undercut and destroy the building guilds. The potential of a democratic building organisation under workers' control had been clearly demonstrated. The tragedy of the development of system-building, which takes all responsibility away from the building worker, is that it moved in a direction never anticipated by innovators like Lubetkin. It was never the intention of the Tekton group that builders and designers should be anything other than united in a regenerated building process, and this is demonstrated by the key roles Lubetkin and Skinner – another member of the practice – played in the Architects and Technicians Organisation (ATO), which included building workers as members. Lubetkin and Skinner had a perspective which embraced the democratisation of design and the involvement of a skilled and respected workforce in architectural considerations. They saw the need for a unity of purpose to replace existing divisions of labour in the industry and were thus diametrically opposed to later trends which actively sought to replace skilled labour with factory-style system-building. In naming their group Tekton, they revived the Greek word for builder, emphasising building as an integrated activity which was to transcend the barriers between architect and builder.

Over this century, however, the divisions have gradually deepened. Gropius's guild of craftsmen and Tekton's vision of building as a socially useful activity have been suppressed by industrialised building techniques; to my mind this is one of the primary reasons for the myriad failures in modern buildings. Within the traditional building process, it is anathema to construct a building which fails to perform its practical functions of keeping out the weather and standing up to the rigours of use and climate. It should have been possible to graft new techniques on to this tradition so that the the centuries of practical experience inherent in the building trades could inform these new techniques with a respect for the principles of good building practice. But that would have required the involvement of site workers in evaluating and developing these techniques. A scientific approach to building technology excluded the workforce as scientifically ignorant, thereby reducing highly-skilled people to mere functionaries and paving the way for continuous and expensive failures.

Lubetkin was profoundly disturbed by what he saw going on around him, and gave up architecture in the 1950s. A recent interviewer was perceptive enough to remark that Lubetkin anticipated architecture's descent into the 'kind of fashionable merry-go-round' which it has become. Lubetkin remains a disillusioned old man, convinced that the world is in a tragic state and given to quoting Bertold Brecht's famous saying, 'If you see a light at the end of the tunnel, jump aside, it's the express train coming in the opposite direction.' He is right of course, because it is the corruption of the intentions of modern art and architecture that is at fault, not the endeavours of its originators. The central problem is, as Lubetkin calls it, the 'universal abandonment of reason'.[5]

At a gut level the rational world of modern industry and science fails to make sense to an increasing number of people, yet we have no theory of art or architecture which can cope with this dilemma. It is increasingly apparent to me that only by uniting the original utopian and humanitarian objectives of modern art with the practices of much older traditions of skilled and autonomous work, can we begin to construct the theoretical basis for a democratic architecture capable of rebuilding and renovating our cities. We can either go on building tomorrow's slums, with all the best intentions in the world, or we can begin to revive skill and responsibility within the building industry. If we are to solve these problems the choice is as stark as that. I am convinced that there is no middle road, for if we abandon our cities to fate, the whole infrastructure of society will collapse around the Victorian sewers and post-war tower blocks which are already so shamefully neglected and ignored.

9
Bridging the Gap between Art and Life

To many people modern art is meaningless and incomprehensible. In this chapter I try to give some clues as to why contemporary art and modern artists appear so lost, and how the initial impetus of radical change and challenge which characterised modern art at the beginning of the century has fizzled out. Art and architecture have become trapped in a blind alley, a philosophical dead-end, where wit and style are no substitute for content and intention.

If art is to become valid and relevant again, our attitude towards it will have to change. It is time to break down the division between hand and brain by bringing art and work together again as activities and attitudes that can no longer remain mutually exclusive.

Modern art always comes across as a difficult subject, as if we need to understand very complex aesthetic issues before we can begin to appreciate it. Emphasis is placed on understanding rather than enjoying, and this serves to intimidate in the same way that museums and galleries do, by implying that most of us are ignorant. I have never found modern art difficult, not because of any superior intellectual ability, but because, like the child in *The Emperor's New Clothes*, I was too naive to join in the game or to realise that anything other than enjoyment was asked of me. As a teenager, I visited art galleries with enthusiasm, walking around saying: 'I like that ... I don't like that.' I never felt a need to understand some obscure mystery. Gradually I learned to look beneath the surface and search for reasons, to ask why artists had produced the works I intuitively liked.

In the early twentieth century many artists saw themselves as part of an innovative international movement. They experimented furiously in their attempts to expand the frontiers of art and, if questioned, would have agreed that there was no one way of proceeding. It is this very unity of intention that is fundamental to modern art, allowing artists to see themselves as part of a broad movement unified by its collective commitment to change and diversity of experiment: a purpose which individual styles and isms obscure.

In this sense, modern art was always revolutionary, and as such could be fully realised only in the context of revolutionary change. The chief reason why so-called 'modern' art and architecture seem irrelevant now is because the social changes ushered in by the twentieth century were not those for which modern art was preparing. Modern art lost its *raison d'être* as the revolutionary fervour of those early years failed to give birth to a socialist Europe. The Soviet Union turned away from the idea of international revolution and reacted against the new art, retreating into a sterile state academicism. The experiments of the Weimar Republic were swept away by Nazism and pioneering European artists fled to America. But although the early visions of a creative generation faded, enormous areas of artistic activity had been opened up and advances made which remain relevant today.

The direction taken by Western society after the early years of the twentieth century – the commitment to industrial production and materialist values on both sides of the Iron Curtain, and in the West in particular the growth of consumerism – was to create an impasse for many artists. Forces outside their control were aggressively shaping and structuring society in ways often alien to their utopian visions of the future. At the beginning of the century, artists had grasped at an intuitive level the role creativity should play in shaping that future, but had no real idea of how to be effective in practice. They awaited a revolution, a dramatic social upheaval to recognise the importance of their contribution and call them in from the wings of history, but instead the enormously powerful forces of profit and greed brushed artistic ideas aside and set about creating a world of material wealth built on growing industrial and technical power.

At first artists tried to steer this new technical capacity in the direction of a classless utilitarian society, but in the end they were betrayed by their own belief in the progressiveness of science. The feeling among artists and designers in the 1920s and 1930s was that they were leading technological change and could therefore control and direct it. This may have been true for a few years as artists experimented with new materials and techniques – laminated plywood, concrete, glass and plastics – but mass production demanded a centralisation of control. Images and the image-makers were sucked into promoting the mass products of industry, and as the growth of military strength in Germany in particular further reinforced the centralisation of power, industrial production became the first priority throughout the Western world. Instead of giving us a world shaped by art and constructed for human enjoyment and fulfilment, the second machine age ushered in a new social order in which materialist values predominated and artists were once again isolated in their aesthetic concerns. Money was poured into building armies and armaments factories instead of hospitals and housing, and the socially useful design projects of the 1920s remained ideas on paper.

The rise of Nazism and Stalinism, and the tragedy of the Second World War, effectively closed a period of experiment which had seen few of its ideas realised. The industrial consumer society that grew up after that war had little sympathy with the original objectives of the modern movement in art and architecture, but was happy to incorporate those elements which suited its purpose and could give its products the 'modern' styling which advertising soon linked to progress. The profit motive triumphed, regenerated by advertising's exploitation of the powerful new media of radio and television, which created artificial habits and desires that the addictive products of modern industry would never truly satisfy.

Under these adverse circumstances, art did not die away completely but was once again forced to stand outside the mainstream of life. Art and work did not combine into a creative shaping of the world; instead work retained its unpleasant connotations and the concept of leisure, of not-work, was introduced to fill the void creative work could have occupied. Over this period artists became increasingly introspective, leaving commercial art to develop the skills of drawing, representation and the handling of materials, while fine artists moved into the inaccessible field of the gesture – abstract expressionism – protecting personal vision and sensitivity from exploitation by the commercial world, hiding behind obscurity and widening the gap between art and life.

The art market responded to a financial world which saw in art objects a sound investment option with high yields to those who could predict its movements with some accuracy, and was quick to embrace each new stylistic development. The result is that artistic success is now almost entirely a question of marketing, and art has been drawn effectively into the arena of commodity production, a rarified and very special commodity, but a commodity none the less, which is bought and sold speculatively and confers status on its owners by virtue of its value. To own a particular work is to make a specific statement about yourself or your company, a statement about wealth, taste and style, and within this convention very little is understood or asked of the artist except that she or he be famous, be recognised. As Andy Warhol said:

> To be successful as an artist you have to have your work shown in a good gallery ... you need a good gallery so the 'ruling class' will notice you and spread enough confidence in your future so collectors will buy you ... No matter how good you are, if you're not promoted right you won't be one of those remembered names.[1]

The radical content of a Grosz or a Magritte now lies hidden behind its status as a valuable object, and images have lost their power to affect us at gut level, to seize on our feelings and change the way we see and experience the world. This ability of art to act as a lens through which we see the world, forming, informing and challenging our perception, has been taken over by the media and by advertising, and in that process the ability of art to challenge our day-to-day assumptions about the world has been subverted.

Despite the constant attempts of artists to achieve that 'shock of the new' which is the stock-in-trade of the *avant-garde*, art works have lost any real ability to shock. No longer amazing objects confronted in daily life – the icon in the church, the ritual mask – no longer acts of prodigious, magical skill, vision and power, art works are reduced in status to bland objects by the contexts in which they are encountered. Gallery and museum, arts centre and office building, all conspire to deny the power of art to transform our understanding of ourselves and the world we live in, and so modern art is now firmly established as an adjunct to polite society.

Potent images are channelled into every home and ruthlessly controlled by the vested interests of capital and authority. Our knowledge and understanding of the world, our images of ourselves, our aspirations and desires, our models and morals are all handed down to us through the filters of TV and technology: an anti-culture serving only to isolate and manipulate. Real cultural activity takes place outside the media, when people come together to shape their own identities in a collective process, when they challenge the narrow conformity inflicted on them by the ethic of consumption, and discover identities which can only be invented in celebration and protest. In the past, denied the ability to participate in shaping the world, artists became increasingly involved either with the production of seductive objects for the rich and powerful, persuasive images of wealth and status, or with the exploration of a personal reality seen with fresh and critical eyes. Some, like Goya, managed to walk a tightrope between the two, making regal images of the Spanish ruling class, and simultaneously exposing the vanity and horror of the social structure they upheld. Others were sucked into that system as they became dependent on the patronage of the rich.

In a sense the same persistent dilemma faces artists today, for while art remains separate from everyday life it cannot be sustained and supported as part of common experience, nor can it play a part in the economics of daily life. It can never therefore be of direct significance to more than a tiny minority of the population and must remain dependent on either the state or that minority for patronage.

In Russia, the triumph of conservative state capitalism over the surge of experimental energy that followed the revolution of 1917 had disastrous consequences for the potential development of a new art of the people. Discussions about the nature and form of an art that would be popular, modern and relevant to the new Soviet order, were constant and intense, trying to visualise a practice which could integrate production and technology within a humanising aesthetic. Differences of opinion were enormous, and the whole debate was seen as crucially important at a time when the Russian people were trying to throw off the tyranny of bourgeois habits and ideas. Artists saw the revolution as their great opportunity to become at last contributing members of society, bridging the gap between art and life.[2] However, the series of conservative steps which brought an end to creative freedom and established an academic and barren form of art servicing the defensive Russian state – Socialist Realism – was coupled with the dashing of hopes for an international revolution across Europe. This meant that by the early 1930s experiment in Russia had virtually ceased, and similar European experiments found themselves isolated. Without radical changes in the nature of production itself, moves towards a democratic, anti-individualist art in the West were frustrated and remained divorced from economic life as esoteric and apparently obscure aesthetic movements. Unable to change the underlying motive of industrial production – profit – the great European experiments in new art forms, the De Stijl group in Holland and the Bauhaus in Germany, found their ideas and products taken up by a society unsympathetic to their intentions and vision.

In the end, capitalism's ability to absorb isolated challenges paved the way for the domination of the media by industry and finance, which in turn made possible the structuring of desires by advertising. Thus the radical experiments of the 1920s and 1930s provided the very images of modernity used to promote the myth of technological progress and to usher in a form of totalitarianism masquerading as free choice – consumerism.

When things started to go wrong, particularly in housing and architecture, the very same radical experiments and their protagonists could be conveniently blamed for the mess. The discrediting of modernism is part of an attempt to divert the blame from the excesses of a consumer system obsessed with exchange values at the expense of use values. It is therefore not at all surprising that Post-modernism has emerged as a witty eclecticism, mocking the seriousness of the modern movement while providing, all too often, little more than a chic veneer for a new phase of consumerism.

At first sight, primitive and modern art appear as opposite poles in a steady development, but they are not even remote points in what we call history. The fact that we call certain forms of art 'primitive' tells us something about our reaction to things we do not understand; it also conditions our reactions to them. As a result, we look at the artefacts of aboriginal and prehistoric societies as forerunners to what we call art, dissociating them from their function as socially useful objects whose meaning derives from the integration of ritual and daily life. But by divorcing objects from the contexts in which they functioned and had significance, we catch ourselves up in the most basic of misunderstandings. An African mask in a museum is really no different from the tiger's head above the manorial fireplace – a trophy transformed into a symbol of superiority, an object devoid of any cultural context other than that of its collector. The lay-out of most museums reinforces this impression. Objects are displayed in that inexorable progression from ancient to modern, primitive to sophisticated, which assumes 'primitive art' to be an embryonic impulse from which our great culture has grown.

There are extensive similarities of appearance between some modern art works and so-called primitive art which point to the profound influence artistic traditions outside the mainstream of Western art have had on modern artists, as well as the absurdity of calling often highly-sophisticated and finely-wrought objects primitive. The strong abstract elements used in the decoration of baskets and textiles, the powerful image-making, observation and realism all apparent in prehistoric and tribal art, make any developmental theory of art suspect. Divorced from their original contexts such objects struck modern artists so forcibly as form and image pure and simple, if inscrutable, that they found in them a new formal basis for experiment. But once we begin to look at them in a social context, as objects for use, and approach them without concepts derived from our own idea of art, they present not simply a challenge to that idea but, perhaps more importantly, they call into question the quality of the objects with which we surround ourselves.

Cave paintings of animals at Lascaux and Altamira show such accurate observation, evidence of an established tradition of drawing skill, that they must disprove any suggestion that such skills grew up slowly alongside the development of what we call civilisation. Daily familiarity with the subject matter cannot account for the graphic skill displayed in these cave paintings, as anyone who has grappled with the problems of drawing will know, for realistic drawing of such quality requires a perceptual leap few people are capable of nowadays.

Human beings have been able to create realistic and symbolic images of great skill and imagination throughout the whole of social history. Within the very diverse achievement of so-called primitive societies, there is clear evidence that realism, symbolism and abstraction, the supposed invention of modern art, have been constant features. In place of a theory of progress, I would suggest that cultural achievement reaches peaks which are relatively equivalent, and that these peaks are closely related to the development of practical skills. By contrast, the prevalent tendency to debase skill and separate art and culture from any valid role in everyday life has promoted a sham and shallow modernity which fails to stand up to comparison with supposedly primitive cultures.

The significant conclusion we can therefore draw from an examination of so-called primitive and prehistoric art objects is that our modern conception of art as something divorced from use is inconsistent with the evidence of traditional societies. The real challenge of these artefacts is to the anti-traditional zeal of consumerism and its disregard for any values which cannot be encompassed within the dubious notion of progress or the discipline of the market place. All such objects are typified by their use value not their exchange value, for they were put to either ritualistic or practical use, and in the societies which produced them no separate category of useless objects – art – existed.

Indeed, works like the bronzes and ivories of Benin and the temple carvings of India challenge the greatest works of the Renaissance and reveal the essentially patronising nature of a value system which justified the exploitation of a vast empire of subject nations by labelling them 'primitive'. But the mental contortions colonialism demanded were not only applied to the restless natives of schoolboy adventure books and B movies. They have come to permeate our thinking about all those aspects of our own society which the Victorians found threatening. The working class living in their foetid urban swamps were subjected to the same patronising rhetoric and given a place on the Victorian tree of life which was perhaps even a little lower than that occupied by the occasionally noble savage.

All these hierarchies have distorted our perception of cultural difference, reducing it to glib and terrifying assertions of superiority and inferiority, the substance of fascism. But, by distorting our understanding of other cultures, they have also undermined the usefulness of concepts like art, for our understanding of what art is has been built up out of the very same theories of Western cultural superiority that fired the Victorian missionaries. Rather than having an understanding of the luxurious and vital diversity of culture which thrives on our planet, we have inherited a narrow historical justification of a Western civilisation that is assumed to have grown out of the Renaissance and developed into the edifice of modern society.

Faced with the fact of a consumer society with little time for a rogue art, what can be preserved from the remnants of what was once a proud tradition of creative labour? I do not see the future as altogether barren; creativity is a deep instinctual process and difficult to suppress. It surfaces in the critical stance of the artist as someone who objects to society, someone who can see through its pomposity and assumptions, and is prepared to say so in no uncertain terms. For although artists are vulnerable and easily coopted, although they are rarely prepared to analyse a society they can never wholly endorse, this particular ability to see with unjaded eyes is priceless. The ability to point a finger, to mock, to debunk, to joke, to ridicule – the ability to see and say that the Emperor has no clothes – is a vital skill without which we have no hope of altering the course of events. It is a skill with a long tradition of cartoonists and caricaturists, of stand up comics and travelling players, of *commedia dell'arte* troupes, of pop singers and balladeers, of street theatre and graffiti to its credit. It is a tradition of protest taken up and made vital by the quality of the imagery which has also made it unforgettable; an essentially popular art which refuses to accept and do as it's told.

Behind all this lies the ability to see afresh, without preconceptions, the ability to free-associate, imagine and invent, which provides us with the reservoir of creativity from which all these images emerge. It is also the capacity to see through humbug and pomposity, by which – nourished with humour – people have preserved their innate ability to mock authority in all its forms. I see art as a creative potential spreading like a leaven through society, informing work, changing our relationship with the world, surrounding us with beauty, and developing within us the will to resist oppression and refuse compromise. I look forward not to a society of artists but to a world in which art, as a distinct activity, ceases to exist. There is, however, one final area of life so complemented and completed by art that I can see no way it could ever be absorbed into everyday life without obvious trace. I refer of course to joy and celebration.

From the landscape sketch that talks of wonder and a fascination discovered face-to-face with nature at its most changeable – wind, weather, light and constant movement – to the elaborate festivities organised to mark a significant social event, joy, wonder and celebration have found an outlet in collective and individual activities since the days of our earliest societies. Often one of the most intangible forms of expression, characterised by song, ritual and dance, celebration – with its emphasis on spontaneity and direct emotional expression; on the moment perceived and experienced to the full – manages to achieve an immediacy that is timeless. How can we record the experience of a moment, the experience of being there, except in the sense that it might change us and our perception of the world? So celebration has perhaps the least accessible history of all the arts.

Preserved only where it appears as an object – the drawing that attempts to trace a moment, the painting that grasps at a fleeting effect of light, the carnival mask – celebration is rarely documented, and never seen for its true nature because it can only be experienced. All we are left with is the debris, the costumes and masks, some sketches for the scenery, a few snatches of song. But it is this immediate, of-the-moment quality which makes celebration perhaps the most typical and enduring of all art forms: a collective experience outside the structures of our consumer culture, with its audiences and artist-heroes, an experience in which we, the performers, are our own audience, and the result is truly cultural.

Whether we march in protest against society's crazy values, or walk the pilgrimage routes in search of ecstasy, as long as there are human beings on the face of the earth, the procession and the dance, the performance and the ritual – celebration in all its forms will be significant and unifying.

Art, once freed from the constraints of the art market and the dubious role of artist, once redefined as the outward manifestation of an instinctive creativity we all share, can become a liberating force. The secret, as Alice would have said, is to follow the principle and see where it takes us. Creativity offers us two things. First, the glorious, child-like ability to see the world afresh and engage it with a sense of wonder. It is potentially both revelatory and revolutionary, not in a destructive but in a constructive sense, suggesting that we can exchange the alienation of roles and assumptions for authenticity and a reality which cheerfully accepts our intimate involvement with one another and the natural world.

Secondly, it offers us a new involvement with work. Once we step outside the idea that work is a way of producing things, and begin to see it as an essentially creative process through which we interact with the world about us, constructing our entire environment from social structures and relationships right through to the objects we use and the food we eat, we can recognise work as a way of choosing the shape of the world we live in. We can begin to see it as something beyond time exchanged for money, and begin to determine the quality not just of our surroundings but of life itself.

If we invest work with joy and excitement, if we make it creative in human rather than material terms, we may also begin to discover in work itself a joy and pleasure which will eventually be reflected in our surroundings, and spread into our social relations. In this way I believe we can discover new forms of art, and new forms of work which have the potential to escape the stranglehold of material production and come together as an honest and sympathetic relationship with the natural world in the beginnings of a new productive process that would be both material and cultural, essentially creative and genuinely economic.

10

Useful Work versus Useless Toil

The title of this chapter is taken from one of William Morris's lectures, in which he sets out his understanding of the difference between work which retains qualities ascribable to art, and work that is devoid of all such qualities and therefore of no intrinsic worth. Here I examine Morris's thinking on this subject and trace in part his influence on later developments in the arts and recent changes in attitudes towards work. If art has lost its way, so has work. Both activities have come to seem relatively bereft of meaning, while excessive consumption does not appear to fill the gap in our lives which creative activities once occupied. Morris's ideas are especially relevant now, faced as we are with an urgent need to reassess our attitudes towards art, work and technology.

Normality in any society or culture can be described as the uniform of the dominant value system. Any deviation from the set pattern is, of course, instantly recognisable. But normality is more than a series of conventions; it is a complete reality produced and reproduced in the daily acts and events which together make up the complexity of relations which constitutes a common culture. Anyone who challenges that collective value system, either because of what they are, or what they think, is immediately seen as unusual and suspect. By the same token, anyone who is seriously critical of the world they are born into will realise, sooner or later, that to change that world they must confront an entire and extremely confident value system. Political power is not in itself sufficient to bring about real changes in our everyday lives because it is this complexity of relationships which has to change if everyday life is to change.

This realisation inspired not just early socialists and theorists like Marx and Engels, but all practitioners of socialism; the clubs, corresponding societies and self-help groups which sprang up in the second half of the nineteenth century and laid the foundations for the labour movement of today. In that period, socialism was essentially practical and experimental: a body of ideas put into practice by masses of working people who organised their own cooperatives – including what we have come to think of as 'the Co-op' – building societies and trades unions, who educated and cared for themselves, buried their dead with dignity, and combined in a solidarity which finally changed the face of nineteenth-century wage slavery. The relevance of early socialist thought is too easily lost sight of in an era of sophisticated theory, but when that theory has failed to stem the resurgence of a semi-fascist right, it is worth re-examining some of the ideas and the vision which gave birth to socialism in this country.

Now that the welfare state, and many of the other gains of organised labour, are under savage attack, it is appropriate to return to such ideas and see what relevance they still have in a period when socialism seems unable to put forward a viable alternative. In the nineteenth century, since the struggle for socialism was recognised as the struggle for an alternative value system and a new order of society, socialists like William Morris were not afraid of the implications of such a proposition. Morris says:

> Even when we explain that we use the word revolution in its etymological sense, and mean by it a change in the basis of society, people are scared at the idea of such a vast change, and beg that you will speak of reform and not revolution. As, however, we Socialists do not at all mean by our word revolution what these worthy people mean by their word reform, I can't help thinking it would be a mistake to use it, whatever projects we may conceal behind its harmless envelope. So we will stick to our word which means a change in the basis of society.[1]

By that 'change in the basis of society', Morris implied not simply a change in power or the relations of class but a complete reversal of social motivation. Usefulness, not profit, was to be the fundamental objective of a new productive system, and social usefulness in this sense did not refer simply to the end products of an industrial process, but to the nature of the process itself. Work had to change and take on some of the qualities of art, so that as an activity it might be rewarding and creative in itself, a pleasure and not merely an obligation.

The problem people like Morris identified was the need for society as a whole to change from one which produced waste and misery into one which could produce true economy and happiness for all. As they saw it, a radical change in the nature of work and production could create conditions in which a new society might develop, but such a change could be achieved only with radical changes in social relations, and in how people think and feel about themselves and one another.

Morris had a profound grasp of the social and cultural implications of industrial labour processes, and his insights are still relevant today, faced as we are with the industrialisation of mental labour. Marx elaborated his theory of alienation in work, first from the products of labour, and secondly from any involvement in the structuring of social relations through work, but, not being practical, Marx never came to the crucial understanding of working processes which Morris acquired through his physical involvement in work. Morris was a wealthy man by birth, and so escaped the demands of economic necessity which permit of very little choice and control over our working lives. But for Morris, because of his practicality, work was a concrete reality, whereas for Marx it remained an abstract concept. Had Morris elaborated his ideas in a dry theoretical way his influence might well have been greater, but that was part neither of his nature nor intention. Morris hoped for social change, not intellectual acclaim, and his apparent lack of lasting influence is indicative of the problems surrounding the relationship between theory and practice in political thinking.

Morris extended Marx's ideas by recognising work as a creative activity which had to be restructured to fulfil its function of shaping the world around us, not eliminated as mere labour carried out by slave machines. He raised, and tried to answer, the same questions about the place of work in life and the relationship between art and utility which gave birth to the enormous experimentation and discovery in Russia after the revolution. These issues have influenced debate since then, but debate has failed to stem the growth of industrialised mass production for profit. Morris's concerns, however, still give us an insight into crucial and pressing problems surrounding the future of art and skilled work.

Morris based his thinking about art and creativity on an analysis of society both impassioned and thoroughgoing, spreading his ideas through a series of lectures and talks, pamphlets and articles, in which he contrasted what he saw around him with alternatives which history and common sense suggested. In 'Useful Work versus Useless Toil' he sums up ideas in a way which, to me, is the nearest any writer has come to a democratic theory of art.

> Thus worthy work carries with it the hope of pleasure in rest, the hope of pleasure in our using what it makes, and the hope of pleasure in *our* daily creative skill.
>
> All other work but this is worthless; it is slaves work – mere toiling to live, that we may live to toil.[2]

In essence Morris's critique of society is materialistic. He judges societies by their products, but he also sees in those products qualities essentially non-materialistic: values which should rightly be called use values, and which originate in the deep pleasure and sense of personal worth found in useful skilled work. Indeed he expressed fears that an over-zealous utilitarianism might strip the world of beauty and pleasure, even under socialism.

I have always believed that the realisation of Socialism would give us an opportunity of escaping from that grievous flood of utilitarianism which the full development of the social contract has cursed us with; but that would be in the long run only; and I think it quite probable that in the early days of Socialism the reflex of the terror of starvation, which so oppresses us now, would drive us into excesses of utilitarianism.[3]

So Morris moved beyond the materialism of what is now thought of as a conventional Marxism, to judge society by the *qualities* inherent in its material products. Measuring them against a non-utilitarian standard – art – he identified a non-elitist 'Popular Art' which he found inherent in all unalienated work.

the chief source of art is man's pleasure in his daily necessary work ... nothing else can make the common surroundings of life beautiful, and whenever they are beautiful it is a sign that men's work has pleasure in it, however they may suffer otherwise. It is the lack of this pleasure in daily work which has made our towns and habitations sordid and hideous, insults to the beauty of the earth which they disfigure.[4]

By asking why popular art was denied in industrial production, Morris arrived at his own instinctive critique of capitalism, which was confirmed in discussion with fellow socialists. But the way he approached the issue – judging a society by the quality of life to which it gives rise – was rooted in a very English tradition originating with the Romantic poets and their revulsion at an emergent industrialism: grim city slums, scarred landscapes and sweated labour in factory and mill. This reaction was moulded into a coherent position by Pugin and Ruskin, two critics who were to have a profound influence on Morris. But it was Morris's ability to ground his thinking in the commonplace of popular art, the quality of the surroundings and details of everyday life, which makes his insights relevant for the future in a way Pugin and Ruskin could never be.

In Morris's utopian novel, *News from Nowhere*,[5] we are constantly aware of the quality of the environment and indeed of everyday life. Morris's time traveller marvels that everything he sees – objects, housing, clothes, the banks of the Thames, the landscape itself – glistens and sparkles from the careful and considerate touch of human hands. Everywhere is gentle beauty. Not puritanical utilitarianism but fittingness for use and a source of pleasure in the making and using which hallmarked Morris's alternative world. Indeed, a constant theme of his political writings and lectures is this conversion of quantity production into the production of quality in an everyday, egalitarian socialist life.

It is worth following some of Morris's ideas as he weaves together the themes of socially useful production, the art of work and the quality of everyday life with a more conventional class analysis of social relations and production. Morris was clearsighted enough to see beyond what is by now a deep-rooted obsession with economics and the politics of distribution which has bedevilled socialist theory in this century, and to recognise that work, the exercise of skill, might be something people could find fulfilling for its own sake. It was the beginning of a much needed politics of production, and an examination of how and why we make things and engage in what we call work.

In his political writings and lectures, Morris's intention is clearly to distinguish between two social systems and the type of work to which each gives rise; between work which is productive in terms of real needs, and work which can only satisfy artificially created needs. One sort of work carries with it 'the hope of pleasure in rest, the hope of pleasure in using what it makes, and the hope of pleasure in our daily creative skill.' This form of work is creative and useful, the other is alienating in every way – useless toil.

The origins of this alienation of work from its true nature lie in the class divisions of society and the exploitation of class by class. Morris accepts a classic Marxist division of society into a ruling class which does no work and is totally parasitic, a middle class which produces little and consumes much, caring nothing for work itself, and a working class which

produces all that is produced, and supports both itself and the other classes, though it is placed in a position of inferiority to them; real inferiority mind you, involving a degradation of both mind and body. But it is a necessary consequence of this tyranny and folly that again many of these workers are not producers. A vast number of them once more are merely parasites of property, some of them openly so, as the soldiers by land and sea who are kept on foot for the perpetuating of national rivalries and enmities, and for the purposes of the national struggle for the share of the product of unpaid labour.[6]

From here Morris goes on to develop his ideas about the nature of wealth, contrasting the material wealth and property of capitalism with the commonwealth of socialism, asking what it is that constitutes real wealth as opposed to the charade of material wealth, and pointing out the extent to which the working class, because of its material poverty, is obliged to manufacture shoddy goods for its own consumption, thereby producing the means of its own degradation. He sums up:

concerning the manner of work in civilised States, these States are composed of three classes – a class which does not even pretend to work, a class which pretends to work but which produces nothing, and a class which works, but is compelled by the other two classes to do work which is often unproductive.

Civilisation therefore wastes its own resources, and will do so as long as the present system lasts.[7]

Having displayed the wasteful nature of unnecessary and unworthy work in a class society – useless toil – he considers how the situation might be reversed; 'For us to sit hopeless and helpless then would be a strange folly indeed: be sure we can amend it.'[8]

Morris regarded machine production as evil in so far as it is used to multiply the quantity of useless toil performed and the quantity of useless shoddy articles produced, and to sentence workers to a life of boredom and drudgery. Remember his emphasis on the pleasure to be derived from our 'daily creative skill'. These ideas are dealt with at length in 'Work in a Factory as it Might Be', from which the following quote is taken:

> Furthermore machines of the most ingenious and best approved kinds will be used when necessary, but will be used simply to save human labour ... since, profit being dead, there would be no temptation to pile up wares whose apparent value ... does not rest on the necessities or reasonable desires of men for such things ...
>
> Well, the manufacture of useless goods, whether harmful luxuries for the rich or disgraceful makeshifts for the poor, having come to an end, and we still being in possession of the machines once used for mere profit grinding but now used only for saving human labour, it follows that much less labour will be necessary for each workman; ... so that the working time of each member of our factory will be very short, say, to be much within the mark, four hours a day.
>
> Now next, it may be allowable for an artist, that is one whose ordinary work is pleasant and not slavish, to hope that in no factory will all the work ... be mere machine-tending: and it follows from what was said above about machinery being used to save labour, that there would be no work which would turn men into mere machines; ... the attractive work of our factory, that which was pleasant in itself to do, would be of the nature of art.[9]

In this way Morris begins to introduce the idea of a different way of producing the world around us, a mode of production whose end is undoubtedly wealth – not wealth in money extracted from the work process as profit, but 'commonwealth', a common wellbeing within which it is unacceptable to reduce work to mere machine-minding. The principle of pleasure in working to produce beautiful and useful things is seen by Morris as a primary goal of social organisation and a way of measuring the relative value of societies. This humane and, as we would now describe it, ecological approach to making things is contrasted with what Morris disdainfully calls 'manufacture'.

For understand once for all that the *manufacturer* aims primarily at producing, by means of the labour he has stolen from others, not goods but profits, that is the *wealth* that is produced over and above the livelihood of his workmen, and the wear and tear of his machinery. Whether that *wealth* is real or sham matters nothing to him. If it sells and yields him a *profit* it is all right. I have said that, owing to there being rich people who have more money than they can spend reasonably, and who therefore buy sham wealth, there is waste on that side; and also that, owing to there being poor people who cannot afford to buy things which are worth making, there is waste on that side. So that the *demand* which the capitalist *supplies* is a false demand. The market is *rigged* by the miserable inequalities produced by the robbery of the system of Capital and Wages.[10]

Moving with ease from such clear-cut Marxism to a more intimate understanding of the nature of work, Morris looks for ways in which work can again become a pleasure and not a life-sentence: 'We must begin to build up the ornamental part of life – its pleasures, bodily and mental, scientific and artistic, social and individual';[11] how it can be varied and extended by education and the learning of other skills: how work can again aspire to the status of art.

One product of Industry which has suffered so much from commercialism that it can scarcely be said to exist, and is, indeed, so foreign from our epoch that I fear there are some who will find it difficult to understand what I have to say on the subject, which I nevertheless must say, since it is really a most important one. I mean that side of art which is, or ought to be, done by the ordinary workman while he is about his ordinary work, and which has got to be called, very properly, Popular Art. This art, I repeat, no longer exists now, having been killed by commercialism. But from the beginning of man's contest with Nature till the rise of the present capitalistic system, it was alive, and generally flourished. While it lasted, everything that was made by man was adorned by man, just as everything made by nature was adorned by her. The craftsman, as he fashioned the thing he had under his hand, ornamented it so naturally and so entirely without conscious effort, that it is often difficult to distinguish where the mere utilitarian part of his work ended and the ornamental began. Now the origin of this art was the necessity that the workman felt for variety in his work, and though the beauty produced by this desire was a great gift to the world, yet the obtaining variety and pleasure in the work by the workman was a matter of more importance still, for it stamped all labour with the impress of pleasure. All this has now quite disappeared from the work of civilisation. If you wish to have ornament you must pay specially for it, and the workman is compelled to produce ornament, as he is to produce other wares. He is compelled to pretend happiness in his work, so that the beauty produced by man's hand, which was once a solace to his labour, has now become an extra burden to him, and ornament is now but one of the follies of useless toil, and perhaps not the least irksome of its fetters.[12]

He goes on to outline his vision of a just and equitable society founded on the principle of useful and creative work shared and enjoyed by all. But achieving this is another matter. Far from displaying the romantic naïveté he is so often credited with, Morris was fully aware that the privileged classes will never willingly relinquish that privilege. Although he states that peace is essential if we are to develop new social forms – 'It is peace, therefore, which we need in order that we may live and work in hope and with pleasure ... let us set our hearts on it and win it at whatever cost'[13] – he is careful to say that peace will not come easily, and foresees a bitter struggle for the establishment of his just and equitable society.

It may be that the best we can hope to see is that struggle getting sharper and bitterer day by day, until it breaks out openly at last into the slaughter of men by actual warfare instead of by the slower and crueller methods of 'peaceful' commerce. If we live to see that, we shall live to see much; for it will mean the rich classes grown conscious of their own wrong and robbery, and consciously defending them by open violence; and then the end will be drawing near.[14]

'Useful Work versus Useless Toil' predates by more than a decade Peter Kropotkin's reasoned and lucid exposition of possible forms of a new extended society. In *Fields, Factories and Workshops Tomorrow*[15] Kropotkin explores very similar ideas, but without Morris's emphasis on art. He is more concerned with giving a predominantly theoretical and economic consistency to all these ideas, demonstrating that they are wholly feasible and not mere hopes and fancies. Although Kropotkin's account of a society organised around the integration of small-scale industry with farming and localised production for need is compelling and pertinent reading it does not display the penetrating understanding of the nature of work as a potential expression of instinctive creative urges, nor does it see in work itself the same vehicle for transforming social relations that Morris sees.

What Morris achieved in 'Useful Work versus Useless Toil' was not simply a summing up of his ideas on work and art and their sorry state under the pressures of industrialism, nor was it a picture of their transformation as envisaged under socialism, it was and still is a genuine theory of the role and function of creativity in transforming the world.

In itself this was a significant break with the nineteenth-century aesthetic tradition, but it was also a coherent, viable and comprehensive alternative to that tradition and acknowledged the fact that new social forms would require a radical appraisal of the nature and function of creativity.

> To sum up, then, the study of history and the love and practice of art forced me into a hatred of the civilisation which, if things were to stop as they are, would turn history into inconsequent nonsense, and make art a collection of the curiosities of the past, which would have no serious relation to the life of the present.
> But the consciousness of revolution stirring amidst our hateful modern society prevented me, luckier than many others of artistic perceptions, from crystallising into a mere railer against 'progress' on the one hand, and on the other from wasting time and energy in any of the numerous schemes by which the quasi-artistic of the middle classes hope to make art grow when it has no longer any root, and thus I became a practical Socialist.[16]

The question of the ends to which industrial progress should be directed is, I think, central to an understanding of the development of modern art. It gives us a much clearer idea of the underlying personal and philosophical impetus behind the experiments of modern art, and reveals the origins of a progressive movement concerned above all with escaping the constraints, not of the past but of what was for Morris, and those who followed him, an imprisoning present and an unacceptable future.

In opposition to the morality that justified production for profit, Morris offered a form of social organisation based on production for need. Not a materialist utilitarianism, but an essentially creative utilitarianism under which work and art would shade into each other, nature would be treated with deference and respect, and wealth would be shared. A form of social organisation which would treat violence as a sickness, and never resort to it willingly as a means of resolving social conflict. A democratic organisation of society based on a respect for skill and an understanding of the true value of work, not as alienating labour but as a way of engaging with the natural world and shaping it to meet people's real needs.

There is no doubt that Morris was a driving force in the craft revival which was instrumental in the development of the art school system that we have inherited in this country, and that it was the resurrection of craft skills that made an association between art and industry possible, which in turn gave rise to design as a separate discipline. Unfortunately, modern design could not hold out against the growing pressures of consumerism, so the prospect of a world of creative diversity was overwhelmed by a future dominated by the mass production of things for consumption. This is a development Morris would never have approved and a reversal of his ideal society built on simplicity and freely chosen creative work.

For Morris, that Utopia had to be founded on the discovery or rediscovery of a close affinity between unpretentious art and unalienated work. In a sense the *work* of art was to achieve the transformation of the material wealth of nature into a world fit for human beings, and the *art* of work was to achieve this transformation with grace and sensitivity. Art and work would thus become inseparable and subsumed into activities creative, fulfilling and, above all, freely chosen. It is against the background of such hopes for a new age, and the madness and absurdity pervading the old world, that we have to view the dramatic changes in art which took place at the end of the nineteenth century.

Were Morris and his ideas merely an historical phenomenon, they would be interesting enough simply for the diversity of his achievements – poet, writer, lecturer, craftsman, designer, artist, historian, scholar. But as the advent of information technology and machine intelligence launches us into a period of change comparable to the Industrial Revolution, Morris's emphasis on the nature and quality of work, and his insistence on our right to choose how and why we want to work, are suddenly and pointedly relevant. Just as Morris's political thought originally formed part of the debate going on in the socialist movement throughout England and Europe, and was rooted in the tradition of discussion followed at the meetings of the Social Democratic Federation, and later the Socialist League, so we can see similar ideas emerging from current debates within the labour movement. It is here, at the heart of thinking about the nature and purpose of work, that we discover the true legacy of Morris's thought and practice.

The issue of production for need, not in a materialistic sense but in the more general cultural sense of the idea of useful work, has been central to a particular thread of thinking stretching from the origins of socialism to the present day. It is best understood as the concept of workers' control. The enormous energy Morris poured into building socialism, speaking on average at one meeting a week over more than a decade, and editing *Commonweal*, which was without doubt the most impressive socialist magazine of the period, is evidence enough of the profound influence his ideas have had on the labour movement in Britain.[17]

It is important not to see Morris as a divided man. The energy and enthusiasm he devoted to craft production, to William Morris and Company, and to the arts and crafts movement generally, before his later dedication to socialist organising, influenced both the development of design as a discipline and the schools of art and design themselves. Successive generations of designers and educationalists have been influenced by his concern for social values in the broadest sense, and his desire that art and artists should be actively involved in promoting social change. Although it is difficult to trace Morris's specific influence, we can see his ideas surfacing constantly during the early twentieth century. The Deutsche Werkbund struggled with the contradictions of industrial and craft production, and members of the Werkbund went on to found and inspire the Bauhaus in Germany. Some years later in Britain the Artists International Association took Morris's political stance in opposition to the unemployment which scarred the 1930s. There are many such examples, and behind each manifestation of Morris's principles there is some link back to his ideas and practice. Against this background of thought as a diffuse reference both for sectors of the organised labour movement and for artists and designers, we can begin to understand relatively recent events in both fields.[18]

At the end of the 1960s, the English art school system was shaken by an unexpected revolt which was suppressed with surprising ruthlessness. A few years later, under the growing threat of redundancies and unemployment, shop stewards at Lucas Aerospace formed a cross-union committee which argued against redundancies by developing its own alternative plan for the aerospace industry: a plan based on arms conversion and socially useful production. The original revolt in the art schools can be traced back to similar demands coming from students who wanted a more relevant training in art and design methods which could begin to tackle real social problems. These demands were framed by students in further education who, thanks to the post-war Education Act, were no longer as exclusively middle class and privileged as they had been. Coming from a much broader class background, they began to insist that their training equip them to deal with what they saw as the real and pressing needs of society.

These ideas did not die with the crushing of revolt at Hornsey and Guildford art schools, but were kept alive in colleges throughout the country, surfacing as a respectable corpus of opinion and practice some eight years later, at a conference held in the Royal College of Art in April 1976. The conference was entitled 'Design for Need: The Social Contribution of Design', and perhaps the most lucid and constructive speaker was Mike Cooley of the Lucas Combine Shop Stewards' Committee.[19] A few years later, on the occasion of William Morris's 150th anniversary, the Institute of Contemporary Arts held an exhibition called 'William Morris Today', in which the ideas of the Lucas workers featured. At the same time the GLC, now committed to the objectives of socially useful production as outlined in the Lucas workers' alternative plan, was looking into ways of saving the threatened handblocking workshop at Sanderson's Horsenden Lane site in Perivale, where Morris's original wallpaper designs are still manufactured by traditional craft methods.

In all these events we can see Morris's concept of work and production as a cultural process re-emerging as perhaps the only viable alternative to an aggressive and ruthless monetarism which smacks so sharply of the nineteenth-century profit grinding and the Victorian values that twentieth-century commerce would dearly love to revive.

The coming together of all these strands of thought is not fortuitous, but is the result of the working through of a constant opposition to the oppressive nature of production for profit. And as people from both poles of this process – the designers at their boards and the producers on the shop floor – start to question the validity of production for profit, Morris's vision of a society built around production for need becomes increasingly relevant. The remaining issue is how to achieve that objective.

The extent to which Morris's ideas have been instinctively proven in practice by the working-class movement can perhaps best be put by Mike Cooley speaking of efforts by the GLC and other metropolitan authorities to put the Lucas Aerospace workers' experience and initiative into practice.

> Many of the things we are doing now arose from a ferocious industrial relations battle at Lucas Aerospace over the right of people to determine what they make and how they make it. Now this struggle was not particular to Lucas, it was part of a general questioning by people in production of what they were doing and why. In Australia workers refused to destroy buildings that they and the community thought important. In Italy there were battles around the quality of products and the nature of work. In West Germany there was a big campaign about the humanisation of work.

> We may have lost the immediate battle of Lucas, but the paradigm we created has caused people to rethink their values, and local governments representing twenty million people in Britain are trying to implement some of those ideas. And all this was an outgrowth of practical struggles, so it seems to me that any idea that we can simply solve such issues by replacing a right-wing bureaucracy or controlling elite with a left-wing equivalent is totally spurious.

> I think the process one uses to effect change is important in itself, just as the labour process is – the end product will be an outcome of that specific process – and so I believe it is incredibly important that masses of people are involved in these activities and that they learn through these processes. It is not a question of handing down knowledge or political theory, but of actually developing that knowledge and theory as you go along. To engage in this people must first have some vision of what the future might hold: exemplary projects, which in embryo show what that future might be like in terms of activities and processes that

people feel at ease with and in which they can interact with each other in creative and co-operative ways.

So part of the struggle – as I see it – is to initiate these sorts of projects, and I regard this as profoundly political ... We have a responsibility to struggle for a future which can begin to match up to some of the basic human expectations of work that William Morris stated so clearly a century ago.[20]

11
The Impossibility of Art

As this book is as much about the practice of art and work as it is about theory and history, I have allowed myself this chapter – which is unashamedly autobiographical. In it, I trace my own attempts at grappling in practice with some of the issues dealt with in this book. How can we reconcile the seemingly opposed objectives of art and work; how can someone like myself, coming from a working-class or artisanal background, find a way of making sense of their experience within the constraints of an 'art' largely defined by and reflective of the values and concerns of people with whom they share neither cultural, nor class allegiance?

Against this background, it is possible to understand developments in the arts during the 1960s and 1970s, when other people like myself tried to change the shape and relevance of artistic activity. My own experience led to a more or less complete rejection of art in favour of work as a valid field of activity. This book, and especially the final chapters, is an attempt to retrieve a validity for art and creativity by locating its own centre more firmly within the everyday world of work.

In the 1960s I was a student at Edinburgh College of Art. At first I did well, winning prizes and a scholarship, but gradually I began to question the underlying values which were integral to what I was being taught in the studio. As I voiced my doubts I was met, not with interest and concern, but with opposition from the staff. The only audience that seemed to exist for the kind of art expected of me was the very same audience William Morris despaired of and the Dadaists despised: a polite, middle-class elite who considered themselves superior in their ability to appreciate the finer things of life – one of which was of course 'art'.

I was never very impressed with the idea of great art, and have always seen the hallowed atmosphere surrounding art objects as a pretentious extension of that idea. To me, art has always been much more to do with experience than with objects, and what the viewer – the audience – experiences is what matters in the end, together with the personal satisfaction from making and doing. I felt that if art was to be for people then everyone should have access to it; it should be touched and used. If art objects ended up a bit battered, that was all the better, for there could then be no doubt that they had existed and been experienced as real tangible and part of everyday life. I could see no contradiction between art and impermanence. If something is broken or worn out why not replace it, accept that it was never intended to last for ever? How can we enjoy art behind ropes and glass?

I started making rearrangeable, reproduceable works, which could be manipulated – played with – and this necessary participation became part of the work. These constructions depended increasingly on an audience prepared to drop pretensions and play with my objects. Piles of perspex cubes with pattern elements on them, tiles to arrange, wheels to turn. On their own they were no more than static collections of dead objects, but as soon as someone joined in they came to life. No brass rails and ropes for me! I had taken one step in what was to be a long trek, although at that stage I was still conscious of the fact that I was making 'art', and that art was intended for galleries.

Soon I found myself making decorations for college dances, and later staging short performances – events – for them. A small group of us came together out of interest, and decorative schemes became intricate and elaborate as the profit from successful dances gave us bigger budgets. These arts balls, or 'revels', as they were called in Scotland, have a long tradition in the art schools, and recall the revels and pageantry for which court artists were formally responsible. Our revels supplied a memory of the celebratory public and popular sides of art, of carnival and *commedia dell'arte*: part fair, part festival, part fête.

One quality distinctly lacking in those revels was the self-consciousness which often accompanies art. At the time we didn't think of them as art – although now I could list many parallels and precedents – for to us they were just a good time. The decorations, elaborate as they were, stayed up only for the night, and the whole event was ephemeral. No one took it seriously, yet those revels broke all the rules of art (which our tutors at college would have claimed to be teaching) without trying; a big step forward, although I failed to recognise it at the time.

Later, with the same group of friends – Helen Ford, Al Hamilton, and Dave Churchill – I organised and largely produced the decorations for the new French consul's inaugural 14 July celebrations. We took over the disused Caledonian station in the Centre of Edinburgh, and decorated the inside with huge murals. We had enormous *drapeaux* flown over from Paris and, with bunting and wine barrels, café tables and umbrellas, created a French village square on Bastille Day, complete with singers, musicians, a dance troupe and the crew of a French submarine. Champagne flowed freely, there were speeches, performances and dancing to quintessentially French accordion music. Everyone ended up a little tipsy, and it was marvellous fun. Throughout, I had enjoyed playing the

temperamental Gallic artist the consul expected me to be, and no one –
except perhaps the consul – considered the event, or its creation, art.

When I finished at art school, after battling against almost permanent
opposition to my anti-academic stance, I destroyed everything I had made
as a final gesture of rebellion. With a wonderful feeling of freedom I
turned my back on Edinburgh. I moved to Leeds where I lived with Alison
Fell, a poet, and taught at the art school. Ali and I soon became close
friends with two likeminded anti-artists, Susan Fox and her husband John.
We talked endlessly about art, politics, theatre, popular culture, music
hall, pop music and much more, and eventually agreed on the only way to
proceed. Considering ourselves artists, but looking for a wider, more
involved audience and a more relevant art; being politically committed
and concerned with making large, public images; wanting to appeal and
respond directly to an audience at close hand rather than through the
mediation of objects, the only way to tackle all these ideas would be to
launch a rock/theatre group. I came up with the name 'The Welfare
State', which in a way crystallised our feeling that a whole era of social
provision had degenerated into a patronising and complacent apology for
consumerism.

There were pressing national and international issues – Vietnam,
growing racism in the cities, the ever-present possibility of nuclear
confrontation – as well as personal issues that young people were
increasingly conscious of as the availability of education and a more open
society allowed us to challenge conventional roles and expectations. This
was to be our subject matter – although our intention was to entertain, to
shock, but never to preach – and with a few friends and students we started
rehearsing.

I have long believed – and still do! – that anyone is capable of anything:
that talent comes out of wanting to do things and is rarely a special gift. I
believe that we are all extraordinary, all talented, and that creative
ability is part of everyone's makeup, part of being human. 'Welfare State'
started out with this assumption – a group of equals improvising around
ideas – despite the fact that a few of us played dominant roles in the
group, a confusion which later led to disputes, even though those early
days were enormously fertile.

We developed a series of bizarre shows combining music, theatre,
poetry, puppets, fireworks, elaborate costumes and as many stage effects as
we could cram into one performance. We improvised instruments and
costumes and most of our material, trying to keep to some overall theme
with a human/political significance, without becoming boring or
dogmatic. Organising all this became a complex problem. We staged the
end of the world according to Nostradamus, marched a ten-foot-high

puppet of Hitler through the streets of Huddersfield at an anti-National Front rally, staged street events for demonstrations against the Vietnam war, performed in pubs and dance halls as well as in theatres, and developed our own brand of impromptu performance based on pre-rehearsed sketches, improvisation, stock characters and a pile of costumes, instruments and props. An electric *commedia dell'arte*.

Unfortunately, our original intention of operating as a collective group with no one in charge broke down under the pressure of working and performing. Arguments began about internal politics and roles – writer–director–singer – and particularly over the vexed issue of who made policy decisions, and what philosophy governed those decisions. Throughout, we tried very hard to operate as a group and achieved a considerable measure of success.

John took on publicity and organising – the truth is he was good at it, and the rest of us shied away from the task – and we soon came to rely on him for administration, for our public image, and for all the chatting up that theatre and art thrive on. Inevitably, he developed a possessive attitude towards the group, and thought of it primarily as a vehicle for his own ideas. We all tried to resist this and retain as much of the original spirit as possible, but the increasing pressure of engagements, children and fulltime jobs eventually reinforced the roles we had slipped into. There was never enough spare time or energy left to sort out group problems.

At the time I think we all had the same sense of frustration with what was going on, and the same feeling of being swept along by events and unable to change them, even though our star was certainly in the ascendant. Before long we had completed a recording session, appeared on the John Peel show and released a record, but that was almost the last thing we did as a coherent group. The internal conflicts were, by this time, too great, and acquaintance with the commercial music scene was enough to make me doubt where we were going. We certainly had some good material and potentially good shows which Ali had put an enormous effort into scripting and structuring, and it looked as if a month or two of rehearsals coupled with some good luck would see us performing fulltime. Events took a different turn. John seemed to become ambitious in an individual way, and started playing the impresario – organising big shows with Mike Westbrooke, now a well-known jazz musician and composer. He did it well too, with enormous energy and enthusiasm, and Mike's instinctive sense of collective improvisation was very close to our own way of working, but to my mind we were all being over-organised by John and treated as his property. Both Alison and I felt alienated and decided to leave the group.

The group began to fragment and, although we did come together for a number of shows – *Circus Time, Earthrise* – and one-off events, we had begun working semi-independently and with other groups like Action

Space and the John Bull Puncture Repair Kit. John kept the group name going, partly because it was becoming well known by then, and partly because of the ideas it had come to stand for, which pleased me. In many ways the image-building and the publicity, the paraphernalia of success, split us up. However, I did feel we had proved that a group of energetic, enthusiastic and committed people could produce something new and powerful out of hard work and imagination. We had tried to reject the idea of talent as something special and individual, even if we did retreat a little from our early idealism, but there is no doubt that we tried throughout to resist such tendencies and to my mind the genuinely collective inventions were some of our best.

During the same period, 1968–70, there was considerable local dissatisfaction with the Arts Council's attitude towards regional sponsorship of the arts and its failure to support the new, inter-media arts we were involved in. A pressure group had been set up called Friends of the Arts Council Operative (FACOP), and meetings were held in various regions with the intention of setting up artists' panels through which attention could be directed towards what were then being called 'New Activities' for want of a better name. It was hoped that financial support would follow.

The FACOP meetings brought a diverse group of people together, and as a result gave a sense of collective identity to experimental artists and performers throughout Yorkshire. We set ourselves up as an organisation for the Arts Council to deal with, and called it the 'Yorkshire Open Workshop' – YOW! Our intention was that YOW! should remain an open collective and not become another elitist institution like the Arts Council, and we hoped that it would bring together and represent people working in fields not covered by the conventional categories of art. Al Beech took on most of the organising, and YOW! received a modest grant from the Arts Council with which we decided to stage a festival of New Activities in Yorkshire. Perhaps then the Arts Council would have a clearer idea of what these mysterious new activities were!

Soon after the formation of YOW! a group of us agreed that we needed a physical base to work from, and a centre for our performances, happenings, events and other experiments. We decided to establish a venue that could act as arts-lab, community centre and open workshop. Steve Brookes, Al Beech, John Fox, Alison Fell, Mick Banks, Roland Miller, Jeff Nuttal, myself and eventually a few others rented an old warehouse in Halifax and were given a small grant by the Yorkshire Arts Association. We demolished the old roof, put on a new one, installed some rudimentary heating, lighting and plumbing, and eventually the Northern Open Workshop – NOW! – opened its doors to the world in 1969.

The workshop started off well, despite the fact that the local police took a predictably dim view of it, probably because we were not sufficiently diplomatic, but in those days who was? We tried to finance a full-time administrator/caretaker, but couldn't pay Tim for long, even though he had done so much of the work on the building in the first place. Still, with our festival planned for May and an Arts Council grant to pay some of the expenses, the future looked good, despite the fact that we could have been much better organised.

The YOW! festival, *Awake!*, took place in May 1970. It was a climax to endless thinking and discussion about art and creativity, about popular art and community art, and turned out to be a striking example of what is possible when people work together to achieve a common end. In this sense the festival was a genuine triumph of the imagination. There was a marquee on the grass by the river with a beer tent beside it: in a small town like Hebden Bridge that was an event in itself. There was a grand procession, street theatre all day, poets and musicians performing on street corners and in the pubs, and there were students, freaks, local rockers, girl guides and boy scouts on parade, and hundreds of curious people. There was red, black, purple, yellow and blue ice-cream, masses of flags and bunting, and free entertainment in the marquee. In short, everything from electronic music to a man who offered a fiver to anyone who could climb through a long broom quicker than he could! Everyone seemed to take a turn in the tent, reading poems, singing songs or reciting dimly-remembered party pieces – very much entertaining themselves – and in the evening there were more organised events, including a 'Welfare State' extravaganza-reunion.

A carnival atmosphere settled over the town. The pubs stayed open all day, and no one was arrested! The next morning the landlord of the Swan played host to those of us who had stayed to clear up the equipment. The table in his best room groaned under the weight of gammon rashers, eggs, fried tomatoes and whole loaves of toast. To top it all, after breakfast he opened the bar! The Town Council sent us a very sweet letter of thanks, hoping we would come again next year, and everyone resolved to make it an annual event.

To me it was all a miracle. But after the *Awake!* festival nothing could ever be quite the same, and the collective impetus which had given birth to that event waned. NOW! started to get into financial difficulties and was badly let down by the Arts Council, although in retrospect I think it was as much our own naive dependence on Arts Council money that undermined the venture. Like so many experiments, it was run on a shoestring of enthusiasm, idealism and financial insecurity which depended on collective commitment from everyone involved, but could not survive without a minimum of external funding.

The *Awake!* festival demonstrated the possibility of new and more open relationships between artist and audience, of a diffusion of creativity within communities, and of new forms of art which could begin to bridge the gulf between art and everyday life and perhaps reinvigorate the vital processes of popular culture. By this time, however, I was growing impatient both with the self-appointed *avant-garde* developing around New Activities, and with the enormous amount of time and energy that went into organising and trying to find financial support for our events. I was also annoyed at the lack of social and political awareness around me, and the liberal or apolitical nature of so much of the art being produced. People seemed content to be outrageous or obscure, or hide behind a fashionable nihilism which to me was just an easy way of avoiding the real issues facing art and artists in a climate of growing political awareness. For a group of self-styled radical artists, we seemed incapable of making any real analysis of either our own situation or our place in society; and were drifting back into an individualism that the *Awake!* festival had briefly transcended.

I had begun printing posters, organising special theatrical events for demonstrations and thinking hard about dramatising social and political issues in a more direct way than 'Welfare State' had done. In short, I was trying to understand in practical terms how art and politics could be related.

In July 1970 I moved to London, into the heart of the beast – as Jeff Nuttal described it – but continued teaching at Leeds for the next year. I was keen to finish off a project I had started before going to London: a landscape event which was staged at a popular beauty spot in the Yorkshire Dales, 'Malham Cove', in which some of my students and most of the NOW! people took part. There were climbers on the rockface; earth, air, fire and water rituals; balloons; flags that made noises; and of course a firework display on the cliff-top at night. The river below and the lake above were stained in bright colours with edible dye, and river sounds were amplified and broadcast across the valley. Monster kites flew high above the cliffs, carrying people, and there was a procession with music, singing and dancing. All manner of incongruous goings-on occurred that day and well into the evening, with the surrounding landscape as both backdrop and subject of the events spread across the valley from the village and up to the hills beyond.

As a grand finale we strung a great chain of fountain fireworks across the cliff-face. That night the cliff – which had sported a waterfall at the end of the ice-age, though now the river ran underground to emerge at its foot – spouted a waterfall of fire while torches burned on the hill behind. The real audience was all the day trippers and hikers, the kids with their mums and dads – all the people who stumbled unexpectedly on this strange surreal world – and the locals. They all thought it was marvellous fun, as did the people who took part. Predictably the man from the Yorkshire Arts Association, who gave us some money towards it, managed to miss most of the fun and probably all the point. He was too busy looking for art. It worked out well, I thought, but by the time it was over I had lost interest in the egotism of staging large events. I was becoming disillusioned with all forms of art and increasingly suspicious of anyone who called themselves an artist, myself included.

The more I thought of the problems involved in developing a genuinely popular art, the more surely I came to the conclusion that modern society itself was a major obstacle, and that it was impossible for the kind of art I envisaged to flourish in this competitive world. The very artiness of the events organised by even the most progressive artists showed that they still saw themselves and their work as an elite – as somehow special. Nor could I sympathise with people who wanted to form an artists' union or, to give a more proletarian ring to it, an art-*workers'* union. To me such pretence served only to emphasise the split between art and everyday life which I saw as the central problem.

The idea that artists could somehow operate outside the class-divided world we live in, or that so called radical art at the ICA or the Roundhouse could transcend or transform these institutions, made no sense to me. Seeing art increasingly as simply a middle-class pretension, I had little choice but to give it up, reject my identity as an artist and end a love affair which had lasted more than ten years. I was convinced the world would have to change before art could exist in any form that I could accept. Until then I would have to sleep in a lonely bed.

I decided to set about trying to change the world through political action. I had certain skills, and could acquire others. At college, I had already learned the basic printing techniques – lithography, silkscreen, etching, woodblock and linocut – but only as art media, and that was not enough to equip me for what I had in mind. So off I went to Manchester to spend a period of time helping out and learning the ropes at Moss Side Press – darkroom work, process photography, machine offset printing and production printing in general. Back in London, I squatted an empty shop with a group of friends, and started a community press in the basement. A positive step across the line between art and life.

I turned to politics with relief and enthusiasm. Like Mayakovsky in the wake of the Russian Revolution I would claim: 'We do not need a dead mausoleum of art, where dead works are worshipped, but a living factory of the human spirit – in the streets, in the tramways, in the factories, workshops and workers' homes.'[1] But as I suppressed the artist in me, involved almost exclusively as I was in political activities – squatting, printing tenants' papers, handbooks on claimants' rights, meetings and discussions – I watched the spontaneity which had originally fired me disappear under a dreary blanket of earnest dogma. Endless meetings dominated by an overriding insistence on having the correct position on each and every issue (a shallow disguise for power struggles) smothered the alternative politics of the 1970s, and gave rise to an inevitable polarisation between the 'blameless' – the earnest politicos, many of whom, I gradually discovered, were the children of the very elite they despised so fiercely, with public school educations hidden under quickly acquired working-class accents – the hedonists – with their revolution of sex, drugs and rock 'n' roll – and more determined people like myself who wanted to build some sort of viable alternative.

The initial energy of alternative politics, with its vision of a liberated and egalitarian society rejecting both conventional politics and the morality of an unbearably *straight* older generation, was not enough to draw the moral and political revolts of the 1970s into a coherent movement. The hoped-for new society, rising from the rubble of the old, proved to be a fantasy. For those who could not face reality, the alternative was to turn to drugs or religion for an answer to life's emptiness. The illegality of drugs brought with it a polarising attitude towards authority and the law which temporarily unified the alternative movement in a politics of liberation focused on the celebration of non-conformity.

For a while refusing to conform was seen as revolutionary – in a sense it was, as people threw off the strait-jacket of convention – but fighting labels with labels avoided the deeper issues as powerful economic forces shaped a very different world. Instead of developing a clear-sighted understanding of the way society structures and moulds us all, instead of trying to develop a culture which could eventually challenge mainstream ideology, the alternative left was content and even proud to remain a minority, often guilty of the same narrow-minded bigotry as the right, particularly in its intolerance of anyone who questioned its dogma and assumptions.

As a movement, the alternative politics of the 1970s was never more than a very loose alliance of individuals and groups who either felt specifically oppressed by society or found it repressive in a general sense and wanted to change it. It was the diversity of this youth culture that gave it such enormous creative energy, but the irreconcilability of all its sub-groupings left it with no unifying objectives other than a nebulous and undefined glorifying of 'revolution' as an end in itself.

The instinctive solidarity of the late 1960s and early 1970s fragmented into self-interest groups, and the politics of what had at first been a broad-based rebellion against a repressive conformity retreated, in a potentially introspective move which meant that any relationship with traditional class politics and working-class movements became increasingly tenuous in practice. Indeed, an important and unacknowledged element of contradiction which undermined the solidarity of a politics of liberation was the fact that so many of its advocates were middle-class kids who could not finally admit to their class origins. The politics they espoused so anathematised the family, wealth, privilege and their own class background that they were forced to carry an impossible burden of class guilt which could be exorcised only in 'revolution'. Libertarianism, Trotskyism, International Marxism were all the politics of young city people, mainly students and ex-students: politics from the universities and colleges grafted on to a new morality of sexual freedom and a new sanctimonious moralism inspired by class guilt.

The revolution they aspired to was not something predicted by their analysis of capitalism, but an essential element in their internal dynamic, generating a level of tension which justified their millenialist polemic. But the male, warrior-hero mould that this 'revolution' was cast in became its own undoing, as feminism shifted the focus of political debate from revolutionary ends to egalitarian means.

Ideas of self-importance, genius, virtuosity, aspirations to personal success and fame, were common-place amongst the artistic *avant-garde,* but by now I had a growing feeling that a significant sector of the political activists I knew were behaving as a similar, self-appointed *avant-garde,* with similar but unacknowleged aspirations and an overwhelming belief in their own importance.

By now my activities had less and less to do with art as such: the odd poster, lots of printing for various groups, meetings as always and, most rewarding for me, working with a few specific groups of tenants, trades unionists and ex-prisoners, teaching them to print and produce their own newsletters and papers. Increasingly I felt swallowed up by these processes. I had hoped to escape from the audience-artist dilemma which first drove me to doubt conventional art, but I was rediscovering it in a different guise. By working directly with people, generalising skills and making processes available, my intention had been to democratise the power inherent in knowledge and skill. But as we started printing more specifically political material, including a local paper, the emphasis began to shift from the practical to the polemical.

My early printing had been about squatting, for people who wanted and needed housing, or newsletters for groups who needed the skills and facilities we could provide: grass-roots organisations with little money or resources. As the Community Press was established in a squatted shop, we could provide these facilities at a very low cost and should have been able to build up a vital community resource, but eventually it all became too manipulative, with a small clique dominating the paper and the old divisions creeping in. In such an atmosphere, the sense of breakthrough my early attempts at artistic and political experiment had brought soon vanished.

I found more theory than humanity, and the same sort of people insistently elbowing their way to the front, as I had in the world of art. This time however, I was looking at the divisions from the other side of the fence, and found politics and political people lacking in the sense of life and wonder I had found among artists. Devoid of that keen sense of the absurd which is central to so much art, politics and pomposity made easy bedfellows.

What I had responded to previously in Yorkshire, and especially at Hebden Bridge, was a sense of community I remembered from early childhood, but now found lacking in more affluent London. When I was young, my family still displayed the cohesion which comes from having survived the war in the centre of London. But as I grew up I watched these family ties weaken and atrophy. My education – I was the first of the family to stay on at school past 14 – carried me far away from my relations, and as I formed my own ideas about the world, I often found them at variance with those of my family. Yet still I carry with me a focal memory of the powerful feeling of belonging that permeated my childhood.

The Community Press was, I decided, an attempt to create community and not discover it. It had identified local groups within the community, and responded to their needs, but had eventually been dominated by a different community: the growing network of young radicals who saw themselves as a vanguard separate from the mass of people, and who I found so full of unacceptable contradictions.

As an experiment in community art – the subjugating of artistic criteria and objectives to genuine need – the press was a roaring success and well ahead of its time in that we had abandoned all conventional art criteria, discovering a very different motivation and practice, but that had been our intention from the start, placing the emphasis on use-values. However, we had other standards too. Some of the output was highly imaginative, despite the fact that the primary function of the press was utilitarian, and imagination was part, but not all, of a process intended to release the creative energies of other people.

The groups who used the press soon proved that it was only a lack of facilities that had held them back, and in some cases the press, or rather the ability to print and therefore express themselves, became a focus around which groups formed. A small nucleus of people could print posters and a newssheet, distribute them on their estate, and from this initiative organise a tenants' association; a group of schoolkids could produce their own magazine, free of classroom censorship. Unfortunately, these activities, which were deeply politicising in that they gave people a sense of collective power within their own lives and the experience of organising around their own needs and frustrations, became secondary to what was considered more overtly political and therefore more important by some members of the group, and my hopes of becoming more deeply involved in a local community were frustrated.

In the North I felt that the reverse was possible, and so I moved to Sheffield with two friends, into the heart of a community where everyone knew everyone else. We were outsiders, as people constantly reminded us, but were eventually accepted. We set up a building cooperative, found a couple of local contracts and with very little fuss got on with it. No endless meetings, no agreed policy, no deep theory, just the confidence that we could do it. Although none of us had much experience, we relied partly on our own aptitude, partly on what we knew – Mat and Andy had trained in architecture – and partly on advice from local friends in the building trades, but we had to do a lot of learning very quickly.

I have always thought of Sheffield as a warm, almost magical town. People are friendly to the point of being nosey. They talk to strangers at bus stops, ask personal questions the first time they meet you, and are happy and ready to pass an opinion about virtually everything. The mixture of dense, backyard living in cramped terraces and the ever present hard life of work in steelmills and mines, coupled now with the threat of unemployment, were such common threads to life in Sheffield that they bound people together in a recognition of shared experience. The feeling that 'we're all in it together' gave a common bond to communities which was neither exclusive nor parochial. In crowded pubs people would signal you in, shove up along a bench, 'make room for a little 'un', and include complete strangers in conversations and card games.

Pitsmoor, where I lived, is just up the hill from the now silent steelworks which ran for a mile down to Wincobank. A busy, noisy, dirty mile of industry drawing the locals down the hill to work. Pitsmoor was a scruffy mixture of old terraces, some empty and boarded up, and council flats. The population was very mixed, and had been for a long time as successive waves of workers were attracted there by the promise of decent wages and a secure future. The extended family, white, black and Asian, was the norm, and friendships spread out from that base into a network of relationships and feuds which were the life-blood of the area. Class antagonisms were few as Pitsmoor was overwhelmingly working class, but a mixture of distrust and tolerance marked relations between the different racial groups. Over and above that, friendships existed on a personal level, and through friendship we quickly came to know an enormous number of people, while everyone found out all about us.

In a short space of time we were roped into the local pressure group – campaigning for play facilities in the area – and a local newspaper, the *Pitsmoor News*. But, unlike London, the lead in all these activities came from the community itself, where the natural network of pub, club, shop, work, backyard and street gathered its strength around such local issues. It was generally agreed that an adventure playground would be a good idea for the kids, and that the ideal site was up on the hill by the cemetery. The Play Facilities Group was already involved in a local youth club where we ran a weekly disco, outings for the kids, a summer play scheme and other *ad hoc* activities. The playground campaign took off from there, and became something of an extended and impromptu version of the *Awake!* festival.

The adventure playground campaign released an enormous surge of creative activity: a collective creativity for which we, the outsiders, might have been catalysts, but were never responsible. Given a glimpse of what is possible and a way to achieve it, people will respond with enormous enthusiasm, which is exactly what happened in Pitsmoor. In three months we raised £3,000, had it matched pound-for-pound by a local charity and, with the unbelievable sum of £6,000 in the bank, the city had no choice but to donate the site we had earmarked. Suddenly the playground was a reality.

I was becoming increasingly embarrassed by the lack of skills within the building group, which had grown to some size by then. Although we had set up a workshop with machinery and were improving all the time, we lacked the real depth of skill that surrounded us in Pitsmoor. In Sheffield, the trade skills are practised and maintained at a very high level and, although the building trades may no longer aspire to being the guardians of the art that they once were, the basic competence of most Sheffield tradesmen would put a Southerner to shame. This, coupled with the fact that I had let myself be drawn into running the playground and anxiety about tensions within the building group, precipitated a personal crisis and I left Sheffield.

My experience in Sheffield, however, led me to think seriously about the whole question of skill, and about the links between skill and art, about the ways in which we shape our environment through what we call work. Why was work referred to in the pub as a four-letter word – 'We'll have no swearing round here!' – and banned as a topic of conversation? Why, when work is so obviously and inescapably the medium through which we shape the raw materials of nature into the world we live in, so obviously a fundamentally creative activity, should we be so effectively alienated as to hate all that it stands for?

I realised that art is inextricably linked with skill, and the next period of my life was absorbed in understanding this fact practically. I set myself the goal of becoming genuinely skilful in at least one trade. I chose woodwork because it is part of building – a central building skill like brick work – but goes beyond building to include design and many other skills and qualities I was not aware of at that time.

I have always had considerable practical ability, absorbed in childhood from practical parents and with little apparent effort, so I was not intimidated by the prospect of learning a skill thoroughly. I read avidly, and taught myself to be a competent carpenter and joiner, but the practical arts cannot be learned in isolation without suffering a considerable debasement. To consolidate my skills, I had to seek out older men who taught me the depth and humility which characterise the trade. Maurice Claydon, Tommy Atkins, and above all Roy Ford who turned a government training scheme into the most thoroughgoing learning experience of my life.

Learning joinery gave me a new understanding of my relationship with the world at large. As I learned to differentiate between timbers and read the shipping marks on the end of planks, I began to recognise the subtle differences between wood grown in the frozen forests of Siberia, and the same species grown in Sweden or Finland. As I began to appreciate these differences – the unique qualities of timber from specific regions – I began to ask why, and so began to understand more about climate, soil and rates of growth. I also came to appreciate the very special appropriateness of certain timbers for specific jobs, as well as the variety of timber available: the diversity and singularity of the products of nature.

As timber from the world's forests passed over my bench and I became intimately acquainted with wood, I developed a strong sense of myself as part of a complex planet, and could feel for all those trees, for the people who tended, planted and felled them. Inevitably I came to resent the enormous waste of this natural capital when the skills and sympathetic understanding of the woodworker are ignored in the production of shoddy articles – windows and doors which last barely ten years, chipboard furniture which scarcely outlasts fashion.

I became acutely aware of the abuse of skill and raw materials that so much modern production is, conscious that it is not just the anti-traditionalist bias of modern society which is at fault. Modern machine methods could, and sometimes do, produce useful, lasting products, but an overwhelming zeal for profits and productivity which takes no account of the growing scarcity of raw materials and the limited capacity of the world to recover from the damage, has favoured production of the 'cheap and nasty', or the 'pricey and pretentious', at the expense of useful and long-lasting products.

In seeking an alternative tradition, I was drawn to the work of Gerrit Rietveldt, the Dutch furniture-maker-turned-architect, who hand/

machine made surprisingly modern objects in the early years of this century. He produced objects which defy classification either as sculpture or furniture, craft or machine production, objects which elude the narrow boundaries of conventional definitions and for a moment give us a glimpse of an alternative direction the technological society might have taken.

Rietveldt used the techniques available to him – some hand, some machine – and the skills he had acquired through practical training and study, and this is the key to his importance. He was not caught up in a narrow conception of what art, craft, furniture, sculpture or later architecture ought to be. Instead, he used the skills and techniques he knew and understood to make objects for the future as he envisaged it, and was remarkably successful. Taken up by the intellectuals of the De Stijl group in Holland, he is too often seen as an impractical stylist, but this is a misunderstanding of his achievement. Rietveldt was able to *make* objects about which the other members of De Stijl could only speculate, for he arrived at his furniture designs by combining the nature and methods of production available to him with the practices of the trade he was apprenticed in and with his own ideas about designing for production.

I was never sucked into the mystique that surrounds the 'fine crafts', but as my skills developed I was increasingly involved in artisanal, if not craft production. Living by then in Lincolnshire, with a workshop full of hand and machine tools – nothing so large that it denied personal involvement – and making bespoke furniture and joinery, I eventually found myself confronted with the same dilemma that had precipitated my quest for new art forms over 15 years earlier. I was working increasingly for wealthy people because that was apparently the only way in which I could practise the skills I had struggled so hard to acquire, but I had little sympathy with my customers. I felt I had never been so thoroughly patronised in my life, and so the work lost the magic that had made it satisfying. Luckily for me another event triggered a series of realisations which pointed a way out of this dilemma.

I was living and working with an architect turned builder and pig-keeper, Frances Holliss, and when an old friend of ours, Rachel, contracted multiple sclerosis she determined to do something practical to help. After considerable pressure, Camden Council's social services department agreed to have Rachel's kitchen – which was utterly impracticable for anyone confined to a wheelchair – replaced with a new, purpose-built one. We surveyed available equipment, assessed the problems and designed a kitchen for Rachel. A one-off solution admittedly, but capable of being adapted for other people and other situations. Not a clinical, institutionalised kitchen which said *disabled* all over it, but a stylish modern kitchen which was the envy of her block.

At the same time, both Frances and I had come to the conclusion that we could not carry on making tasteful joinery and furniture for tasteful people. Before actually making the kitchen we moved to Cambridge – a very expensive town after the rural wastes of Lincolnshire – and I had to take a job with a local builder so that we could pay our bills. I worked as a joiner and wood-machinist during the day, rushing through boring production runs of bonus work, with the odd quality job – the balcony doors – thrown in as light relief, and working on Rachel's kitchen units with Frances in the evenings and at weekends.

The contrast between the three forms of work; mindless, frantic bonus work; careful, challenging joinery and restoration work – for wealthy people again; and the enormous satisfaction of using my skills to produce a special kitchen which might change Rachel's life, was an object lesson I will never forget. In that experience I had suddenly found a valid reason for making things, and for applying my skills to the shaping of a world of which I could approve. Not a romantic world in which no one is ever ill or deformed, but a world in which practical steps could be taken to come to terms with such realities. I had seen the possibility of something beyond art and craft, something which could account for both ideas, and yet required none of the humbug associated with art and craft to justify it. What Fran and I had made was more than an object, it was an environment, and in no way useless. On the contrary, it was pre-eminently and specifically useful, well made, well designed and, above all, a source of pleasure for Rachel to *use* because of the freedom and independence it gave her.

I realised that I could also apply artistic criteria to the kitchen we had made – it definitely could have looked better – and I could criticise it in the terms of the craft and skill involved in its making, and how it performed in use. Such criticism was constructive rather than destructive and spoke of how it could be improved on, what the next one would be like. In other words, I found myself using all the criteria, all the self-criticism skilled workers have subjected themselves to for centuries, and which can rightly be said to underpin art, but this time it was directed to a practical and useful end and pointed the way towards a future I could approve.

I could suddenly see the possibility of a new way of working which would deny nothing that I considered art, and nothing that I had loved so dearly yet rejected at such personal cost, a way of working that could stand against all the squalor and degradation William Morris had railed against 100 years ago, and which still permeates the clinical twentieth century in new guises. A way of working that neither approves nor disapproves of machinery and technology, of mass-production and computerisation; that does not accept or reject handwork, craft production and traditional skills, but simply asks how useful they are, how relevant, how appropriate, and to what ends they are employed.

12
Freely-chosen Work

In this chapter, I try to pull together some of the threads that appear in other parts of the book. My intention is to propose some ground rules for a new attitude towards work: neither a shunning of work nor an endorsement of it in its present form, but a basis for the value of work, its purpose and the use we make of it. Like William Morris, I suggest that one of the reasons for working must be the satisfaction of work itself. This leads to a questioning of the product of work – surplus value – and how we express that surplus.

I see a primary need for people to choose the nature and content of their work and in so doing, to choose ways of working that are at present available only to a privileged minority, including those people who call themselves artists.

Technology, the power to change and exploit our environment, has developed far beyond our ability to grasp the overall implications of the changes it makes possible. We are, even now, barely coming to terms with the effects of nineteenth-century technology and the systems of work organisation it required and, unless we can find some way of closing the gap between capability and understanding, we run the risk of self-destruction in any number of ways. Our chief adaptive ability is a capacity for creative thinking which the most intelligent machines lack. Unfortunately, this ability has taken second place to our logical, linguistic, linear abilities: scientific, abstracted knowledge has triumphed over tacit, practical understanding. The implications of the suppression of 50 per cent of our mental and intuitive capacities are enormous, for these very faculties are a specialised, adaptive capability which we neglect at our peril.

Only by recognising the importance of our creative potential – the ability to challenge assumptions and break down rigid thought patterns – can we begin to bring science and logic into balance with traditional and intuitive modes of understanding and producing. We still have enormous respect for the great artists of the Renaissance. One of the things they all had in common was the ability to combine art and science in their creative activity. The other stemmed from the fact that they were all trained in the workshop tradition of the medieval trades and crafts. They placed

140

the centre of gravity of their lives squarely in the middle of work, and their achievement was enormous. But work for them was not the alienating, self-denying, anti-autonomous activity that we see. It was a truly creative form of art work which developed human potential, both practical and intellectual, to the full.

This world we inhabit as human beings is not the apparently chaotic world of nature, nor is it in any sense given, as air and water are. It is created, shaped and moulded day by day, by our collective presence. The medium through which this creative process operates is work. By actively constructing our physical environment – fields, hedges, factories and streets – work conditions and structures our lives, defining the context in which we exist. But its influence is more profound than this because work, or rather the manner in which we experience the world in its natural state as we work on it, is central to our understanding of both nature and ourselves. If we live in an environment where we only ever meet pigs as pork chops in plastic trays, our understanding of pigs is very limited. In this sense then, work is a defining activity, shaping the way we experience the world around us. More than a physical act, work is also deeply cultural in its implications, for through work we construct not only the physical, but our social and cultural world. This is a process which is irreducibly creative – the counterpart of reproduction – and gives rise to the dense complexity of our social environment.

We need some idea of what the world is like, and how we stand in relation to it, if we are to begin to change and shape it with any purpose. We acquire this understanding by probing and exploring – at first with the random enthusiasm of childhood, later with more constructive intentions. We actively explore the world around us and thereby inevitably change it – physically by our presence, and more subtly by thinking and projecting our ideas on to the world, making it as much an environment of ideas and collective assumptions as one of physical objects. It is this complex and continually changing interaction between physical facts and abstract ideas which constitutes the world. Before and beyond separate ideas like work and leisure, however, the simple project of survival involves us in a direct contact with nature, with a reality not divisible into separate activities which can be called either productive – work – or cultural – art, leisure, philosophy.

I go camping in the marshes with my son and our dog. We gather driftwood, make a fire, pick samphire on the beach, perhaps catch a rabbit or crabs from the pools. Together we go about the magic ritual of living moment by moment, and as we do a profound sense of belonging settles over us. We gradually establish a presence and build up a relationship with our surroundings which in no way changes them radically. Like fish swimming in water, we move over the marshes and exist in them as if they were our element, which indeed they are for that short time. The experience is deeply cultural, and 'normality' is thrown into sharp relief by it. Returning to normality requires a cultural reorientation; suddenly we are aware of how this normality – the everyday events of life – shapes and conditions us, not just physically but also emotionally.

Tribal societies still preserve that essential feature of ritual and adventure, where every act becomes significant, in one sense an act of survival, and in another a cultural statement. The objects and artefacts of these societies are typically mediators between the people who use them and the world they live in. Defined in ritual use and decorated with symbols – all of which serve to bind individual to tribe and tribe to nature in an elaborate mythology which accounts for the perceived facts of existence – such objects and the ways they are used acquire a significance far beyond what could be regarded as their immediate usefulness. In an essay entitled 'The Plight of Culture', Clement Greenburg pointed out that:

> In societies below a certain level of economic development, everybody works: and where this is so, work and culture tend to be fused in a single functional complex. Art, lore and religion then became barely distinguishable, in either intention or practice, from the techniques of production, healing and even war.[1]

In this context every act becomes a statement about complex relationships between individuals and nature, and there is no way in which art can be divorced from either craft or work. Art, science, religion and work are all equivalent and integrated in a concern to understand and define ourselves as part of the world. But work becomes increasingly detached from nature as we type instructions into computers and press buttons to initiate extensive processes in which we have little or no direct involvement. In a similar way, knowledge and understanding become increasingly abstract and separate from nature, which is in turn swamped by a barrage of figures and formulae. This distancing has eroded some of our most intimate, instinctive and subjective responses to the world and to one another, relegating the warm emotions of nurturing and caring, of love and collective sympathy, and at the same time favouring those aggressive, competitive, individualistic drives which promote success in a world dominated by power and possessions.

We no longer live an animal existence, browsing and grazing or hunting and killing in a world over which we have little or no control. Instead, human beings fall into a separate category of creatures who modify their environment to favour survival. This instinctual urge is the source of our creativity, and the point of application for this instinctive creative activity is exactly at the interface between ideas and reality: between the world of nature and the reality into which we shape it either through physical work or by perceiving and interpreting it. Creativity is not a separate activity, but an attitude which can potentially inform all activities with significance. It is a means to inventing new ways of working on and with our environment and new ways of describing and accounting for it.

The ways we have invented for working on nature are by now highly efficient, but they are also destructive. As the Lincolnshire countryside, with its bleak, haunting beauty, is systematically stripped of its few remaining trees, hedges and farmhouses and relentlessly ploughed into an arid agro-chemical desert, and as work is systematically stripped of its content, I am convinced that in exchanging creativity for productivity we have lost touch with an essential part of our nature.

At times in my life I have had different identities – artist, craftsman, tradesman – and in each phase of that life have experienced sharply the reality which surrounds each persona. Locked in one identity, we may be happy and fulfilled or utterly desperate, trapped and alienated from what we feel to be our true selves. As individuals we shape this world, but seem to have no real control over the process. We work on the raw materials of nature, but exercise very little choice in how we do this. Our work is mapped out for us, ordered and organised to such an extent that we often feel powerless and incapable of making the world conform to any idea we may have of what it could or should be like.

There have been times when I have been miserably conscious of the apparently inescapable paradox which imprisons us all as agents of processes outside our control, and other times when I have felt joyously free of constraints and capable of choice. But my overriding impression is that as individuals we have little actual freedom, little choice and very little power. As a joiner, employed by a building firm, I felt thoroughly divorced from my own creativity. Everything I made was preordained, designed, described in full and completely outside my control. I neither bought the timber I used, nor was I allowed to select it from stock; I just had to make do with what turned up. I had very little control over how long I could take on a job, or what standard to work to. That was defined by the bonus system and my own financial needs. As joiners are poorly paid and often bound by invidious bonus systems, I could rarely afford the luxury of deciding that a particular job or detail needed special attention and extra time. Instead, I developed an eye for the clock and a keen sense of what was acceptable, what I could get away with.

Working as an independent craftsman gave me more freedom and control. I could set my own standards and to a large extent my supply of work depended on them. I could determine my own hours too and, although I worked for myself, I felt that I also chose how and when I worked. Designing most of the work myself meant that I could decide how to go about it, and so could choose the materials with great care, investing my work with a whole range of qualities I thought it ought to have. But at the same time my customers were prepared to spend only a certain amount of money, often less than the work was worth, so I ended up exploiting myself much of the time – working long hours for little financial reward, worrying about money and the quality of my work, and trying to balance the pressure of bills against my own desire to work creatively.

The contradiction bites deep. We appear to gain control over our lives only to lose it in the process. When I behaved as a creative craftsman, as an artist of a sort, I lost money and could not afford to work! Lacking a private income, I had to choose between lowering my standards to compete with the shoddy mass-produced goods which still set price levels, even for hand work, and going stoically bankrupt. What underlies this is the fact that we confuse and obscure concepts like art and craft under a fog of romantic preconceptions. Craft in particular has been idealised as a fulfilling and unalienated way of working. At one level its practitioners style themselves artist–craftsworkers in a vain attempt to knit together the worthy aspects of both traditions, justifying high prices by their claim to artistic originality and status. At the other end of the spectrum, people are exploited in scruffy workshops which would never pass the factory inspector. Arts, crafts, skilled trades and plain work are all modes of production and as such are part of a continuum stretching from prehistory to the present day. Art became craft, which in turn became skilled work and eventually degenerated into plain four-letter work. At each stage the process became less intimate and less complete, output increased at the expense of content, and so the productive process itself has gone through a series of critical changes which have affected and structured our lives to the point where the vast majority of people seem to have no control over their work at all.

This paradox permeates our lives. We believe in freedom – freedom of choice – and yet on examination the choices open to us are almost exclusively to do with consuming and not with producing. We experience the world by consuming it, and for those of us lucky enough to have work, the choice is one of either going to work to earn money or being denied the choices outside work to which money gives us access. Consequently we accept enormous limitations in the control we have in shaping the world, in exchange for what appears to be freedom to choose what and how we consume. Thus, what was once an essentially creative activity in which people came to an intimate understanding of the world around them and structured from it an environment of their own choosing, has become an ordered, controlled and logically determined activity in which creativity is as a bug to be removed from the system. As Fredrick Winslow Taylor, the father of systematised production management once said: 'In my system the workman is told precisely what he is to do and how he is to do it, and any improvement he makes upon the instructions given to him is fatal to success.'[2]

Realising this is the first step to resolving the paradox. There is no doubt that the enormous qualitative leap forward taking place at the moment in the productive processes could free us all from arduous toil and make a life of fulfilment a possibility. There is, however, a factor which is ignored in all discussions about production and technology, a factor which William Morris was perceptive enough to recognise 100 years ago. For him production was more than the mere manufacture of commodities, it was production in the broadest sense; that is to say, the production of a world worth living in through work which is healthy and fulfilling. From this perspective we can begin to talk of art as freely-chosen work, as skill allowed its full expression, and suggest that art, in this new sense, could inform production. The meeting of human and social needs could replace profit as the driving force of a truly humane and creative society in which technology, the ability to shape the resources of nature, would be valued, not because it was modern but because it was appropriate.

The origins of art lie in the production of surplus value, and the uses we make of it. All work produces a surplus of some sort, otherwise it is counter-productive and uneconomic. But in the simplest and most direct forms of work – hunting and gathering and rudimentary agriculture – the surplus produced by a group can only be measured collectively over all its activities. This surplus is most frequently expressed in the few surviving tribal societies we know of as free time, that is to say it is not stored in any obvious way. In those societies, productive work as such typically occupies only a short part of the day.

Surprisingly enough, the most apparently primitive of societies – the African Bushmen for example, and the Australian Aboriginals – live not in a state of scarcity, but in what for them is considerable surplus and freedom from want,[3] particularly if we accept that poverty is as much perceptual – feeling deprived – as it is physical. How else can we explain their ability to survive, in marginal areas of the globe, for longer than any other culture, and how can we explain the complexity and cohesion of the cultures they have developed?[4]

The simplest expression of surplus may be free time, but time in which one is free to do nothing can be experienced only as excruciating boredom, as an utter *waste* of time, and so in preindustrial societies surplus value was usually spent in social activity, in investing objects and acts with significance. Rituals abound around activities we may well regard as work, whereby a large percentage of free time is taken back into work to make it more significant: a ritualised, social and cohesive activity which is part of a natural and instinctive creativity. In this sense work becomes art and art is inseparable from work; consequently skills are developed far above the level of technology required to sustain the social economy, in a complete reversal of our modern conception of economy as the saving of labour and money, rather than the constructive use of time. In societies we insist on calling primitive, surplus value is predominantly expressed as skill and expertise, which in turn endows all aspects of life with significance in a process utterly different from what we call work.

Under this system, surplus is invested directly in cultural activities. Where we trivialise life and divest work of any importance other than its exchange value, societies like those of the American Indian built a world of enormous and complex significance around them which was integrated with the natural world in the most intimate way. Their culture was supremely skilful and aesthetic, almost gratuitously so, and they were quite rightly proud of what and who they were. In such societies, there was no special category of labour or activity which approximated in any way to what we call work, nor was there a corresponding category of labour which was considered art, for surplus value was not hoarded as material wealth and property, but expressed as culture.

The dominant mode of production in such societies was undoubtedly art – skill exercised well beyond the levels demanded by economic necessity. The consequent level of cultural development was astonishing, comprising as it did a dense mythology expressed in ritual, story, dance and artefacts of often exquisite beauty. Add to this the fact that life itself was significant, moment by moment, and we have a picture of a culture far richer than our own. It is not my intention to romanticise early forms of society, but in comparison with our own they undoubtedly exemplify attitudes and values we could well rediscover. What I do want to pursue, however, is the idea that production itself is essentially creative and that art is only one aspect of a productive process which has changed radically over the last few hundred years, a fossil fragment, if you like, of preindustrial production.

Prior to the Renaissance, craft production had been raised to extraordinary levels of skill. Controlled by the trade guilds, standards were set which generally ensured that a fair proportion of surplus could be expressed within the work itself. Skill, decoration and quality were invested in even humble objects, and important collective endeavours – churches, cathedrals and other religious monuments – became a *tour de force* of invention and excellence in which enormous surplus was invested. An additional input of time, skill and work was made, over and above that demanded by function and necessity, and craft production became a vehicle for deep cultural expression.

By the late Middle Ages, however, the hierarchical power of the trade guilds was so institutionalised that little or no autonomy was allowed to workers in the crafts. A reaction to the monopolistic power of the Guild-Masters, coupled with a rejection of the constraints imposed on talented individuals, gave rise to early forms of individualistic *art* as we know it. As the most inventive workers broke free from the restrictive power of the guilds, finding themselves rich, influential patrons among the rising merchant classes, a flowering of cultural production took place characterised by a new interest in the natural world. But by separating art from craft the Renaissance also paved the way for that endless division of labour that typified craft production in the eighteenth century, setting the stage for the replacement of living skills with repetitive machine production.

Once the creative content of productive work had been removed and isolated as a special form of work called *art*, it remained a simple matter to extract the value of surplus production from work as money, and invest none of it in embellishing the product. The shoddy goods of the Industrial Revolution were an inevitable consequence of the separation of art and work, and the production of useless insignificant objects will continue until art and work are once again integrated in new forms of production.

Crafts are specialised and highly skilled forms of work, but this specialisation can limit and constrain the individual worker who is potentially controlled and shaped by the craft in ways which can be wholly stultifying. The crafts, as highly skilled work, encompass some of the most amazing of human achievements – the medieval cathedrals, the Bayeux Tapestry – and some of the most alienating forms of work imaginable, as Adam Smith described in this famous passage from *The Wealth of Nations*:

> One man draws out the wire, another straightens it, a third cuts it, a fourth points it, a fifth grinds it at the top for receiving the head; to make the head requires two or three distinct operations; to put it on, is a peculiar business; to whiten the pins is another; it is even a trade by itself to put them into the paper; and the important business of making a pin is, in this manner, divided into about eighteen distinct operations.[5]

What Adam Smith describes can scarcely be called craft production, for it is only factory production without machinery. At root, the crafts are essentially handwork, or work in which if machines are used they are used as tools, as things the worker uses with skill. By the eighteenth century, however, the division of labour in craft production had become such that human beings were turned into machines with no control over their own exploitation. Once the surplus value produced by the crafts was stripped away as profit and reinvested, not in the work itself but in machines to replace skill, the crafts and trades were rapidly and inevitably dehumanised.

As technologically determined work and its products come to dominate so much of our environment, the areas which people feel they can control shrink. Early socialist visions of extended communities sharing facilities and services, controlled by neighbourhood committees and communes, have given way to the mini-environment of the modern home, which has become both an escape from the world and a place where the world is experienced, restructured, through the medium of television. Work is despised in our society precisely because it is not freely chosen, and artists are often admired because they have had the courage, luck, determination or audacity to choose how they work. In the end it matters little if what they produce is trite or inconsequential. The absurdity of being envied and admired for doing something essentially useless is not generally acknowledged, but in a way the major achievement of the artist in modern society is symbolic – a gesture like that of the criminal and the vandal – two fingers to a mundane world with its petty restrictions and posturing.

As a symbol, art points the way back to and perhaps out of our dilemma. When we choose what we make we enter a world where quality exists again, where we can discuss the relative merits of ways of doing and making, where we can choose to make things well or badly, where shoddiness is not masked by ideas like cost-effectiveness and built-in obsolescence, and cost is not the governing criterion. The idea of work, freely chosen for its practical and ritual significance, brings us back to art. We are left with a choice of motive. Profit: something extracted from labour and raw materials via a reductive process in which everything is expressed as money. Or art: a constructive process in which labour and raw materials are converted into complex cultural goods which have the ability to provide for a broad spectrum of physical, spiritual and emotional needs. Paralleling the two primary modes of the natural world – the continual degradation of matter and the complex organisation of life forms – these two diametrically opposed modes of production are ours to choose from.

By extending the idea of freely-chosen work to include the choices we make in perceiving the world as we interact with it, we can discover how conventional work distances and structures our understanding of the world, denying intimate forms of knowledge and replacing them with a dispassionate objectivity, encouraging us to accept the destruction of our environment as a rational and necessary fact of life. A felt response to the natural world could permeate our attitudes towards making things that last and give lasting pleasure: a new aesthetic based on a genuine economy in which products are required to outlive the process of renewing their component materials. We can also look for artists to return to nature as subject matter. Not to naturalism, but to a direct response to nature, attempting to portray it as perceived; an art whose objective is to rekindle a subjective and immediate experience of the world. Artists and designers can begin to come to terms with the problems of structuring and making a world shaped by and for people. Not finalised, finite designs, but open procedures in which people can participate in designing and making their own surroundings. Decisions about houses, furniture, vehicles, clothes, could be returned to the people who produce and use them, in a collective process through which individuals can develop by using skills and imagination without dominating others. When disabled people are involved in the whole business of designing and making, not just their own special products, but common everyday items, then and only then will they gain access to the world of the able-bodied.

It is amazing how 'blind' supposedly normal people are to the world as experienced by the less than able-bodied. Very small changes in the way buildings and vehicles are designed and the way we go about organising the mechanics of everyday life would make a dramatic difference to the so-called disabled who are more often disabled by *our* attitudes than *their* disabilities. When people begin to redefine all those social elements which structure and confine them in roles they feel to be restrictive, or jobs that are soul-destroying, then we may begin to clamber out of those nineteenth-century concepts and attitudes which imprison us just as surely as nineteenth-century housing and twentieth-century household gadgets reinforce specific ideas about domestic life.

By rejecting shoddy goods, and the numbing, alienating, degrading ways in which we produce them, we can begin to visualise a world in which different values could prevail. Not a clinical world of stainless-steel 'appliances' for the disabled, but a world in which utilitarian purpose is no longer synonymous with mean, cold, barren and institutionalised objects – council housing and 'homes' for society's rejects. Surplus value would once more be reinvested in enriching our environment, producing well-made goods which last and give lasting pleasure, and useful objects to alleviate suffering in place of armaments. A simple but inspiring vision of a future we could all acknowledge as worthwhile.

Such forms of socialised production have been argued for since the Industrial Revolution. The Luddites' revolt was not a revolt against machinery itself, but against the machinery of enslavement; William Morris argued that useful work should replace useless toil and some of the most significant artists of the Russian Revolution rejected art in favour of socially-useful production. If we query what forms this socially-useful production might take, we are constantly directed towards the same conclusion – that it will be based on freely-chosen work. When the nature and purpose of work is chosen by those who carry out that work, production will be directed towards social ends determined by use values.

13
Inventing the Future

In this chapter, I set out to describe some practical attempts to develop new ways of working, and examine the problems inherent in such a radical project. I also present some arguments for a new and more creative approach to both work and unemployment. I do think it is possible to invent a future of our own choosing if we have the will and are prepared to take the risks involved.

Summer is over. Yesterday a rude wind blew into the last warm corners of a sunny August which had lingered on into late September, and today, outside the office window, I can see the two plane trees that conspired silently with me throughout the summer, struggling against the blustery wind. In no mood to relinquish their summer greenery, the trees toss and sway wildly. Twigs snap and fly past the windows, littering the street outside.

Inside my bureaucratic fastness all is executive plush, calm and orderly, except for the usual background noise of typewriters and telephone conversations. The drinks dispenser clicks and gurgles. Transfixed by the sound, I feêl isolated. A sudden sensation of movement catches me unawares. It takes me some time to recognise it as that same uncanny moment when the train alongside you at the station moves and it is impossible to tell which train is in motion. For a few seconds all is relative and my first floor office glides silently along the city street.

Here at my spaceship desk I am an alien visitor to the planet, slipping undetected through the city. The bronze-tinted double-glazing – my monitor screen – admits no sound from outside, and the delicious smells of approaching autumn are efficiently filtered out by the air-conditioning system. I can sense a chill in the wind outside, a premonition of winter, but here in my shirt sleeves the alienation is so complete that the spaceship image stays with me. Unable to shake it off, I cross the control room and throw a window catch. Someone shouts: 'What the hell are you doing, Roger. Close that bloody window will you!' A musical roar of sound: moist cold air and thick rich smells swirl into the office, an almost visible cloud of poisonous gas choking my colleagues. Papers fly everywhere, and before I can sit down again Mike 'B' has slammed the window shut and muttered off on a halo of indignation.

'What the bloody hell's eating him today!'

The windows on the other side of the office look out on to a nineteenth-century factory-cum-shop front. It is a typical all-in-one workshop/office/salesroom of Victorian urban industry, a marvellous concoction of coloured brickwork and careful joinery, carved stone lintels and corbels, string courses and dentils; in short, all the exuberant detail of an era convinced by its own sense of self-importance. A name, Atlas Print Works, is carved in gilded Roman lettering on black marble, and runs, frieze-like, above the windows of the street front. White caryatids or herms – take your pick – add a mythological weight to my argument, and on closer inspection turn out to be Atlas, naked from the waist up, sharply muscled and carrying the globe on his shoulders. On this symbol of permanence – as permanent as the world itself, and repeated four times for good effect – rise the upper stories of the building. The only hints of transience on the whole facade trail, wrinkle-like, from the window ledges where generations of London's ubiquitous pigeons have perched, yet even these traces of pigeon shit testify to the building's survival, to its solid and enduring presence.

The language of that building, all its signs and metaphors, speaks of a certainty and self-confidence completely out of key with our rapidly changing world. The Victorians borrowed styles and used them as part of a celebration of their own earthly dominion, but then change, for them, was still partially cyclical and, like the seasons, predictable. The modern world really began only when the last vestiges of medieval culture were buried under the soot of progress. Nowadays change is linear and our architecture bears testimony to this. A sequence of styles sliding back into the eclecticism of the nineteenth century, with critics to enumerate and catalogue them, now exemplifies this progressive principle. There is an essential difference, however, between nineteenth- and twentieth-century eclecticism which, although it may masquerade as a joke – Doric columns in plastic and neon – reflects a similar change in the way we feel and think about the world. Nowadays the trappings of traditional imagery herald an anti-traditional future, and the brittle facades of architecture speak of an impermanence and frivolity which is the counterpart to linear change.

As human beings, we are part of the natural world, and inevitably enmeshed in an emotional, felt relationship with it, but all the signs are that the productive forces we have unleashed will finally engulf us just as they have come to pollute great tracts of this planet. Science is drawn more completely into the process, and the small voice of knowledge which originally inspired scientific investigation is ignored. So, too, are its forecasts of crises precipitated by the exponential erosion of what were once thought to be limitless resources, or by the psychotic exterminism inherent in the weaponry of defence. Scientific fact is now acceptable only if it reinforces the morality of consumption or the aggressive 'defence' of ideology, and so, despite cries of warning from the engine-room of science, we sail on – a technological Titanic – bands playing, champagne flowing, not responding to the wheel until it is too late.

As the managers of this process, we may appear to dominate and organise the natural world, but in our other role as human beings, as part of that natural world, we are enslaved by our own systems. The challenge facing us all now is implicit in the schizophrenia we experience as slaves and masters. Certain individuals, certain classes and social groups, fall more readily into one of these categories, but each of us is potentially both manager and managed, regardless of class, sex or race. The problem is how to transcend this division in ourselves, which is manifest in the way we, as a society, manage the world and consequently ourselves.

There are deep contradictions inherent in our attitudes towards management. As individuals we try to wrest control from impersonal forces and choose a life that accords with our needs and desires, but the survival of any civilisation is directly dependent upon its ability to manage the production and distribution of essential commodities and the infrastructure which supports this – transport, sewage, communications. The temptation to minimise the inevitable conflict between individual and mass needs by managing desire, either through the mechanisms of discipline and control or propaganda and advertising, has led us to the point where the ecological consequences of our organised acts pose the greatest threat to our own survival. We have to begin to recognise and organise those areas of life that have to be 'managed', in such a way that they do not dominate those aspects of life that need to be lived out emotionally and intuitively; and do this without threatening either the delicate balance of nature, or the exercise of those sensitive feelings that reveal us at our most human.

Changing the course of history is no easy matter, but becomes an urgent necessity as thermonuclear destruction and the waste of natural resources vie with each other as harbingers of Armageddon. Faced with this urgency, I become increasingly convinced that social change can come about only through progressive change at an individual level. The sum total of individual acts and choices will, in the end, determine the course of history. As individuals, choosing to confront the colossus of materialism may appear to be an impossible, futile, romantic gesture, but it is the only real choice open to us, and recognising that we are not alone in making this choice is perhaps the first step towards changing the course of history. Refusing to accept our allotted future becomes a powerful gesture not because it is the final romantic choice on which heroics are built, but because it is potentially the driving force of evolutionary change.

In my office, I spend my time plotting against the inertia of the world around me. Working in a socialist bureaucracy which has taken on the almost impossible task of 'shifting the balance of industrial power from the hands of capital into the hands of labour' – the GLC – I am organising community building groups and Technology Networks, experimenting with new ways of working and with new products and services designed to meet social need which we hope will lead to new and worthwhile jobs. Ironically or appropriately enough, we start in Islington, home of the Community Press. The cycle begins again.

This time, instead of confronting authority in the shape of council, law courts and police, I am working with it. But rather than feeling capable of achieving my objectives, armed as I am with executive power, I find my hands tied. At least as squatters we could say – 'We live here, this is our home, go away!' – and the bureaucratic process, with all its endless delays, filing trays, committees and reports, worked in our favour, widening the gap between thought and action and leaving a space in which we could organise. Power it had, but was powerless to cope with the immediacy of our acts.

Now I 'progress' my ideas through bureaucratic channels. A year of organising has passed and still a lengthy sequence of committee cycles and legal opinions stands between me and my original objectives. I look across the office at the Atlas Print Works and realise that at this end of the twentieth century the only thing we have which can claim anything like the immutability of the Victorian certainty that could build a print works on the back of Atlas, is bureaucracy itself. Only bureaucracy has the same sense of permanence and the same indifference to any imperative other than that of due process.

In the Victorian era, thought and act were more intimately connected. Now a yawning gulf seems to separate thought and deed. But creativity is born of an intimacy between thinking and doing, in the moment when thought and action combine to shape the world around us. The musician improvises, the skilled worker thinks by doing – like this, or like this? – the dancer dances, and lovers surrender themselves to the moment. Bureaucracy, however, insinuates itself between thought and action, dividing the space in between into an infinite number of events. As each bureaucrat interfaces with the next by phone or letter, committee or protocol, a delay occurs. Like the paradox of Achilles and the tortoise, if we continually sub-divide what is essentially a continuous process, thought can never be transformed into action, nor theory into practice.

So part of the problem consists of trying to find ways to break through the inertia of convention, expectation and bureaucracy: ways of building up that critical mass of activity, enthusiasm, optimism and initiative that once realised can achieve the most unexpected results. I do not see the critical mass of atomic theory as an isolated phenomenon, for it seems to me that a similar process is at work in all sorts of animal and human behaviour. Beyond a certain density, a collection of dwellings suddenly becomes a village, a community. At that point changes in mass, in quantity, initiate qualitative changes and people behave differently.

A flock of birds is not simply a collection of individual birds, it behaves differently and recognisably, it has its own identity and habits. The same can be said of human endeavours. In Lincolnshire, the Council for Small Industries in Rural Areas (CoSIRA) agent had a rule of thumb for success – below five and above twenty-five. Five people working together can normally service themselves. They do not need bookkeepers and secretaries, delivery van drivers and sales people. All those roles can generally speaking be shared among the workforce or carried out part time, often outside working hours. Be it small business or cooperative, the rule seems to hold true, for once more than five people are involved in an enterprise all the additional jobs which have to be done, and done well if the enterprise is to survive, place an impossible burden on the productive workforce.

Cooperatives tend to try to share out these administrative tasks, perhaps taking them in turn. But that disrupts work and often means that jobs are not done as well as they could be, so non-productive work begins to erode the profitability of the enterprise. Approach 25 people and the equations begin to work out favourably again as a balance between administrative and productive work is reached. But these critical thresholds apply to more than the organisation, they affect the motivation, relationships and energy of people within organisations. When the balance is right, people feel effective and enjoy their own sense of achievement. When the balance is wrong, they feel they are struggling against impossible odds or engulfed by uncaring structures over which they have little or no control.

To effect change, alternative forms of organisation will have to achieve these critical thresholds of scale and collectivity where quantity becomes quality. A few cooperatives, isolated across a large city, are vulnerable, surviving by chance where they can secure the advantages of sympathetic custom – whole foods and radical books. But add other cooperatives working in related fields – printing, book distribution, typesetting – and group design, wood and metal work around that nucleus building, and the potential for mutual support is there. Merge those cooperatives into a federation which can begin to supply its own members with specialist advice and services, economies of scale in purchasing, and eventually its own banking and promotional services, and what at first sight seemed a lunatic fringe activity could establish itself as a viable, secure and consequential alternative, pointing a way forward.

This is exactly what the people of a small Basque community – Mondragon – did. Over a period of some 30 years, they have progressed from one small cooperative manufacturing paraffin stoves to a complex federation of cooperatives employing in excess of 18,000 people and offering a level of social provision unheard of elsewhere, entirely financed from the proceeds of cooperative enterprise.

The Mondragon group actually started in 1943 with a few classes at the lowest level of technical education for the training of unemployed young people; in 1956 a small workshop was opened for the manufacture of cookers and stoves; and in 1959 a credit cooperative opened its first branch office. All this happened in Mondragon, a small town in the province of Guipuzcoa – one of the Basque provinces in the north of Spain. According to the Guipuzcoa census for 1970, Mondragon then had 22,421 inhabitants and the province as a whole approximately 631 thousand.

Since those beginnings in the 1950s, huge expansion has occurred in three directions: education, industry, banking. By the end of the 1970s there existed in the province a modern cooperative system of technical education, 70 cooperative factories with a work force of more than 15,000 cooperators, and a credit cooperative bank with 93 branches and 300,000 deposit accounts.[1]

Add to that a highly advanced research and development institute, a social security system, housing cooperatives on a considerable scale, and a growing consumer cooperative with its own laboratories for monitoring the quality of goods it sells, and we can begin to get some idea of what is possible. Despite high levels of unemployment in northern Spain, typically 25 per cent in the Basque provinces, the cooperatives have followed a no-redundancy policy during recent years of recession and their ability to sustain this is proof of the economic strength of this remarkable development in workers' control.

As a phase of production dominated by heavy industry and large-scale factory production draws to a close, putting millions of people out of work, the new industries, occupations and ways in which work is organised (those which achieve this critical mass) will be influential in defining the shape of society for a considerable period of time. So it is important to do more than theorise about social change, more than insist on there being any one ideal form of organised work, for the society that emerges from this period of social and industrial change will be shaped by those forms of organised work which are successful in the near future.

I think the struggle for new forms of social organisation is by no means lost, but there is no doubt in my mind that time is running short. Within the next 20 years, social patterns and productive forces will be established which will exert a powerful influence over the coming decades. One of the chief reasons, I think, that William Morris's writings should appear so apposite now is because they were written at a similar moment of change, when enormous forces were shaping a mode of production which is only now petering out. What Morris pointed to were the social consequences of productive processes shaped expressly to generate the maximum surplus value extracted from work as profit. What the example of Mondragon demonstrates clearly is the effectiveness of organising production to ensure that the surplus generated is invested to the benefit of the working community. Perhaps in the future we can elaborate new forms of work organisation which will allow some of that surplus to be reinvested in the work itself, as Morris would have counselled.

Modern technologies are well suited to high precision, small-batch production. I can see them opening up a future of varied and highly-skilled work, just as readily as a future of automated alienated non-work. The choice is ours and we still have the time in which to make it, but that choice will emerge only as the sum-total of individual acts and choices. If we leave all these choices in the hands of financial and political vested interests, the future will be no better than the past. We have reached a point in our technological development where the amount of work required to satisfy our basic needs, to remove the imperative of survival, has been dramatically reduced. The concept of full employment is now in question, and raises the more crucial question of what production is *for*. Nowadays most work is devoted to the production of non-essentials, but, by reassessing our priorities, we could release enormous quantities of time which could then be devoted to improving the quality of life. Although there is no doubt that technology could, with sensitive application, free us from material need, the reverse seems to be true and an abundance of things brings with it alarming areas of poverty, even in the heart of the affluent West. Need has been confused with desire to the point where a lack of consumer durables is experienced as a fierce poverty, and it seems that the only way out of this modern more-equals-less paradox lies in the direction of a radical reassessment of wealth.

The early socialists were good at this. Individual wealth, they felt, must be replaced by 'commonwealth' – by a universal entitlement to an equitable share in the products of labour. A common*wealth* of quality, not quantity. A reassessment of wealth which recognises a host of needs outside the material necessities of life. Peace, affection, empathy with the natural world, are not compatible with the ever-quickening pace of material production which fails to remedy the lack of clean water, unpolluted air, adequate clothing and shelter, food even, which is a daily reality for millions of people. But if Western society were to renounce its attachment to *things* – its ponderous materialism – massive resources of time, energy, materials and creative ingenuity would be freed, and could be applied to supplying the real needs of the rest of the world and eliminating the poverty that exists in the heart of our cities.

Communities no longer operate as they used to. People are isolated in their rooms and houses, and the networks of family relations and neighbourhoods have broken down in all but a few rural and working-class communities. In the cities, people talk glibly of community art, community politics and community spirit, but community is more than a physical area, more than a ghetto, it is a sense of having something in common: a network of interlocking personal bonds cementing a community into an identity that can sustain its members through adversity and unite them in celebration. A genuine commonwealth affirmed and reaffirmed in collective cultural events: dance, song, parties, outings, mourning and rejoicing.

There are few communities left in our villages and fewer still in the cities. In the prosperous South-east of England people now talk of 'working' villages, which are becoming a rarity, and residential villages, populated by wealthy commuters and retired professionals. The demands of material production require that old established communities be broken up, and the working class is now a hindrance to modern industry which avoids the growing poverty of urban concentrations. The essential ingredients of a common culture no longer exist, although the urban planners grudgingly acknowledge the need for it by leaving the pubs standing whenever they demolish a neighbourhood: lonely guardians of a local culture that somehow survives in spirit until the last pub is bulldozed to the ground.

The physical destruction of our communities is only a final, symbolic act. The real damage was done years ago, but in a sense the regeneration of these communities could be but a small step away. A creative step, involving the transformation of quantity into quality, which begins as all human endeavour begins, in self-interest, but this time in self-interest expressed through collaboration. In the centres of our large cities, housing cooperatives, service cooperatives and producer cooperatives have only a little way to go before they achieve the critical mass that could give rise to a self-sustaining cooperative economy, in which collective organisation and mutual aid would grow out of individual choice, with surplus time used to develop communal facilities – nursery, workshop, club – run not by the municipality but by the community. Not given by the state, but hard won by people working together.

Achieving this would require an extensive commitment to real democracy on the part of central and local government; handing over buildings and empty land to local community ownership instead of insisting on managing them centrally; supplying materials and expertise rather than money; helping people establish their own forms of self-government and their own local banks and development agencies. Beyond that an educational framework is needed, within which people can learn the practical and organisational skills to allow them to take responsibility for their own lives and break the patronising cycle of bureaucratic delay. Add to this the concept of a minimum national wage to replace dole and social security payments, and time already freed by unemployment could be used constructively.

Self-organisation happens all around us, but has to be learned by experience, and cannot occur on a large scale without certain preconditions being met. Time and resources are both important, so mechanisms for redistributing wealth as free time and access to resources are necessary. It is absurd that some of us should spend our lives working overtime while others have nothing but boredom to fill their days, when an intelligent reassessment of the extent to which work is actually necessary, and not just useless toil, could pave the way for a redistribution of work and wealth. Nothing could be more pleasurable than a morning of useful productive work, an afternoon spent looking after children, and an evening passed in conversation, study, or the careful making of some item of clothing or furniture, with the results of each occupation contributing to a full life in harmonious surroundings. An old theory but a pertinent one.

Our cities are full of old and decaying buildings, and the cost of refurbishing these will be enormous. Most of the work involved is inevitably labour intensive. An expedient solution is to abandon them and build anew on green-field sites along the motorways, easily accessible but close to the charms of the countryside. The 'Birmingham has no future, so we will abandon it to its fate' theory makes sound economic sense of a sort, for in money terms there is little doubt that such a solution would be cheaper and more profitable – as long as the social costs don't have to be counted – but if we free social reconstruction from the imperative of a profit-and-loss accountancy which makes no attempt to assess the social costs of deprivation, all our cities could be gradually and lovingly restored. We have the necessary labour to hand, but paradoxically the 'logic' of modern management and monetarist economic theory requires that a skilled workforce be kept idle on the dole while the fabric of the country's buildings and services rots.

I recently calculated that it would cost the national economy little more than £40 per week, over and above the present total costs of keeping someone unemployed, to put them back to work productively, renovating the country's buildings; the value of each person's output would be somewhere in the region of £200–£400 a week. The current cost of unemployment represents a huge disinvestment of the country's human and financial resources, but such is the myopia of economic theory that the small additional expenditure necessary to reverse this state of affairs is not allowed. Money currently wasted on unemployment could be put to work in a profitable way. Unfortunately, investing £40 per head in improving the country's housing stock would be profitable only in human terms, not in immediate financial ones, although it would generate an enormous capital asset that could be used to finance further economic activities, particularly in the inner cities. But, because no one seems prepared to take account of the true costs of unemployment, the investment goes unmade.

By all accounts, there is well in excess of £20,000,000,000 worth of work that should be carried out with some urgency if our building stock is to be put in a satisfactory condition, and that figure rises every time another building system failure comes to light. Spending this money over ten years would generate enormous employment; the combined effects of reduced state outgoings in unemployment and allied benefits, rate rebates and so on, added to increased returns from income tax and the knock-on effects of increased spending power, would result in the treasury recouping 70 to 80 per cent of the money spent.

Nothing is done because neither the political will nor the all important infrastructure exists to implement such a programme. I am convinced, however, that a coordinated, self-managed solution would work, and that by utilising time freed by unemployment amongst skilled and unskilled people a commmunity-based programme of renovations could succeed where all other strategies have failed. This sort of programme would not require elaborate bureaucratic organisation, and would, in all probability, be massively cost-effective, although it would involve imaginative and innovative financing from private and public sector. Experimental schemes suggest that this could be the beginning of a viable solution to the issue of unemployment.

Under these conditions the nature of work itself would change dramatically. People would be involved directly in decisions about what they would perceive as their own buildings and, because the work would be organised within the community and not from outside, women would not necessarily be excluded from it as they are today, nor would learning and discovery be regarded as inefficient ways of using labour. Thousands of people could embark on a voyage of discovery similar to Maurice Claydon's: the world could be a richer place, culturally as well as financially.

The same principles can be applied to a thousand activities, all essential to our well being, and similar conclusions wait to be drawn. If it is possible to collectivise and enrich the ordinary activities of daily life, of work in and outside the house, what happens to all those activities we call art? I have suggested that by introducing a creative element into work we can enrich it and make it more art-like. I have also envisaged work as a collective activity, a way in which individuals and communities can organise their environment to suit their own purposes. But there are more intimate areas of life where we create personal environments, where feelings for ourselves and concerns for others come into play. These two parts of life overlap considerably, as do the activities appropriate to them, and in the same way that it is possible to envisage the enrichment of work in the outside world, it is possible to look to the enrichment of a more intimate, personal world.

Food for example has to be grown, preserved, prepared and cooked. Freeing time will allow us to set store by how well we do these things, and they could become once more the arts they undoubtedly were. Freeing time also allows us to develop skills above the level demanded by economic necessity. I could spend a fortnight of evenings making a table, say, and invest it with all the love, care and attention the task and the materials deserve, knowing that it will give lasting pleasure for a century, perhaps longer. I could never expect to be paid for all that labour, but why should I be if I can think of it as free time?

The production of commodities in this freely-chosen way would release them from the demands of profit, from the ever-pressing need to compete for custom by reducing expensive labour content – and our daily lives would be enriched by a revival of the traditional idea of art: of skill enjoyed. Once again we would be surrounded by objects invested with significance, personalised and humanised to give pleasure in the making, and lasting pleasure in use.

This is not idle daydreaming; it could become economic reality with remarkably small changes in attitude. As this present phase of the Industrial Revolution gathers pace, it is obvious that manufacturing is going to follow the pattern of dramatic labour reduction which has characterised agriculture over the last two centuries, during which time the agricultural labour force, which once numbered above 80 per cent of the working population, has fallen to under 2 per cent. New technology creates new forms of employment, but is not at all labour intensive. The fully-automated factory is already a reality, just as the automated field is an ever present fact of life – sprayed by aeroplane and cropped by machines. There is absolutely no reason to believe that unemployment will go away unless we change our attitudes towards work.

During the early days of the Industrial Revolution, labour freed from the fields was directed into the growing clutter of factories and sweatshops which characterised eighteenth- and nineteenth-century cities, but today there are no new labour-intensive industries springing up. Instead human labour – work itself – is being replaced by a growing army of robots, and millions of people are no longer required by the conventional manufacturing economy. Work itself is becoming obsolete, and people view this development with alarm. Their security is threatened by it and they clamour for 'work'. But work as we have known it – human labour bought and sold to make a profit over and above the costs of employing it – a four-letter word for the regimented prostitution of the production line – will never again be available in quantity, despite the fact that material production continues at an ever-quickening pace.

What this really indicates is that we have finally reached the point where huge quantities of time can and are being freed from the daily imperative of drudgery, and this should give us enormous hope for the future. It is nothing more than an intransigent puritanism that forces us to see this time in a negative way, as 'unwork', unemployment. The practical problems involved in converting the useless dead time and capital of unemployment into a productive force for social regeneration are not insurmountable. In fact the financial burden of maintaining a growing pool of useless people will soon become intolerable unless mechanisms are found to utilise that pool of human skills and resources in a productive way.

Unfortunately, contemporary economic theory has no way of coming to grips with the problem because it is overwhelmingly concerned with the production of quantity. Output, productivity, profit, viability, competitiveness are all ways of measuring performance in terms of quantity, of money. Expressed as ratios and percentages they are no measure of quality. The growing mass of unemployed people is in itself a very costly *product* of mass production, and as people in quantity are no longer necessary to produce goods in quantity the only way everyone can re-engage in work is through an expansion of activities not conventionally or obviously economic, but which serve to improve the quality of life.

These facts are recognised at a certain 'voluntary-work' level by most people, but the idea of putting gangs of people to work tidying up derelict sites smacks so offensively of Victorian paternalism and army-life inanities that it is completely unacceptable. People want to be productive, usefully employed and adequately rewarded for their contribution to society. They have no wish to be slaves or to live useless lives, but are anxious to contribute and participate. In the end there are only two assumptions that stand in the way of the growth of useful work. One is the idea that all work should generate profits and therefore be carried out on a conventional business model. The other is our failure to recognise the costs of unemployment as part of the costs and consequences of automated production. We tend to blame people for being unemployed, and then, to make matters worse, insist that they make themselves available for work which does not exist – in other words, we deny them the right to put their unemployed time and skills to use in a meaningful way.

As I have already suggested, only relatively small amounts of money are required to unlock the vast resources of time and talent contained by unemployment. Investing in the use of time freed by unemployment could give enormous returns measured in output value, in socially useful work that is ignored as unprofitable by conventional business. Taxing the new technological industries, and looking critically at our dependence on an aggressive, essentially suspicious stance in international relations, reducing our investment in weapons and war-preparedness, would supply the financial catalyst needed to convert enforced inactivity into self-determined activity.

My Utopia of freely-chosen work could start tomorrow. It is an economic possibility, and simply needs to be recognised as perhaps the only alternative to social and economic disaster in one form or another, an alternative to the unpredictable havoc the apocalyptic social forces unleashed by the technological revolution of automation and consumerism will wreak, if they are not balanced by a reassessment of the objectives of production. Freely-chosen work could begin to challenge our assumptions about the nature of work, because freely-chosen work would be work chosen for its own sake, for the pleasure in it, or the pleasure that could come from it. Faced with enforced non-work, people would have to do more than pine away, they would have to decide what to do with their time. Those choices would perhaps have more to do with social well-being and enjoyment than with economic necessity, in which case work might finally cease to be a four-letter word.

One of the biggest flaws in the political arguments of the left is that they are all too often based in morality, in the puritanism of the religious movements which assisted at the birth of socialism some two centuries ago. They indignantly scorn the pragmatism to which most people respond. The utopian alternative I am proposing is not a romantic fantasy, but a way of steering essential pragmatism. Indeed, I would argue that progressive social change is not merely possible, but essential, and an instinctive way of adjusting to changes in the social and economic environment. It is the frustration that comes when this process is denied by vested interest – be it bureaucratic socialism, the competitive anarchy of the free-market economy or physical repression by militaristic regimes – that all too often erupts as social disorder. For the social stability and peace desired by most of us can come only when this urge for progressive change is encouraged and not denied.

I can hear some armchair radicals puffing at this – it sounds too compromised, too liberal – but then they often suffer from a puritanical sense of outrage at any suggestion that does not fall in line with their dogma, and are likely to miss the point altogether. What I am arguing for is a realisable socialism, a caring socialism, going back to essential ideas about securing the means of production and distribution in the hands of the community, and trying to confront the very real problems involved: a socialism committed to creating the practical conditions under which its egalitarian goals can be achieved. A socialism that respects, and is prepared to learn from, the practical and organisational achievements of the nineteenth century labour movement; above all a socialism built on the vision and practicality of creative people who can live with the contradictions and apparent compromises the process of social change involves.

What becomes increasingly clear, as the welfare state and nationalised industries are dismantled and turned against the very people they were intended to sustain, is that it is impossible to legislate for social equality: political power is not enough. Extensive changes will have to come about in our attitude towards work – in the way we produce and reproduce the world around us – and these changes will be secured for the future only if they involve people in organising their lives and communities for themselves, not through the agency of state, bureaucracy or ideology. Not in the fantasy world of purified doctrinal socialism, but in a real and contradictory world where the dialectical process of Marx is confronted in practice.

But my arguments carry little weight if I cannot propose a viable alternative, a different way of producing and distributing wealth and of measuring it. I would begin by going back to William Morris's definition of wealth, back to what nature gives us and what we can reasonably make of it – 'The sunlight, the fresh air, the unspoiled face of the earth, raiment and housing necessary and decent, the storing up of knowledge and the power of disseminating it ...' – a very simple and surprisingly contemporary demand. Morris placed constant emphasis on the quality of life, contrasting this with quantity production and its effects on people's lives. If we take this as a starting point – how to increase the quality of life in general and reduce the disparity between material wealth and poverty – we can begin to build an intriguing picture of a society motivated by different economic principles.

Unfortunately, redistributing wealth in a conventional sense – taxing the rich and patronising the poor with welfare – is only a way of avoiding the real issue of the quality of life that redistribution causes. Indeed, this century has been dominated by the politics of distribution at the expense of the development of any coherent politics of production. What we produce and how we produce it is of crucial importance, especially when the social fabric is so threatened by our ability to produce things without people. Poverty is finally to do with how rich or how poor we feel, and beyond the point of material necessity it only reflects cultural expectations. The problem of affluence rests in the inability of the things we produce with such ease to satisfy a deeply-felt and universal need for meaning in daily life.

There is without doubt an enormous and real poverty in our society. People live in substandard homes, without basic amenities; the elderly and disabled are institutionalised for want of the often simple equipment and appropriate housing which would give them independence and self-respect. There is much that could be made and done to improve the quality of people's lives, and as a consequence a very considerable 'social' market exists outside the conventional market economy of consumerism.

But that social market is not supplied with goods and services because there appears to be little profit in it. Poverty means deprivation for the poor, but it also deprives the country of economic activity: it reduces our purchasing power and consequently our productive output, breeding unemployment, deprivation and social need, and stoking the miserable cycle of human wastage. Trying to satisfy these real needs could become the most positive solution to unemployment, and it could also bring about the sort of social changes that would herald an acceptable future.

The prospect of building a successful economy around this social market is not as farfetched as it seems; I have already mentioned the staggering quantity of work to be done if our housing stock is to be brought up to an acceptable standard, and a similar quantity of work exists in other less obvious fields, spreading through the whole infrastructure of society, such as transport, the sewage system, the low-tech end of medicine and so on. The problem of catering for the ever-increasing number of old people will sooner or later bring home to us the fact that virtually everyone is physically or mentally handicapped at some point in their life.

Until recently, prescriptive design and high technology were heralded as the solution to all these problems, but things haven't worked out as expected. Designers are obliged by the market economy to work on profitable projects, so unprofitable, social 'problems' are left to fend for themselves, or set as student exercises rarely to be realised. We lack the mechanisms both for researching and designing in these fields and for manufacture, production and distribution, so a whole range of essentially labour-intensive economic activity is neglected simply because it cannot be quantified as profitable; we lack a social cost accounting to tell us the real costs of economic choices like unemployment.

Not to have these facts is an example of gross mismanagement at a national and international level. As any management consultant will tell you, an enterprise which fails to count the real cost of production and ensure that it is covered in the selling price of its goods is headed for bankruptcy. For a national government to lack this basic management information is inexcusable. It is a supreme irony that we can squander some £19 billion on high-tech defence, spending massively on imported weaponry and increasing our dependence on an economic system that creates poverty, while knowing that the same amount of capital could service the social market I have described and generate not hundreds but hundreds of thousands of worthwhile jobs and new forms of work.

The tragedy is that this could all be reality with a little will and commitment. Thousands of schoolchildren follow craft design and technology courses, but spend most of their time reinventing the wheel, while art and design students at college are sucked into the glossy world of style and consumerism, largely because the practical subjects have always been tainted by an association with manual labour. Practical research in applying existing technology by designing around social problems has never been given the credibility which leading-edge academic research has achieved, and so is neither organised nor coordinated in the same way. Product designers rarely see themselves as pushing forward the frontiers of research in the way academics do, and the majority of research is concentrated in the profitable fields of defence and consumerism, dominated by the mystique of 'new' technology, when many pressing social problems can be solved simply and at a low cost.

It is surprising – or not surprising, depending on your point of view – that so called 'ordinary' people, in their everyday lives, see the need for and come up with endless inventions and designs which are not taken up by industry unless they are obviously profitable. But then, what is so surprising about seeing ways in which machines and techniques could be used to meet the needs that we, or people we know, so obviously have? Or again, what is so strange about a building worker inventing an efficient wallpaper stripper, a woman office worker inventing typing correction fluid, a kitchen worker inventing an onion peeler, or nurses specifying the precise sort of equipment they need to provide the level of care we all hope to receive? So much invention, ingenuity and talent, so many ideas that could generate useful work making useful products that in their turn could truly improve the quality of life for everybody, are ignored and remain undeveloped by an economy which devotes an increasing proportion of its resources to the production of weapons and a wealth measured according to profit-and-loss accounting which ignores human misery and wastage in its narrow monetary calculations.

Under the threat of future (now accomplished) redundancies, the Lucas Aerospace Combine Shop Stewards Committee drew up an alternative plan for their company based on the idea of socially useful production, as an alternative to the wastage of human skill and potential which contraction in the aerospace industry would inevitably bring. Not only was this idea of the possibility and form of work in a technically-advanced society imaginative in itself, but the alternative plan documented hundreds of potential products with positive social-use value. These were not simple outline sketches, but considered and developed designs envisaging alternative uses for existing plant and skills, all produced by people in full-time work, elaborating their ideas in tea breaks and lunch hours!

The committee sent letters to 180 organisations and individuals with reputations in the field of alternative technology – academics and designers with the massive resources of research time, money and laboratory equipment available to them. Only three people responded. Who then are the real inventors, the real designers, the real artists?[2]

This ability of so-called 'ordinary' people to invent and originate, to arrive at useful, practical solutions to a multitude of problems is not in any sense new, it has been obvious to some people for a long time. In *Fields, Factories and Workshops Tomorrow*, written in 1898, Peter Kropotkin tellingly observed:

> Is it not striking, indeed, that the steam engine, even in its leading principles, the railway engine, the steam boat, the telegraph, the phonograph, the weaving machine, the lace machine, the lighthouse, the macadamised road, photography in black and in colours, and thousands of less important things, *have* not been invented by professional men of science, although none of them would have refused to associate his name with any of the above-named inventions? Men who hardly had received any education at school, who had merely picked up the crumbs of knowledge from the tables of the rich, and who made their experiments with the most primitive of means – the attorney's clerk Smeaton, the instrument maker Watt, the brakesman Stephenson, the jeweller's apprentice Fulton, the millwright Rennie, the mason Telford, and hundreds of others whose very names remain unknown, were, as Mr Smiles justly says, 'The real makers of modern civilisation'; while the professional men of science, provided with all the means for acquiring knowledge and experimenting, have invented little in the formidable array of implements, machines, and prime-motors which has shown to humanity how to utilise and to manage the forces of nature.[3]

I would like to see a very different design process emerging from changes in school teaching, and in attitudes towards practical education, which would place greater emphasis on solving urgent social problems and less emphasis on designing fashionable objects. Let me give an example: many disabled people find the places they live in – their domestic environment – at best restrictive, and at worst imprisoning, often for the lack of very minor adaptations. Despite the enormous combined resources they represent, local government departments – social services, housing, building works – seem unable to respond adequately, yet few designers see this as a design problem, when in fact a systematic approach to disability in the domestic environment could be highly fruitful. Since a diversity of domestic aids and equipment already exists, merely cataloguing and evaluating these products would go a long way towards simplifying the task of specifying for individual needs, which local council officers often find impossible.

Charting the sort of difficulties associated with particular disabilities – getting up and down steps, in and out of the bath – working out alternative ways of dealing with them, and devising check lists and survey forms which disabled people can use to assess their own surroundings would be a useful beginning. Carefully coordinated study and research in this area would soon reveal a multitude of specific 'products' that could be designed and made, and these more conventional design 'problems' could then be handed on to schools and colleges where students could work on real design projects, rather than imaginary ones. Background research could be taken seriously and organised nationally to avoid duplication. Of course this would require different people working on the same problem, so the cult of the individual designer would have to give way to the design team that could and should include the people who are designed 'for'. Who knows more about wheelchairs than someone who has to live in one?

Organised in this way, design, and the practical subjects which are still rated a poor second to academic study, would begin to acquire the credibility and status they once had and so rightly deserve. Freed from the association with manual labour as a demeaning and second-class activity, and allied to the concept of caring and concern, the practical subjects would begin to lose their association with harsh, hard *man's* work and be seen as one of the most important activities open to us all. This will require considerable changes in the way we see the world and one another; it will mean abandoning our attachment to intellectual skills at the expense of the practical, accepting that we cannot afford to spend billions of pounds on arms if we cannot stop old people from dying of cold, or if young people have to die because there are not enough kidney machines. It will also mean reducing our dependence on the Third World.

Instead of exploiting the Third World and destroying local economies in exchange for the products of a dubious Western culture, we should be exporting methods based on smaller scale, more localised production that we should try to develop here in the West. By reducing our dependence on high-tech products and production methods, except where they genuinely improve the quality of life, we can gradually reduce the cost of living, and so perhaps choose to work within a stable and varied but less cash-dominated economy where culture will flourish and caring research and production will be organised to meet social need.

In his frequent talks on the Lucas Aerospace alternative plan, Mike Cooley is fond of pointing out that 'the future is not somehow out there, like a continent or a coastline, waiting to be discovered', and I think the same point applies here. The future will be largely determined by the choices, both positive and negative, that people make, and it is up to us all, collectively, to shape that future. I have tried to sketch in a brief indication of the sort of future I hope to see, but in the end it will be up to the designers and makers, the tribe of Daedalus if you like, and the mass of working people, to play their part in defining and structuring a future in which work can again become a meaningful, satisfying and creative activity.

Notes and Bibliography

Introduction – The Fall of Daedalus

1 Robert Graves, *Greek Myths*, illustrated edition, Harmondsworth: Penguin Books 1981, p. 88.
2 S.W. Singer, *Wayland Smith, a Dissertation on a Tradition of the Middle Ages*, London: William Pickering 1847, pp. lxviii–lxvx.
3 R.W. Hutchinson, *Prehistoric Crete*, Harmondsworth: Penguin Books 1963, pp. 300–5.
4 Graves, *Greek Myths*, p. 88.
5 Ibid., p. 89.
6 Hutchinson, *Prehistoric Crete*, pp.113–15.
7 Ibid., pp. 21–2.
8 Arthur Cotterell, *A Dictionary of World Mythology (revised edition)*, Oxford: Oxford University Press 1986, p. 170.
9 Raymond Williams, *Keywords, a Vocabulary of Culture and Society*, Glasgow: William Collins (Fontana) 1976, pp. 32–5.
10 Richard Ellmann, *James Joyce*, paperback edition, London: Oxford University Press 1966, pp. 153–4.

The Art of Work

1 J.A. Bundgaard, *Mnesicles: A Greek Architect at Work*, Copenhagen: Scandinavian University Books 1957, p. 184.
2 Ibid., p. 133.
3 We do, however, know something about how working drawings were made and used, and indeed why so few have survived. For an account of this and a description of a fine and very rare key to medieval working methods see: John Harvey, 'The Tracing Floor in York Minster', *40th Annual Report of the Friends of York Minster*, 1968, pp. 9–13.
4 Bundgaard, *Mnesicles*, p. 138.
5 Ibid., p. 139.
6 Edward Lucie–Smith, *The Story of Craft: The Craftsman's Role in Society*, Oxford: Phaidon 1981, p. 15.
7 Quoted by J.J. Coulton in, *Greek Architects at Work: Problems of Structure and Design*, London: Paul Elek 1977, p. 15.
8 For a discussion of this point and an intriguing account of changes in building forms and their significance, see Richard Krautheimer,

'Introduction to an Iconography of Medieval Architecture', *Journal of the Warburg and Courtauld Institute*, vol.5, 1942, pp. 1–33.

9 Ibid., p. 20.

10 John Summerson, *Georgian London*, London: Barrie and Jenkins 1970, p. 70.

11 John Harvey, *The Master Builders: Architecture in the Middle Ages*, London: Thames & Hudson 1971, p. 13.

12 Ibid., p. 13.

13 P. W. Kingsford, *Builders and Building Workers*, London: Edward Arnold 1973, p. 26.

14 Summerson, *Georgian London*, p. 34.

15 Harvey, *The Master Builders*, p. 38.

16 In Japan, carpentry – the art of housebuilding – survived as an intact tradition until very recently, in a way it has not in the West. Such skills were highly regarded in Japan, and their practitioners had considerable social status. Japanese tools and working methods are subtly different from ours, preserving a sensitivity to materials rarely seen outside fine woodworking circles in the west. For an interesting and well illustrated introduction to this subject see Kiyosi Seike, *The Art of Japanese Joinery*, New York/Tokyo: Weatherhill/Tankosha 1977. The quotation in the text is from pp. 17–18: 'The Carpenter's *Dògu*, or Instruments'.

17 From a contemporary account by the monk Gervase of Canterbury, 'History of the Burning and Repair of the Church of Canterbury' (1185), which is given in full in *Literary Sources of Art History*, selected and edited by Elizabeth G. Holt, Princeton: Princeton University Press 1947, pp. 48–58. Later published as *A Documentary History of Art*, by Doubleday (Anchor Books).

18 Ibid., p. 52.

19 Ibid., pp. 50–1.

20 Ibid., p. 53.

21 See Jean Gimpel, *The Cathedral Builders*, Wilton: Michael Russell 1983, pp. 85–6, for an account of some of the closely–guarded secret skills of the medieval masons. Gimpel's book is also one of the best and most readable introductions to the builders of the great Gothic cathedrals and their working methods and traditions.

22 Robert J. Clements, 'Michelangelo on Effort and Rapidity in Art', *Journal of the Warburg and Courtauld Institute*, vol.17, 1954, pp. 309–10.

23 Ibid., p. 304.

24 John James, *Chartres, The Masons who built a Legend*, London: Routlege & Kegan Paul 1982, pp. 34–40.

Further reading

As well as the books cited in the notes, C. Hewett's *English Historic Carpentry*, London: Phillmore 1980, gives a real insight into Western traditional building skills and methods. For an insight into Eastern tools and working methods see Henry Lanz, *Japanese Woodworking Tools, Selection, Care and Use*, New York: Sterling 1985, and Yasuo Nakahara, *Japenese Joinery, a Handbook for Joiners and Carpenters*, Washington: Hartley and Marks 1983.

The Pig

1 The most evocative, atmospheric, yet detailed and accurate account of a traditional trade in all its complexity and intricacy that I have come across is given by George Sturt in *The Wheelwright's Shop*, Cambridge: Cambridge University Press 1923.

Further reading

Marshall Sahlins, in his book *Stone Age Economics*, London: Tavistock 1974, argues the case for an original 'affluent society' of hunter gatherers, characterised by domestic production.

Assumptions

Further reading

R.L. Gregory, *Eye and Brain: the Psychology of Seeing*, London: Weidenfeld & Nicolson 1966, deals with the mechanics of visual perception in an accessible way. Robert M. Pirsig, *Zen and the Art of Motorcycle Maintenance*, London: Corgi Books 1976, deals with the philosophical problems of perception and knowledge in a very readable way. His discussion of skill as a way of knowing the world is relevant to what I am discussing in this chapter and throughout this book. Betty Edwards, *Drawing on the Right Side of the Brain*, London: Fontana 1982, is arguably one of the most enlightening and interesting books on artistic perception, especially as it takes a practical, how–to–do–it approach to the subject.

It's not Normal

1 R.D. Laing and D.G. Cooper, *Reason and Violence: a Decade of Sartre's Philosophy, 1950–1960*, London: Tavistock 1964, p. 20.
2 Jean Genet, in the introduction to: *Soledad Brother: the Prison Letters of George Jackson*, London: Jonathan Cape 1971, p. 23.
3 Quoted by Franklin Rosemont in: *André Breton and the First Principles of Surrealism*, London: Pluto Press 1978, p. 27.

4 Arthur Koestler, *The Ghost in the Machine*, London: Hutchinson 1967, pp. 166–7.

The Work of Art

1 D.S. Chambers, *Patrons and Artists in the Italian Renaissance*, London: Macmillan 1970, p. xxvi.
2 John Berger, *Art and Revolution: Ernst Neizvestney and the Role of the Artist in the USSR*, London: Writers and Readers 1969, pp. 22–3.
3 E.H. Gombrich, *The Story of Art* (1950), Oxford: Phaidon 1984, p. 232.
4 Andrew Wilton, *J.M.W.Turner, His Art and Life*, Secaucus: Poplar Books 1979, pp.16–17.
5 Chambers, *Patrons and Artists*, p. xxv.
6 Edward Lucie–Smith, *The Story of Craft: the Craftsman's Role in Society*, Oxford: Phaidon 1981, p. 41.
7 Joseph and Frances Gies, *Life in a Medieval City*, London: Arthur Barker 1969, p. 53.
8 Nicolas Pevsner, *An Outline of European Architecture* (1943), London: Allen Lane 1973, p. 200.
9 Gombrich, *The Story of Art*, p. 221.

Further reading
While D. S. Chambers's book, referred to above, gives a clear and detailed picture of the relationship between artists and their patrons during the Renaissance, William Morris is possibly the most interesting and informative writer on the broader issues touched on in this chapter. The two most readily available selections of his writings are: *William Morris: Selected Writings and Designs*, edited with an introduction by Asa Briggs, Harmondsworth: Penguin Books 1977, and *Political Writings of William Morris*, edited by A.L. Morton, London: Lawrence and Wishart 1984. Raymond Williams, *Keywords: a Vocabulary of Culture and Society*, Glasgow: William Collins Sons & Co. 1976, discusses the changes in meaning which words like art and artisan have gone through since they first entered the English language, providing a key to the cultural shifts that have accompanied these changes in meaning.

In Pursuit of Reality

1 E.H. Gombrich, *The Story of Art*, 1950, Oxford: Phaidon 1984, ch. 24. pp. 376–94.
2 Nicolas Pevsner, *Pioneers of the Modern Movement, from William Morris to Walter Gropius*, London: Faber & Faber 1936, pp. 69–95.
3 Gombrich, *The Story of Art*, p. 376.
4 Ibid., p. 403.

5 Hans Richter, *Dada: Art and Anti-art*, London: Thames & Hudson 1965, p. 25.
6 Ibid., p. 9.
7 Ibid., p. 25.
8 William Morris, in *The Letters of William Morris, to his Family and Friends*, edited by Phillip Henderson, London: Longmans Green & Co. 1950, p. 187.
9 For a discussion of Gropius's declared intention of reviving traditional craft practices, and the medievalism inherent in the name Bauhaus, see Paul Whitford, *Bauhaus*, London: Thames & Hudson 1984, pp. 29–30. The quote in the text is from Gillian Naylor, *The Bauhaus*, London: Studio Vista 1968, p. 50.
10 Camilla Gray, *The Great Experiment: Russian Art 1863–1922*, London: Thames & Hudson 1962, p. 10.
11 Teresa Newman, *Naum Gabo: The Constructive Process*, London: Tate Gallery 1976, p. 25.
12 Richter, *Dada*, plate 62, facing p. 128.
13 Richard Wollheim, *Art and Its Objects*, Harmondsworth: Penguin Books 1970, pp. 168–9. To my mind Wollheim's book exemplifies the aesthetician's dilemma, which is to account for the fabulous monetary value works of art have acquired without referring to it directly. The aesthetician, therefore, has to discern some intrinsic value artists embody in the objects they produce which could possibly be valued so highly, hence the focus on the material work rather than on the social and historical context in which it arises.

Further reading

Perhaps the best known alternative approach to art history is Arnold Hauser, *The Social History of Art*, London: Routledge & Kegan Paul 1951, which was the first thorough attempt to relate art to its social context. T.J. Clark's *Image of the People: Gustave Courbet and the 1848 Revolution*, and *The Absolute Bourgeois: Artists and Politics in France. 1848–51*, both published in paperback by Thames & Hudson (London 1982), are good examples of an art history which gives us the information we need to begin to understand how artists functioned in relation to a particular society. Another equally illuminating book is Gwyn A. William's *Goya and the Impossible Revolution* (1976), Harmondsworth: Penguin Books 1984. In: *Old Mistresses: Women, Art and Ideology*, London: Routledge & Kegan Paul 1981, Rozsica Parker and Griselda Pollack take issue with twentieth-century art history which, they argue, has erased the work of women artists.

From Utopia to Ronan Point

1 John James, *Chartres, The Masons who built a Legend*, London: Routledge & Kegan Paul 1982, p. 43.
2 Berthold Lubetkin, quoted in 'Lubetkin Speaks', *Building Design*, no. 585, 12 March 1982, p. 8.
3 For a detailed account of Tekton's practice, and Lubetkin's thinking on architecture and social change see Peter Coe and Malcolm Reading, *Lubetkin and Tekton: Architecture and Social Commitment*, Bristol: Bristol University for the Arts Council of Great Britain 1981.
4 Colin Ward, *Tenants Take Over*, London: Architectural Press 1974, Appendix III, Building co-ops, pp. 166–7. For a development of some of these ideas, particularly relevant here, see also Colin Ward's excellent new book: *When we Build Again, Let's have Housing that Works!*, London: Pluto Press 1985.
5 'Lubetkin Speaks', *Building Design*, no. 585, 12 March 1982, p. 8.

Bridging the Gap between Art and Life

1 Andy Warhol, quoted in 'Gordon Burn, Master of Art', *Sunday Times Magazine* 7 March 1982, pp. 36–43.
2 Camilla Gray, *The Great Experiment: Russian Art 1863–1922*, London: Thames & Hudson 1962, pp. 241–55. In this book Camilla Gray takes the attitude that a key concern of Russian artists over this period was to bridge the gap between art and life. Chapter 8 deals with the question of utilitarian art, and the factionalism that characterised the early years of post-revolutionary art in Russia. In 'The Genesis of Socialist-Realist Painting – Futurism – Suprematism – Constructivism', *Soviet Survey*, no. 27, 1959, pp. 32–9, she gives a detailed account of the rivalries and conflicting theories that preceded the adoption of Socialist-Realism as the approved state art form in the USSR.

Further reading
Herschel B. Chipp, *Theories of Modern Art: a Source Book by Artists and Critics*, Berkeley and London: University of California Press 1968, gives an insight into the complexities of twentieth-century art theory. John Berger, *Art and Revolution: Ernst Neizvestney and the Role of the Artist in the USSR*, London: Writers and Readers 1969, looks at the work and social role of a contemporary artist under the constraints of the USSR's art bureaucracy. Christina Lodder, *Russian Constructivism*, Newhaven and London: Yale University Press 1983, gives a thorough account of the early years of the twentieth century in Russia and the effects of the revolution on artistic thought and practice. Lucius Burckhardt, *The Werkbund: Studies in the History and Ideology of the Deutscher Werkbund 1907–1933*,

London: The Design Council 1980, gives an account of this movement in Germany which was influential in the development of modern art and design. John Willet, *The Weimar Years: a Culture Cut Short*, London: Thames & Hudson 1984, describes the short flowering of a radical culture in Weimar that was a unique attempt to put into common use the technical and artistic discoveries of the pioneering movements of modern art and design, tragically cut short in 1933 by the rise of Nazism.

Useful Work versus Useless Toil

1 William Morris, 'How we live and how we might live': a lecture first delivered to the Hammersmith branch of the Socialist Democratic Federation on 30 November 1884, reprinted in *Political Writings of William Morris*, edited and introduced by A.L. Morton, London: Lawrence & Wishart 1984, p. 136.

2 William Morris, 'Useful Work versus Useless Toil' (1884), A.L. Morton, *Political Writings*, p. 88.

3 William Morris, 'Socialism and Anarchism' (1889), A.L. Morton, *Political Writings*, p. 211.

4 William Morris, 'The Worker's Share of Art' (1885), *William Morris, Selected Writings and Designs*, edited with an introduction by Asa Briggs, Harmondsworth: Penguin Books 1977, pp. 140–1.

5 For the complete text see William Morris, *News from Nowhere, or an Epoch of Rest* (1890), edited and introduced by James Redmond, London: Routledge & Kegan Paul 1970.

6 'Useful Work', *Political Writings*, pp. 90–1.

7 Ibid., pp. 92–3.

8 Ibid., p. 94.

9 William Morris, 'Work in a Factory as it Might Be', *William Morris, Artist, Writer, Socialist*, edited by May Morris, Oxford: Basil Blackwell 1936, vol.2, pp. 134–5.

10 'Useful Work', *Political Writings*, p. 98.

11 Ibid., p. 100.

12 Ibid., pp. 101–2.

13 Ibid., p. 107.

14 Ibid., p. 108.

15 Peter Kropotkin, *Fields, Factories and Workshops Tomorrow*, edited, with additional modern material by Colin Ward, London: Allen & Unwin 1974.

16 William Morris, 'How I Became a Socialist' (1884), *Political Writings*, p. 244.

17 Eugene D. Lemire, *The Unpublished Lectures of William Morris*, Detroit: Wayne State University Press 1969, is difficult to get hold of, but contains a complete calendar of Morris's platform career, and a

bibliographical checklist of Morris's speeches and lectures, both of which help to give some idea of the enormous dedication and energy Morris brought to various social causes during the later years of his life.

18 For an account of the Deutscher Wekbund see: Lucius Burckhardt, *The Werkbund: Studies in the History and Ideology of the Deutscher Werkbund 1907–1933*, London: The Design Council 1980, and for an account of the Artists International Association see: Lynda Morris and Robert Radford, *The Story of the Artists International Association: 1933–1953*, Oxford: The Museum of Modern Art Oxford 1983.

19 See J.Bicknell and L.McQuiston (eds), *Design for Need: The Social Contribution of Design* (Papers presented to a Symposium at the Royal College of Art), London: Pergamon (for ICSID) 1977.

20 Mike Cooley, in conversation with Roger Coleman and Ian Todd on 10 November 1983, *William Morris Today*, London Institute of Contemporary Arts 1984, pp. 110–17.

Further reading
E.P. Thompson, *William Morris: Romantic to Revolutionary* (1955), London: Merlin Press 1977, is the most complete and balanced life of Morris, dealing extensively with his political and artistic activities.

The Impossibility of Art

1 From *Iskusstvo Kommuni* (Art of the Commune), no. 1, 1918, p. 1. Quoted by Camilla Gray in *The Great Experiment: Russian Art 1863–1922*, London: Thames & Hudson 1962, p. 216.

Freely–chosen Work

1 Clement Greenburg,'The Plight of Culture', in *Art and Culture*, London: Thames & Hudson 1973, p. 32.

2 Fredrick Winslow Taylor, 'On the Art of Cutting Metals', quoted by Mike Cooley in *Architect or Bee*, Slough: Hand and Brain 1980, p. 17 (now in a new, extended edition published by Hogarth Press, London, 1987). Despite his obsession with the rationalisation of production processes, Taylor still referred to cutting metal as an art, a contradiction Mike Cooley picks up when he takes issue with Taylor, pointing out the grotesque social consequences of Taylorism when applied to the mechanisation of work. *Architect or Bee* is a perceptive and incisive exploration of the relationship between human beings and technology, and the dangers inherent in an overly mechanistic approach to it.

3 For an enlightening discussion of the question of surplus value and its

investment in cultural as opposed to material wealth see Marshall Salins, *Stone Age Economics*, New York: Aldine Atherton 1972, particularly 'The Original Affluent Society' pp. 1–39, and the two chapters on 'The Domestic Mode of Production'.

4 For an enlightening and enjoyable account of the complexity of Aboriginal and Nomadic cultures see: Bruce Chatwin, *The Songlines*, London: Jonathan Cape 1987.

5 Adam Smith, *Inquiry into the Nature and Causes of the Wealth of Nations* (1776), edited by Campbell, Skinner and Todd, Oxford: Clarendon Press 1976, vol.1, p. 15.

Further reading
The classic work on the mechanisation of production is Harry Braverman's *Labor and Monopoly Capital: The Degradation of Work in the Twentieth Century*, New York and London: Monthly Review Press 1974. In his early writings, Karl Marx discussed the idea of freely–chosen work and developed the concept of alienated labour as the opposite and destructive form of work. See *Karl Marx: Early Writings*, introduced by Lucio Colletti, Harmondsworth: Penguin Books in association with *New Left Review* 1975, pp. 259–78, and pp. 322–34. Hilary Wainwright and Dave Elliot, *The Lucas Plan: A New Trade Unionism in the Making?*, London: Allison & Busby 1982, describes the radical and innovative attempt by the workers at Lucas Aerospace to define alternative and socially–useful products they would choose to make if they had control of their own industry. Jenny Thornley, *Workers' Co–operatives: Jobs and Dreams*, London: Heinemann Educational Books 1981, describes another tradition of workers' control, and in particular the experience of the British co–operative movement.

Inventing the Future

1 Henk Thomas and Chris Logan, *Mondragon: An Economic Analysis*, London: Allen & Unwin for the Institute of Social Studies at the Hague 1982, p. 1.
2 Hilary Wainwright and Dave Elliot, *The Lucas Plan: A New Trade Unionism in the Making?*, London: Allison & Busby 1982, pp. 95–6.
3 Peter Kropotkin, *Fields, Factories and Workshops Tomorrow*, edited with additional modern material by Colin Ward, London: Allen & Unwin 1974, pp. 182–3.

Index

Gabo, Naum, 83
Genet, Jean, 52–3, 56
Genius, 67
Geometry, 9, 23
Gervase (of Canterbury), 21
Giles, Joseph and Frances, 72
Giotto, 64, 73–4, 85
Goldsmith, 64
Gombrich, E.H., 67, 73, 76
Gothic (style), 14
Goya, Francisco de, 45, 53, 79
Grand Tour, 44, 67
Gray, Camilla, 81
Gropius, Walter, 80, 81, 92, 97
Grosz, Georg, 83
Guernica, 79
Guild(s), 70–2
    Roman, 17
Guipuzcoa, 155

Hamilton, Al, 125
Heartfield, John, 83
Hebden Bridge, 129
High Point, 98
Hockney, David, 54
Hogarth, William, 76
Holliss, Frances, 138
Holy Sepulchre, 13, 23
Honnecourt, Villar d', 19
Housing cooperatives, 155
Hughes, Patrick, 12

Icarus, 2–3
Iconoclasm, 68
Impressionism, 76
Industrial Revolution, 7, 36, 72–3,
    77, 81, 83, 96, 120, 147, 149, 160

Jackson, George, 52–3
Janco, Marcel, 78
Jazz, 15, 68
Jigs, 20
John Bull Puncture Repair Kit, 128
Joinery, 26–9, 37, 65, 87–90, 94, 137

rod, 23, 27–9, 88
setting out, 19, 22–3, 24, 27–9, 94
workshop, 23
Joinery details,
    beads, 28
    check grooves, 28
    curve-on-curve work, 23
    jigs, 20
    quirk beads, 28
    mortices, 19
    mouldings, 28, 58, 61, 88–9
    rebates, 27–8, 89
    stiles, 89
Journeymen, 18
Joyce, James, 7

Kara Sea, 88
Kells (Book of), 69
Kent, William, 18
Keystones, 22
Knitting, 94
Koestler, Arthur, 54
Kollwitz, Käthe, 53
Krautheimer, Richard, 13
Kropotkin, Peter, 118, 166
Labour, *see* Skill,
    division of, 27, 35–8, 147
    value, 62–5
Laing, R.D., 52
Lascaux, 107
Lime mortar, 90–1
Lubetkin, Berthold, 97–9, 100–1
Lucas Aerospace Combine Shop
    Stewards Committee, 165
Luddites, 149

Machine-minder, 42
Malevich, Kasimir, 82–3
Mantegna, Andrea, 64
Marx, Karl, 111, 112–13
Masonry, 9–10, 14–15, 16–17, 19,
    20–22, 24
McCarthyism, 68